GW01495678

# GREAT WESTERN COACHES APPENDIX

## Volume Two

STANDARD PASSENGER STOCK

# GREAT WESTERN COACHES APPENDIX

## Volume Two

## STANDARD PASSENGER STOCK

by J. H. Russell

Oxford Publishing Co.

Copyright © 1984 Oxford Publishing Co.

ISBN 0-86093-154-4

All rights reserved. No part of this book may be reproduced or transmitted in any form or by any means, electronic or mechanical, including photocopying, recording or any information storage and retrieval system, without permission in writing from the Publisher.

Typesetting by:
Aquarius Typesetting Services, New Milton, Hants.

Printed in Great Britain by:
Netherwood Dalton & Co. Ltd., Huddersfield, Yorks.

Published by:
Oxford Publishing Co.
Link House
West Street
POOLE, Dorset

# INTRODUCTION

This is the second portion of a two volume work, dealing exclusively with the carriage stock of the Great Western Railway. This volume deals particularly with vehicles intended for specific duties.

The entire work, entitled *Great Western Coaches Appendix,* is intended to act as a companion and an addition to the previous volumes; *A Pictorial Record of Great Western Coaches Part I (1838-1913)* and *Part II (1903-1948)* which were published several years ago by OPC.

The endeavour has been to fill in the omissions from the previous work, add to the fund of information and to give as much pictorial detail of the coaching stock of the Great Western Railway as possible.

It is hoped that the complete series of four volumes will help the modeller and enthusiast alike, and put on record, for many years, visual data on those interesting carriages, once seen in great numbers at any Great Western station.

*Jim Russell*
*1984*

# CONTENTS

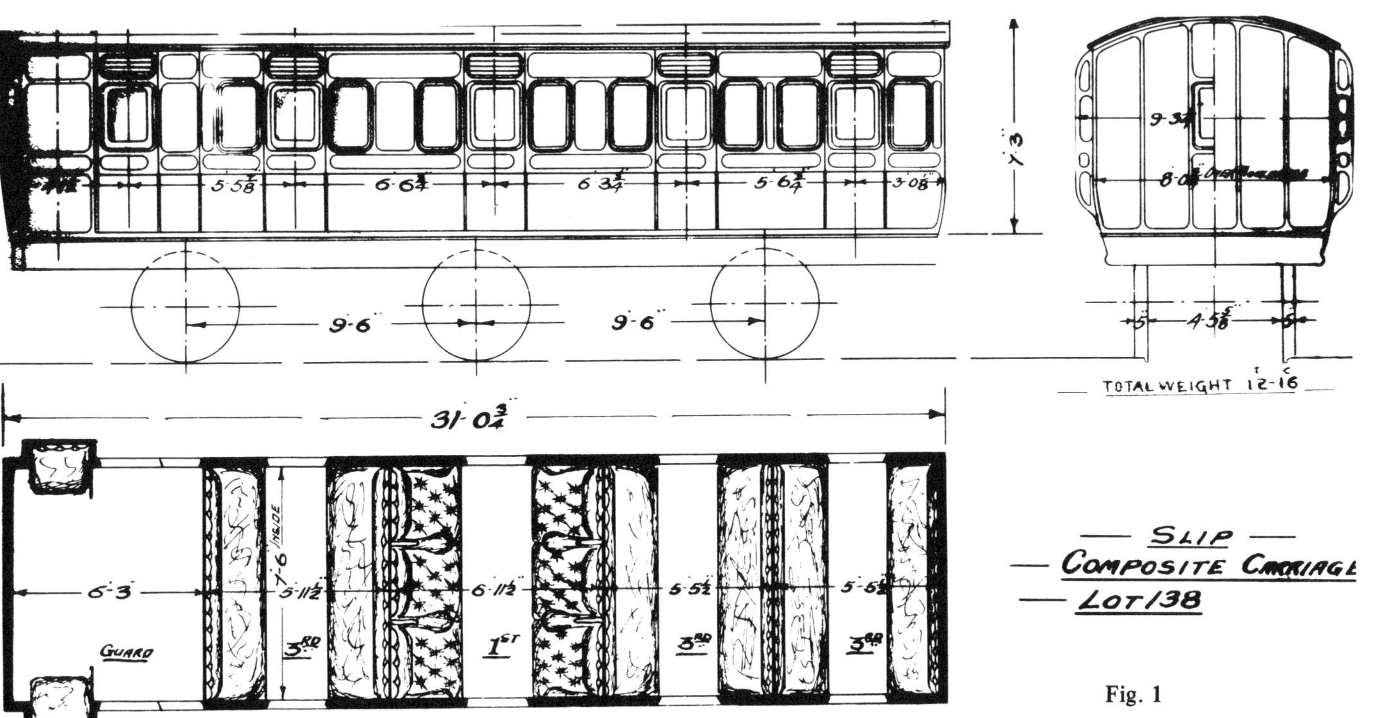


Fig. 1

*DIAGRAMS F19, F18 & F17 (Page 2)*

On this page we have two drawings of early pre-1890 slip carriages. There was quite a range of these four and six-wheeled vehicles which were used as 'slip' vehicles and, although being outside the scope of this work, it was thought that the inclusion of three samples would be of interest of the reader. The examples shown are: in **Fig. 1**, a short-wheelbased six-wheeled, single-ended low-roofed slip carriage, to the early Lot number of 138, built to *Diagram F19* (1st series). **Fig. 2** shows a 31ft. single-ended 'slip', fitted with the long narrow compartment windows. This pattern was constructed to Lot 349 and given *Diagram F18.*

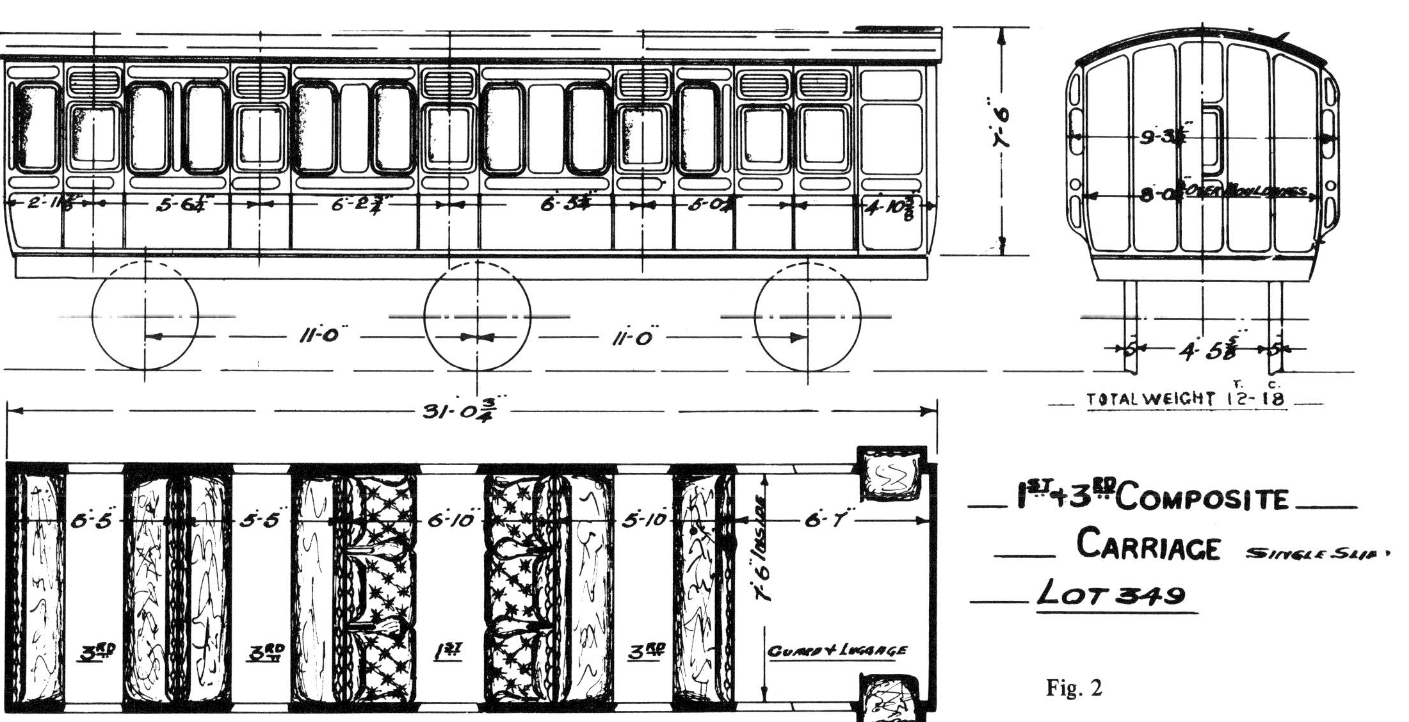


Fig. 2

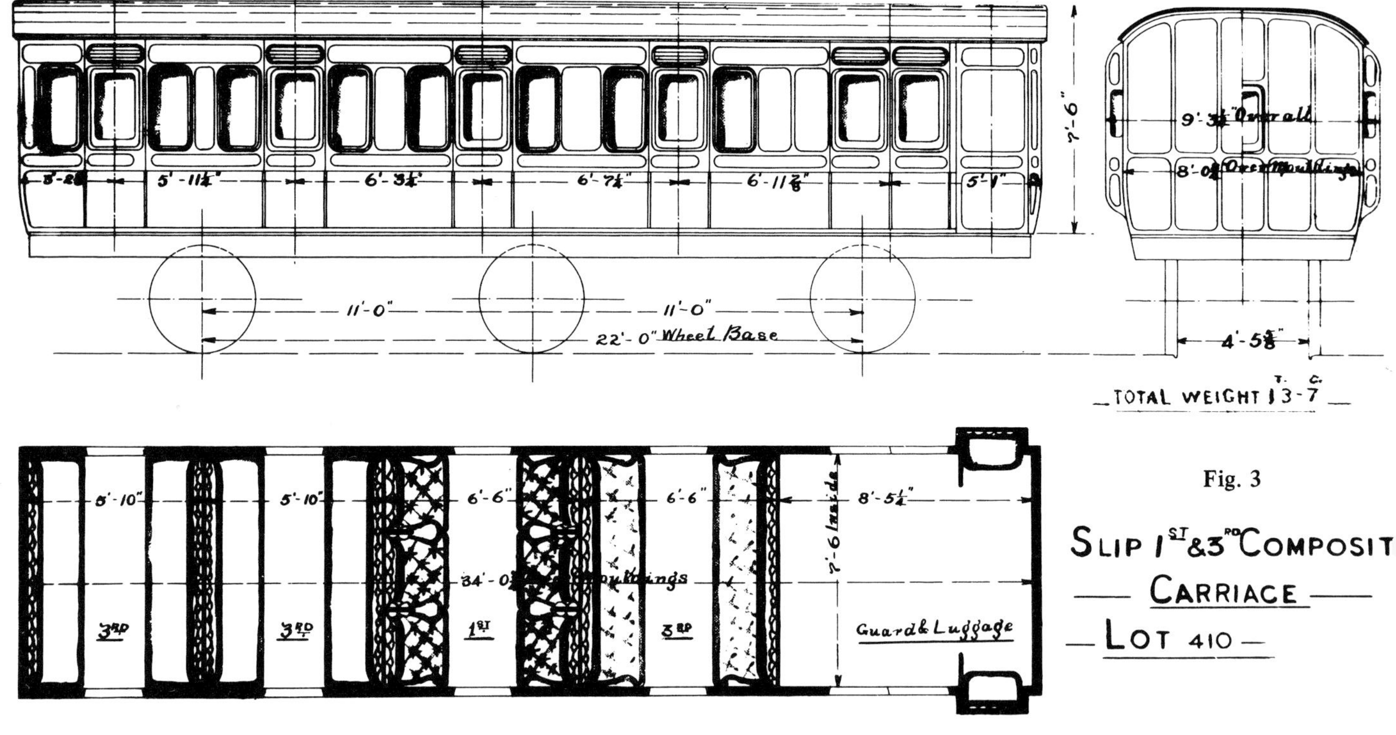


**Fig. 3** This shows the 34 ft. single-ended 'slip', built to Lot 410 to *Diagram F17.*

*DIAGRAM F19*

The only photographs I have been able to find, relating to these early short-wheelbased 'slip' carriages have been loaned to me by the HMRS and are shown on this page. It is No. 388 which was originally one of the *F19* series, which is seen in diagram form on the previous page. The photographs show the vehicle from both ends, **(Figs. 4 & 5)**, and, long after it had ceased to be used for 'slip' working, was demoted, in fact, to a shuttle service between Churston and Brixham, in the 1930s.

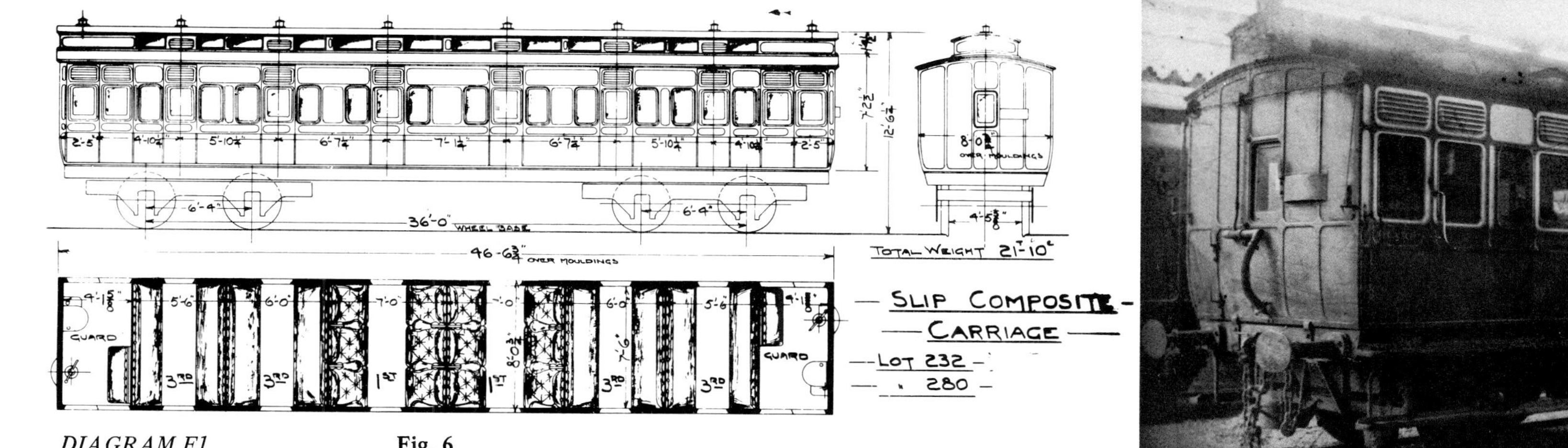


*DIAGRAM F1* **Fig. 6**
Slip Composite Carriage (Clerestory)
Lots 232 & 280
Dimensions: 46ft. 6¾in. x 8ft. 0¾in.

*DIAGRAM F2*
Slip Composite Carriage (Clerestory)
Lot 360
Dimensions: 46ft. 6¾in. x 8ft. 0in.

**Fig. 8**

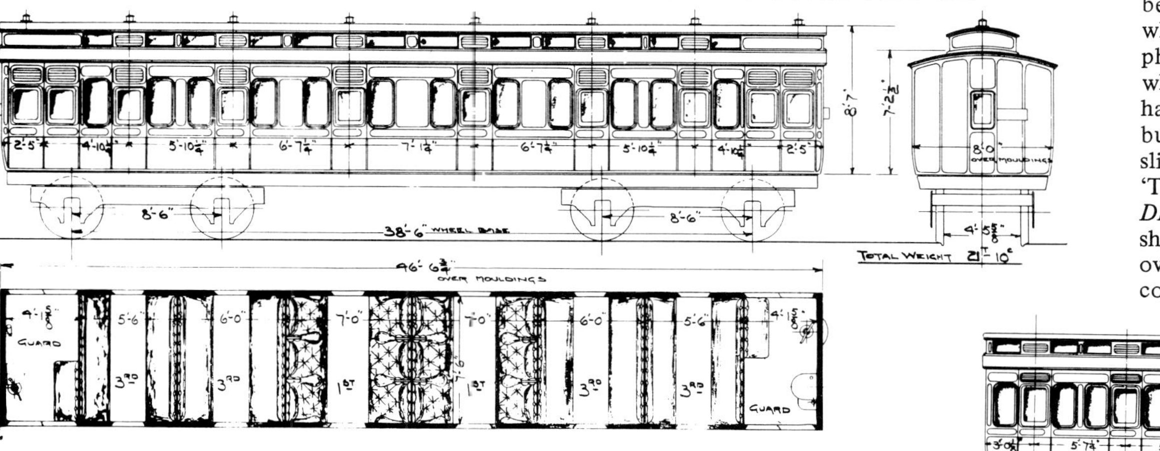


*DIAGRAMS F1, F2 & F3*
Starting with the bogie eight-wheeled stock, the 'slip' series of diagrams were recoded and began again with F1, which saw the demise of the early four and six-wheeled vehicles which are mentioned on the previous two pages. As with the short wheelbase 'slips', photographs are extremely rare, but a good friend has located the view of No. 1016 which is seen in **Fig. 7**. Points to note are the curved guard which allows the handle of the handbrake to be turned, and the linkage for the handbrake, which can be seen below the buffer beam. The fitting of safety-chains is curious as they would make the practice of slipping the coach very complicated if they were coupled up. The destination board reads 'To South Eastern & Chatham Railway'.
*DIAGRAM F2* was similar to *DIAGRAM F1* but ran on 8ft. 6in. Dean bogies and had shallower eaves panels over the compartment windows. *DIAGRAM F3*, while the same overall length as the two previous series, differed by having shallow eaves panels over compartments and doors and by being a single-ended pattern.

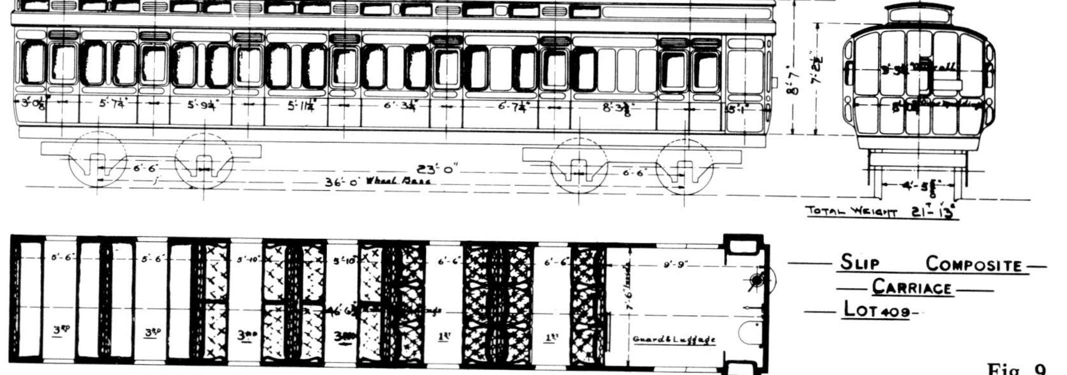


*DIAGRAM F3*
Slip Composite Carriage (Clerestory)
Lot 409
Dimensions: 46ft. 6¾in. x 8ft. 0¾in.

**Fig. 9**

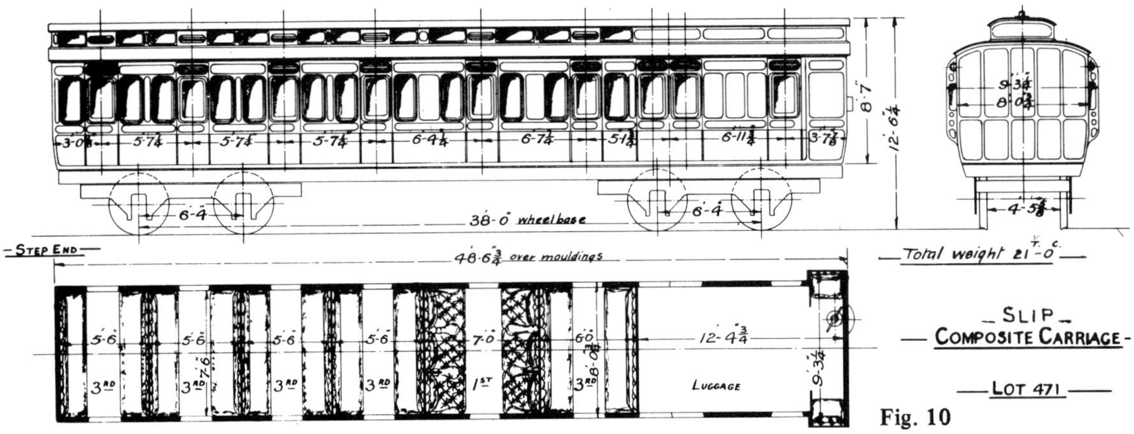

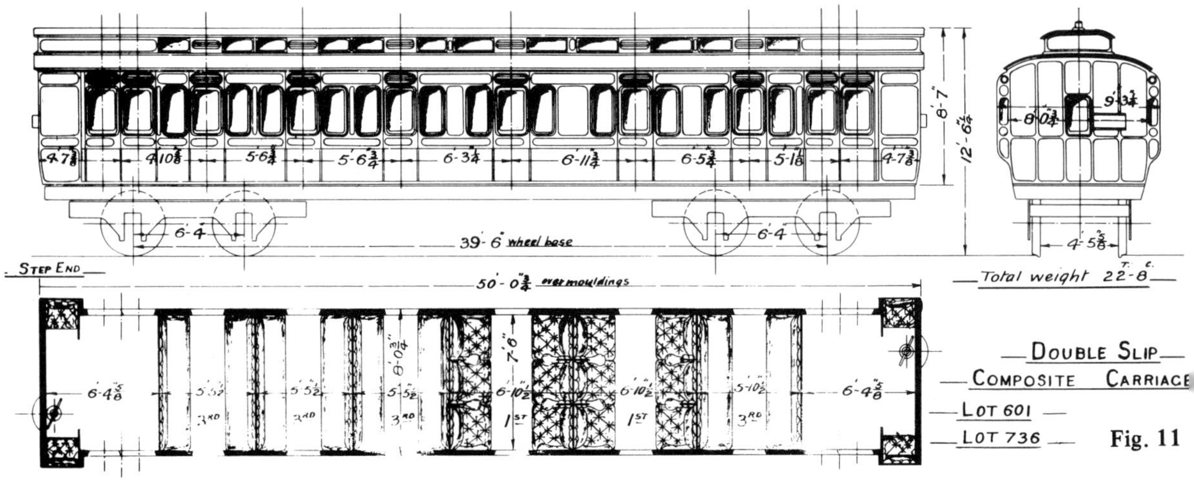

STEP END
48-6¾ over mouldings
38-0 wheelbase
Total weight 21-0
LUGGAGE
SLIP
COMPOSITE CARRIAGE
LOT 471

Fig. 10

*DIAGRAM F4* **Fig. 1**
Slip Composite Carriag
(Clerestory)
Lot 471
Dimensions:
48ft. 6¾in. x 8ft. 0¾in

*DIAGRAM F5* **Fig. 1**
Slip Composite Carriag
(Clerestory)
Lot 601 of 1891
Running numbers:
7065–70
Lot 736 of 1894
Running numbers:
7075–78
Dimensions:
50ft. 0¾in. x 8ft. 0¾in

STEP END
50-0¾ over mouldings
39-6 wheel base
Total weight 22-8
DOUBLE SLIP
COMPOSITE CARRIAGE
LOT 601
LOT 736

**Fig. 11**

*DIAGRAMS F4, F5, F6 & F7*

The next three designs of bogie slip carriages, *Diagrams F4, F5 & F6,* show a progressive increase in length to allow for greater luggage space in the guard's compartment. *Diagram F4* **(Fig. 10)** was a single 'slip' with a single first class compartment. *Diagram F5* **(Fig. 11)** had the first class accommodation increased to two compartments and was a double 'slip'. The vehicles built to *Diagram F6* **(Fig. 12),** however, broke new ground by being equipped with four lavatories and a cunning system of seating, which gave all the passengers access to the toilet facilities. An additional innovation was the fitting of end windows in the first class coupe, giving a compartment with four corner seats. To achieve all this, the length was increased to 56ft. 0¾in. and, as a result of the end windows, the vehicle could only be a single 'slip'. *Diagram F7* was similar to *Diagram F6* but the fitting of diagonal partitions provided more space in the toilets. This variation can be seen in **Fig. 13.**

STEP END
56-0¾ OVER MOULDINGS
48-0 WHEEL BASE
TOTAL WEIGHT 24-2
Cupboard
SLIP
COMPOSITE CARRIAGE
LOT 697

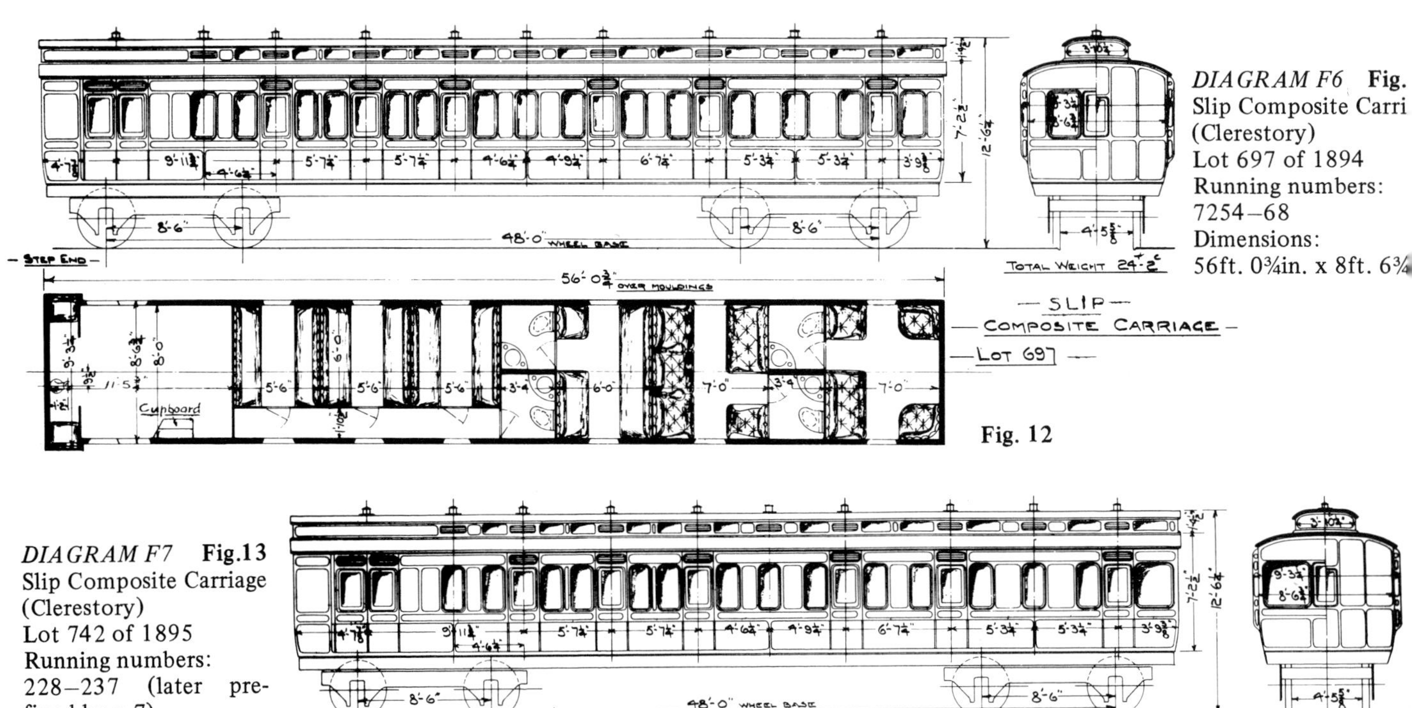

*DIAGRAM F6* **Fig.**
Slip Composite Carri
(Clerestory)
Lot 697 of 1894
Running numbers:
7254–68
Dimensions:
56ft. 0¾in. x 8ft. 6¾

**Fig. 12**

*DIAGRAM F7* **Fig.13**
Slip Composite Carriage
(Clerestory)
Lot 742 of 1895
Running numbers:
228–237 (later prefixed by a 7)
Dimensions:
56ft. 0¾in. x 8ft. 6¾in.

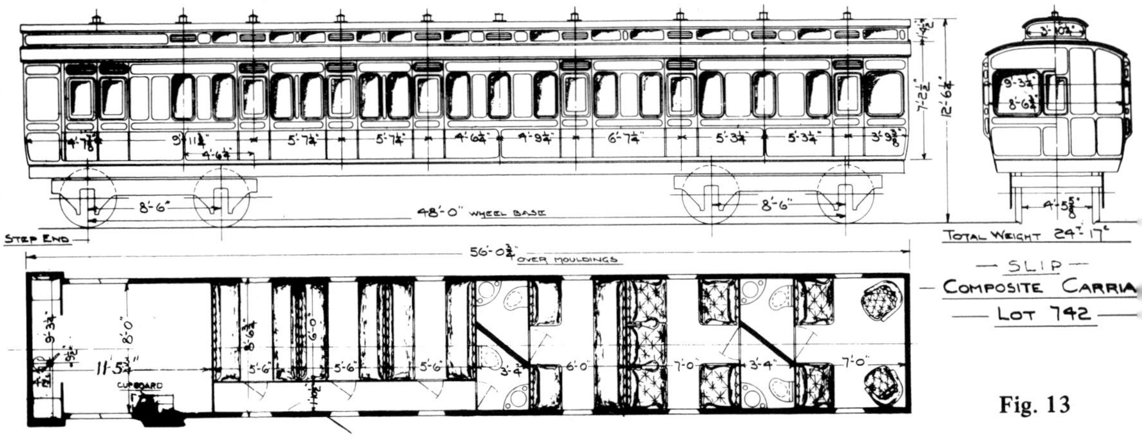

STEP END
56-0¾ OVER MOULDINGS
48-0 WHEEL BASE
TOTAL WEIGHT 24-17
CUPBOARD
SLIP
COMPOSITE CARRIA
LOT 742

**Fig. 13**

Fig. 14

*DIAGRAM F8*

The ten vehicles built to *Diagram F8* finally reached the length of 58ft. 0¾in., which was to remain the standard for the clerestory vehicles until their withdrawal. Fitted with four lavatories and an internal corridor, every passenger could, again, obtain toilet facilities, there being four small and one full width third class compartment, plus two first class at the opposite end to the 'slip' compartment. **Fig. 14** shows one of the series standing at Cardiff Station in the 1920s and gives a good view of the long vacuum reservoirs on the roof. In the lower illustration **(Fig. 16)**, showing a 'slipping' taking place at Slough, the vehicle acting as the 'slip' is one of the *Diagram F6* series previously mentioned.

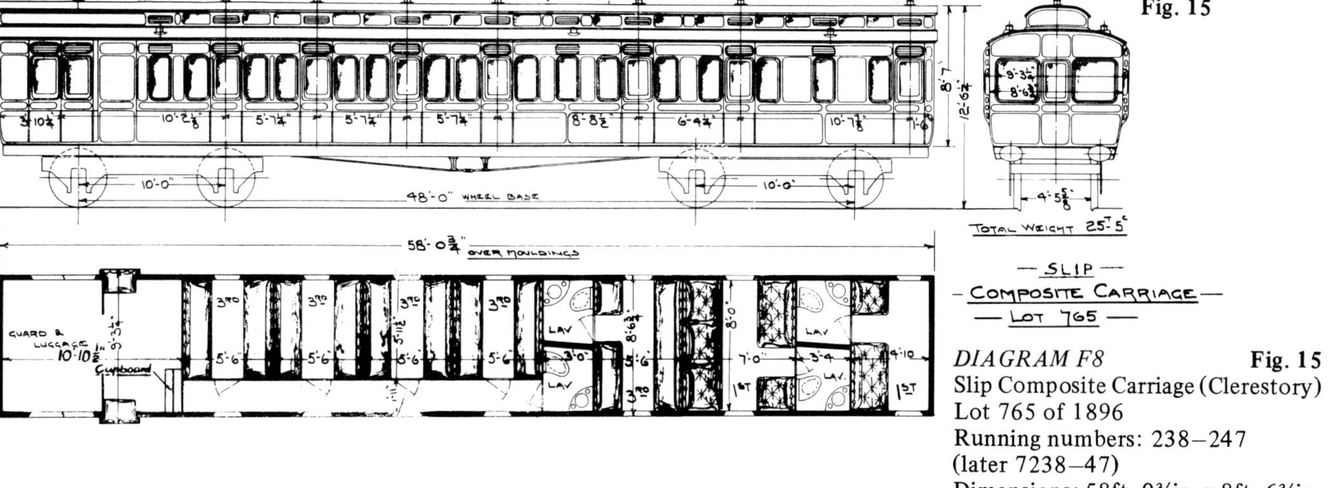


Fig. 15

*DIAGRAM F8* **Fig. 15**
Slip Composite Carriage (Clerestory)
Lot 765 of 1896
Running numbers: 238–247
(later 7238–47)
Dimensions: 58ft. 0¾in. x 8ft. 6¾in.

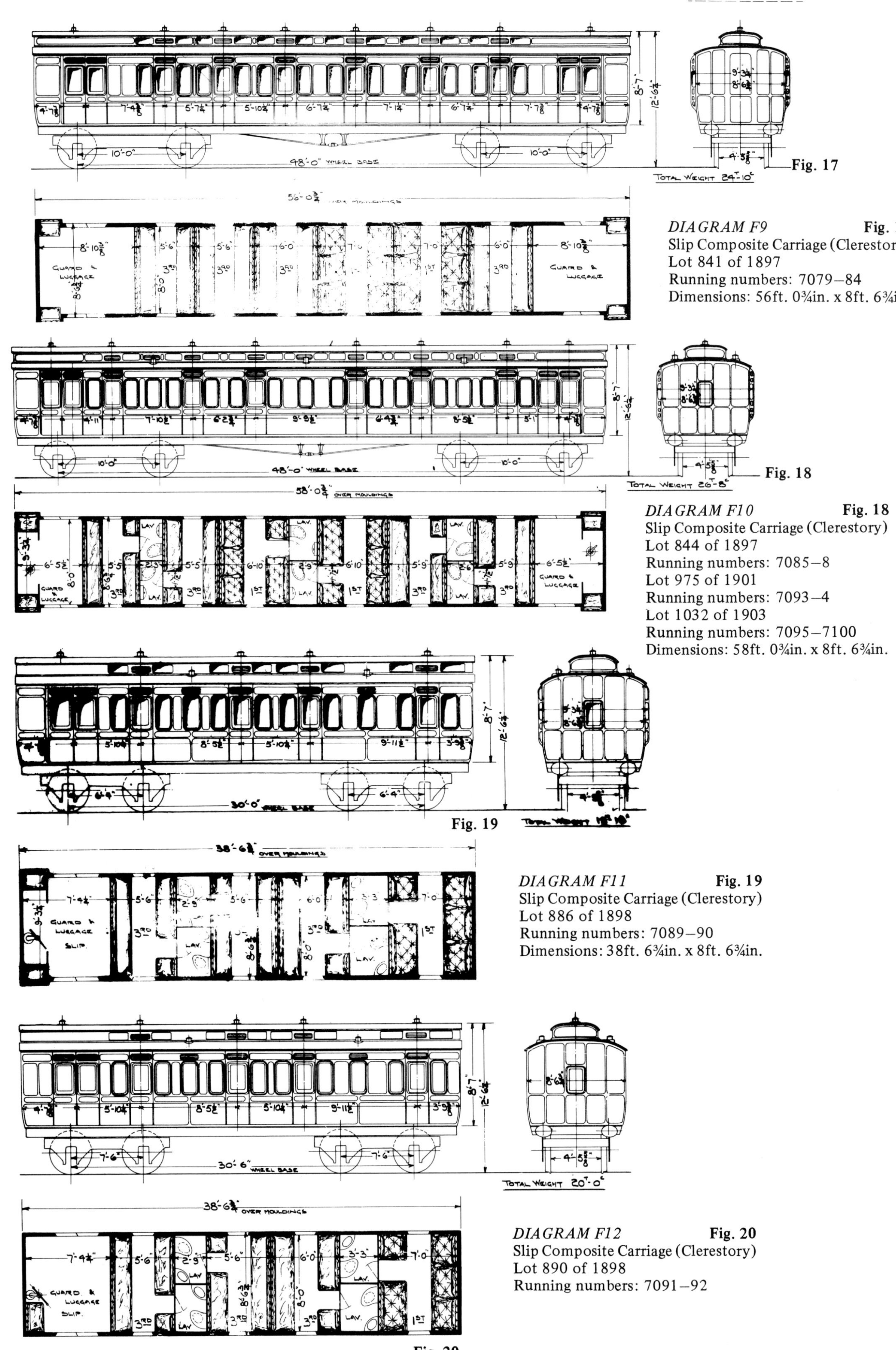

Fig. 17

*DIAGRAM F9* **Fig. 17**
Slip Composite Carriage (Clerestory)
Lot 841 of 1897
Running numbers: 7079–84
Dimensions: 56ft. 0¾in. x 8ft. 6¾in.

Fig. 18

*DIAGRAM F10* **Fig. 18**
Slip Composite Carriage (Clerestory)
Lot 844 of 1897
Running numbers: 7085–8
Lot 975 of 1901
Running numbers: 7093–4
Lot 1032 of 1903
Running numbers: 7095–7100
Dimensions: 58ft. 0¾in. x 8ft. 6¾in.

Fig. 19

*DIAGRAM F11* **Fig. 19**
Slip Composite Carriage (Clerestory)
Lot 886 of 1898
Running numbers: 7089–90
Dimensions: 38ft. 6¾in. x 8ft. 6¾in.

*DIAGRAM F12* **Fig. 20**
Slip Composite Carriage (Clerestory)
Lot 890 of 1898
Running numbers: 7091–92

Fig. 20

**Fig. 21**: This official photograph shows the end view of one of the clerestory 'slip' carriages, and many interesting features can be identified. The droplight window in the centre of the end panel is for the use of the 'slip' guard, who originally had to lean out of this aperture and shut off the vacuum cocks on the flexible hoses, before releasing the 'slip' portion. Two vacuum hoses can be seen, the lower left being for use when the vehicle was marshalled into a non-slipping portion of a train. The higher pipe was the vacuum hose, which was used when the vehicle was being slipped, and the spring-loaded valves were fitted into the end of these flexibles. On the roof can be seen the long vacuum reservoir tanks, which were fitted later in the coaches' life, to enable the vacuum brake to be released again and again, after application.

*DIAGRAMS F9, F10, F11 & F12 (opposite page)*
Four more examples of the clerestory 'slip' design which were built at the turn of the century. *Diagram F9* (**Fig. 17**) was evidently built for short distance use as no lavatories were fitted. In contrast, the vehicles built to *Diagram F10* (**Fig. 18**) had no less than six lavatories, reached by communicating doors from each compartment. The only person without access to the facilities was the guard! (See also *G W Coaches, Part I, page 232*). The two unusually short vehicles seen in **Figs. 19 & 20** were probably intended to serve stations that did not receive a large enough number of passengers to warrant a full size carriage. The differences between the two series are that *Diagram F11* is running on 6ft. 4in. bogies and has a look-out in the guard's compartment, while *Diagram F12* has no look-out and is fitted with 7ft. 6in. bogies.

**Fig. 22**

The problem of recreating the vacuum after applying the brake, when slipping a vehicle from the main train, caused a lot of concern to the design staff at Swindon, and the dilemma was eventually solved by installing large reservoir tanks on the 'slip' vehicles. Thus, when air was admitted into the braking system to apply the brakes, the vacuum could be recreated by connecting up to these large tanks. On clerestory vehicles, the only space available was on the roof in the angle of the clerestory, and **Fig. 22** shows these long reservoirs fitted to No. 7084, one of the *Diagram F9* series. On the larger, more modern, vehicles, the reservoirs were accommodation in the underframe, between the queen posts of the truss rods, and transversely instead of fore and aft. **Fig. 23** illustrates these tanks fitted to one of the *Diagram F13* 'Concertina slips'.

**Fig. 23**

Fig. 24

Two pictures showing the coupling gear necessary between the 'slip' carriage and the main train. In the upper illustration **(Fig. 24)**, the early system of disconnecting the vacuum hoses can be seen. On the main train (on the right of the picture) the hose valves can be seen fitted with the lever cock, which had to be turned off by leaning out of the droplight window. In the lower photograph **(Fig. 25)**, the automatic valve gear is seen fitted, which consisted of spring-loaded ball valves, which snapped into position when the carriages broke away from one another. Note the safety chains which prevented the gear from falling down and fouling the track after release.

Fig. 25

Fig. 26

*DIAGRAM F13*
Slip Composite Carriage (Concertina) **Fig. 27**
Lot 1117 of 1906
Running numbers: 7685–99
Dimensions: 70ft. 0in. x 9ft. 0in.

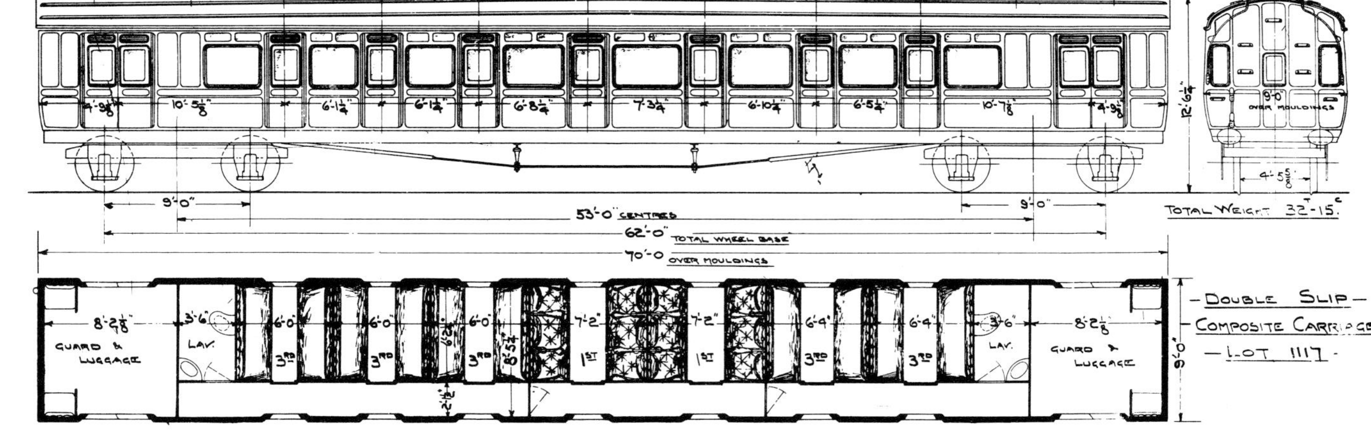


*DIAGRAM F13*
The 'Concertina' 70ft. 0in. stock of 1906 were the largest 'slip' vehicles made for the GWR. Very handsome vehicles, they were nicknamed 'Concertinas' because of the flat doors in a curved tumblehome side. The drawing in **Fig. 27** shows the layout of the carriage, which was double-ended and had a lavatory at each end, with two first class and five third class compartments. **Fig. 26** shows No. 7689 leaving Paddington, No. 1 Platform, in 1946 with the corridor side nearest the camera, and **Fig. 28** gives the official view of the compartment side of No. 6963, one of the 70ft. 0in. toplight series which was given 'slip' apparatus in the 1920s. (See also *GW Coaches, Part II, pages 38 & 39*).

Fig. 28

**Fig. 29** **Fig. 30**

These two official photographs illustrate very well just how the parts of the slipping train would appear immediately after the actual detaching. **Fig. 29** shows No. 7688, one of the *Diagram F13* series, with the hook open and the retaining chain on the steam heating hose. The other picture **(Fig. 30)** shows the last carriage of the main train, minus the tail lamps, of course. The chains which prevented the steam heating hose and the screw coupling from dropping too low and fouling the track, are evident. The gong on the end of the 'slip' carriage was sounded to give warning of the approach of the slipped portion of the train.

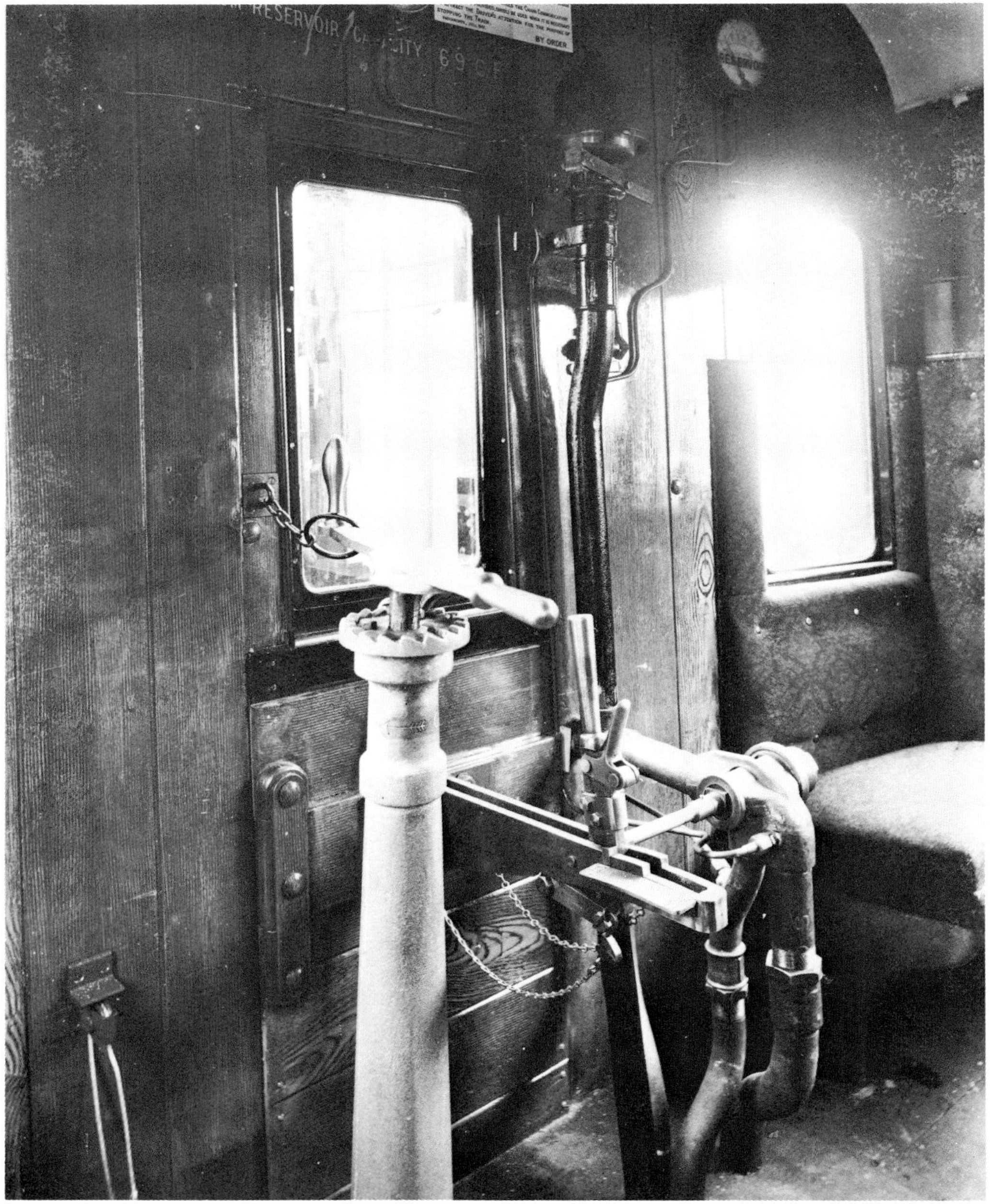

Fig. 31

Fig. 32

Two views showing both inside and outside of the guard's 'slip' compartment. In the interior photograph **(Fig. 31)**, the column and ratchet handle, seen in the foreground, is the vehicle's handbrake, for use if the vacuum brake failed. Immediately behind is the actual slipping handle, shown in the running position, with the gear locked against misuse. To operate the 'slip', the lever was pulled right towards the 'slip' guard, which pulled out the pin on the hinged coupling hook and at the same time allowed air into the train pipe, which applied the brakes. Pushing the lever up to the first notch shut off the air, and by restoring the vacuum from the large reservoirs, so released the brakes once more. To warn railway staff working on the track that a loose carriage was following along behind the

Fig. 33

Fig. 34

*DIAGRAM F14*
Slip Composite Carriage (Toplight)
Lot 1150 of 1908
Running numbers: 7101–2
Dimensions: 57ft. 0in. x 9ft. 0in.

*DIAGRAM F14*
Just two vehicles were built on Lot 1150, single 'slips' to the 'Bars 1 Toplight' pattern. **Fig. 33** shows the rear end of No. 7101 and the compartment side. The official photograph, **(Fig. 34)**, taken in 1908, illustrates the same vehicle from the corridor side. In the lower photograph, **(Fig. 35)**, No. 7102 is seen painted in the BR Strawberry and cream livery. (See also *GW Coaches, Part II, page 57*).

Fig. 35

Fig. 36

This trio of 'slip' pictures show the very moment of detaching the 'slip' portion from the main train. In the upper view **(Fig. 36)** two double-ended clerestory 'slip' carriages are shown, presumably bearing down on the unsuspecting platelayers. The photograph is one of a series of specially posed shots, taken at Old Oak Common, to illustrate the hazards of working on the track, and demonstrates the need for the gong already referred to, although, in this picture, it is conspicuous by its absence. The other two pictures **(Figures 37 & 38)** were taken at Banbury in the late 1930s and show how different the actual spots chosen by the 'slip' guards could be.

Fig. 37

Fig. 38

Fig. 39

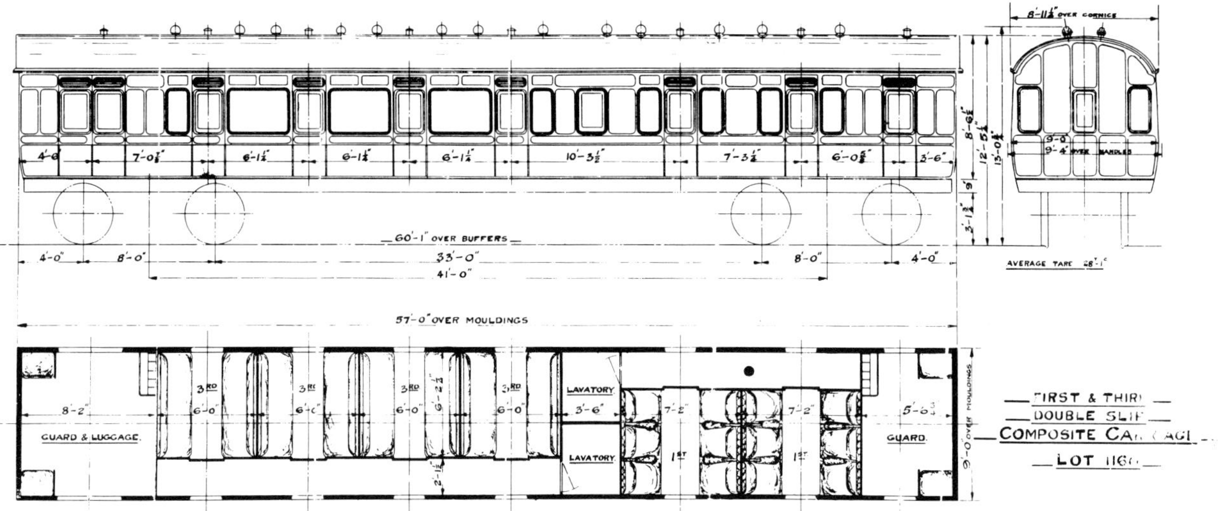


*DIAGRAM F15* **Fig. 40**
Composite Slip Carriage (Toplight)
Lot 1166 of 1909
Running numbers: 71039 and 7994-8000
Dimensions: 57ft. 0in. x 9ft. 0in.

*DIAGRAM F15*
This design was also part of the 'Bars 1 Toplight' series and had four third class compartments and two firsts, with a separate central lavatory for each class of traveller. **Fig. 39** shows No. 7108, while the lower illustration, **(Fig. 41)**, is of No. 7998.

Fig. 41

Fig. 42

*DIAGRAM F15*

These two photographs show the corridor side of the *Diagram F15* series of double-slip carriages. In **Fig. 42**, No. 7109 is seen at Old Oak Common in 1952, whilst in the lower illustration **(Fig. 43)** No. 7995 is depicted as converted to travelling accommodation for the GWR's fire-fighting team, based at Reading during World War II, when incendiary bombs were being used by enemy aircraft. (See also *GW Coaches, Part II, pages 59 & 60*).

Fig. 43

*DIAGRAM F21*

The four double-ended slip coaches built to *Diagram F21* were the only 70ft. 0in. examples of the type and were of the 'Multibar Toplight' design. The extra length allowed for five third class and two first class compartments, with the lavatories at each end. The compartment side of No. 7991 can be seen in **Fig. 44** at Old Oak Common in 1953. The official photograph **(Fig. 45)** shows No. 7993 in all the glory of the full maroon livery used after World War I. The corridor side of the same vehicle is seen again in **Fig. 46**, this time at Penzance, in 1950. (See also *GW Coaches, Part II, page 92*).

**Fig. 45**

**Fig. 46**

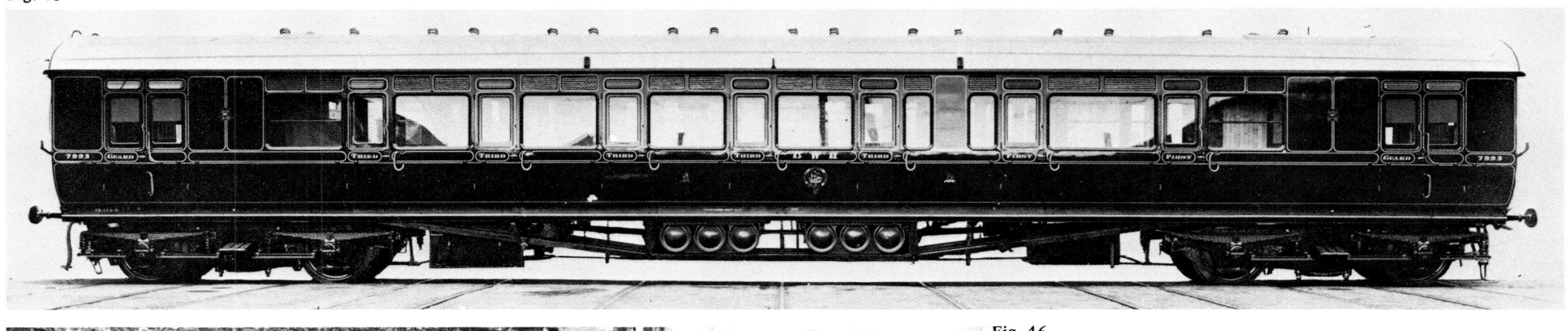

*DIAGRAM F21*
Composite Slip Carriage (Toplight)
Lot 1252 of 1916
Running numbers: 7990-93
Dimensions: 70ft. 0in. x 9ft. 0in.

*DIAGRAM F22*
Composite Slip Carriage (Clerestory)
Originally Lot 697 of 1894
Converted 1924
Running number: 7258
Dimensions: 56ft. 0¾in. x 8ft. 6¾in.

Fig. 47

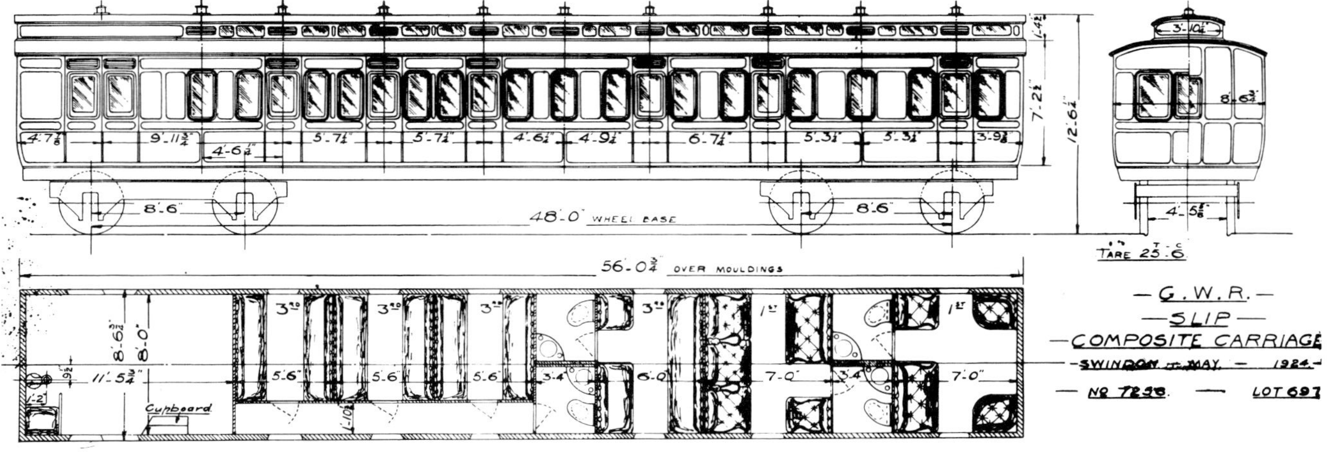


*DIAGRAM F22*
After the ravages of World War I, many older vehicles were restored and pressed back into service. One such vehicle was No. 7258, which was originally built in 1894 as a 'Falmouth Coupe' to *Diagram E39*. It was rebuilt to *Diagram F22* and given a further lease of life.

Fig. 48

*DIAGRAM F23*
In complete contrast were the three new double-ended slip coaches built for the 'Cornish Riviera' in 1929. The two illustrations **(Figs. 48 & 49)** show No. 7898 in the original livery and No. 7899 in British Rail days, on the carriage turntable at Old Oak Common.

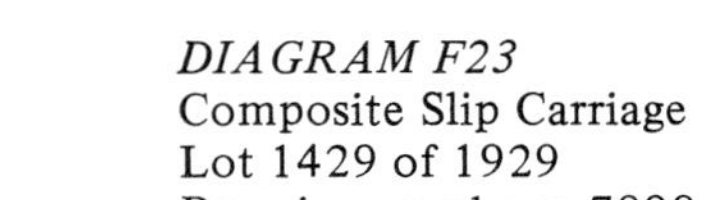

*DIAGRAM F23*
Composite Slip Carriage
Lot 1429 of 1929
Running numbers: 7898–7900
Dimensions: 61ft. 4½in. x 9ft. 5¾in.

Fig. 49

Fig. 50

*DIAGRAM F24*
Composite Slip Carriage
Lot 1597 of 1938
Running numbers: 7069–74
Dimensions: 60ft. 11¼in. x 8ft. 11in.

Fig. 51

*DIAGRAM F24*
The last batch of slip coaches to be constructed before World War II were the six vehicles built to *Diagram F24*. There were four third class and two first class compartments and 'slip' apparatus was fitted at both ends of the vehicle. The official photograph **(Fig. 50)** shows No. 7071 as built with the 'roundel' monogram and with the corridor side nearer the camera. In **Fig. 51**, taken at Old Oak Common in 1952, the corridor side of No. 7069 can be seen.

Fig. 52

Finally, in 1958, three of the Hawksworth brake composites originally built to *Diagram E164* in 1948, were converted to slip carriages. The vehicles concerned were Nos. 7374–76, and the original *Diagram E164* is shown in **Fig. 53**. The two pictures **(Figs. 52 & 54)** show No. 7374 being slipped from the 5.10p.m. Paddington to Birmingham train at Bicester in 1960, the last such operation to take place on British Railways.

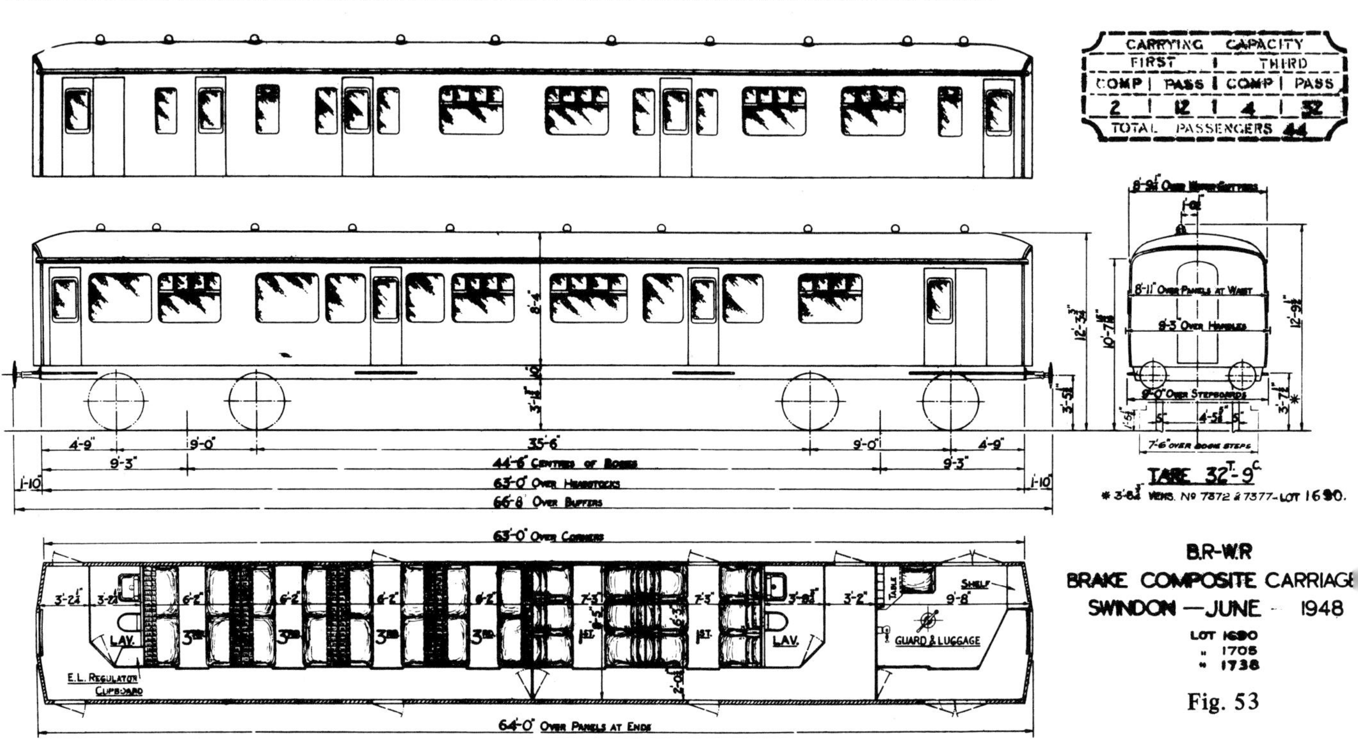


Fig. 53

Fig. 54

Fig. 55

*DIAGRAM G2*
Built in the 1890s, this vehicle had two saloons, one at each end, with an attendant's compartment in the centre. In the large illustration **(Fig. 55)**, the interior of one of the saloons is seen, upholstered in the period first class trim of chocolate and gold. Note the suspended pillar gas lamp hanging from the clerestory roof. The lower picture **(Fig. 56)** shows the exterior of the *Diagram G2* saloon, and was taken at Old Oak Common in 1928, when the vehicle had been renumbered 9044.

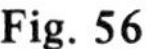
Fig. 56

**Fig. 57**

*DIAGRAM G3*
'Director's Saloon' (Royal Clerestory)
Lot 745 of 1894
Running number: 249
After 1907, No. 9045
Dimensions: 56ft. 0¾in. x 8ft. 6¾in.

*DIAGRAM G3*
This well-known vehicle was extremely well appointed, as might be expected from its designation as a 'Director's Saloon', and it often formed part of Queen Victoria's Royal Train. **Fig. 57** shows the vehicle as built and bearing the ornate livery of the period. In the lower picture **(Fig. 58)**, the vehicle is seen at Old Oak Common in 1928, renumbered 9045. This picture gives a good illustration of the curved end to the clerestory which became known as the 'Royal' style. It is pleasant to record that this carriage is still in existence and is being restored by the Dart Valley Railway Co. (See also *G W Coaches, Part I, page 81*).

**Fig. 58**

*DIAGRAM G3 (opposite)*
These two interiors **(Figs. 59 & 60)** are typical of the early 'Royal' clerestory saloons, and although it is not stated in the official register, I believe they refer to No. 249, the Director's Saloon seen on the previous page. Note the early use of the GWR motif in the scrollwork of the brackets of the luggage racks, and also the engraved glasswork in the clerestory lights and corridor door.

GENTLEMENS
LAVATORY

**Fig. 63**

*AGRAM G4*
st Saloon (Royal Clerestory)
t 840 of 1897
nning numbers: 233–4
ter 1907, Nos. 9002–3
nensions: 58ft. 0¾in. x 8ft. 6¾in.

*DIAGRAM G3*
**Fig. 63** shows the 'Director's Saloon' again, (old No. 249) after being renumbered in the 1907 schedule. Very little has changed except for the fitting of a dynamo and increased battery storage. There is a slight variation in the external painting and lining, with the new number, 9045, carried on the solebar.

*DIAGRAM G4*
The lower illustration **(Fig. 64)** shows No. 9002, one of the vehicles specially built for the Royal Train, as it appeared in 1909 having been renumbered. Once again the outline of the 'Royal' clerestory is evident.

**Fig. 64**

*DIAGRAM G4*
Showing a marked similarity to the previous interiors, are **Figs. 65 & 66** marked in the register as the two separate saloons in vehicle No. 9003, as at 1909. This was originally No. 234, and was later numbered 8234 and finally 9003. The only slight difference between the two vehicles, is that the photographs over the seats are not identical, and an electric fan has been fitted over the door. The keen-eyed will also spot a slight variation in the light fittings. What a superb example of Victorian coach building!

**Figs. 61 & 62** *(opposite)*, are definitely of No. 9045 and were taken to show how the vehicle was re-upholstered in 1909. Both pictures are looking in, towards the centre of the carriage, where the lavatories and attendants' compartments were situated. Several points of interest can be seen. Note the double arm slings, the umbrella or walking stick racks in the gangway, the electric lights, and the diplomatic marquetry on the clerestory bulkheads: a floral design incorporating the Rose of England in a central position, with shamrock, thistle and daffodil emblems entwined.

**Fig. 67**

*DIAGRAM G5*
The illustration on the left **(Fig. 67)** shows the corridor view of one of the 'Royal' carriages, with all the ornate door furniture of the sliding doors clearly shown. Note also the padded panels on the bottom halves of the opening doors, the heavy duty blinds over the corridor side window lights, and the electric lights on the decorated ceiling.

*DIAGRAM G4* **(Figs. 69 & 70)** *(opposite)*
After World War I, the Great Western Railway carriage painting changed from chocolate and cream, to a dark crimson lake, and the Royal Train vehicles received their new decor in due course. These two examples are, in the upper picture **(Fig. 69)**, No. 9003, and in the lower figure **(Fig. 70)**, No. 9002. As already stated, they were both built in 1897 to Lot 840 starting out as Nos. 233 and 234 respectively, were changed to 8233 and 8234, and finally became 9002 and 9003. Notice the solebars were painted in a slightly lighter colour and the wheel tyres were picked out in white.

*DIAGRAM G33*
**Fig. 68** is the drawing room in vehicle No. 225 *(to Diagram G33)*, according to the register, with the usual chocolate cloth first class trim, with mahogany woodwork. The tassels hanging down from the gas lamps controlled the illumination. The pulling of one lit the lamp, and a tug on the other extinguished same. The exterior of the carriage can be seen in **Fig. 91**.

**Fig. 68**

Fig. 71

*DIAGRAM G4*

These two illustrations link up nicely with the previous pictures as they show the interior saloons in vehicle No. 9002. In **Fig. 71** is seen the King's compartment looking towards the vestibule end, and in **Fig. 72** we see the Queen's compartment, also looking towards the opposite end of the carriage. The decor shown is that of the 1920s when the vehicles were painted crimson lake. The ramshackle shed and rubbish, visible through the window, detract from the dignity of the pictures.

Fig. 72

Fig. 73

Two more interior views which contrast the rather austere fittings in the longitudinal compartment of one of the first eight-wheeled saloons which were designed for third class travellers **(Fig. 73)**, with the heavy luxury of the first class saloon in No. 225 in the lower illustration **(Fig. 74)**. This view is the opposite to that on page 26, and is looking towards the coach end.

Fig. 74

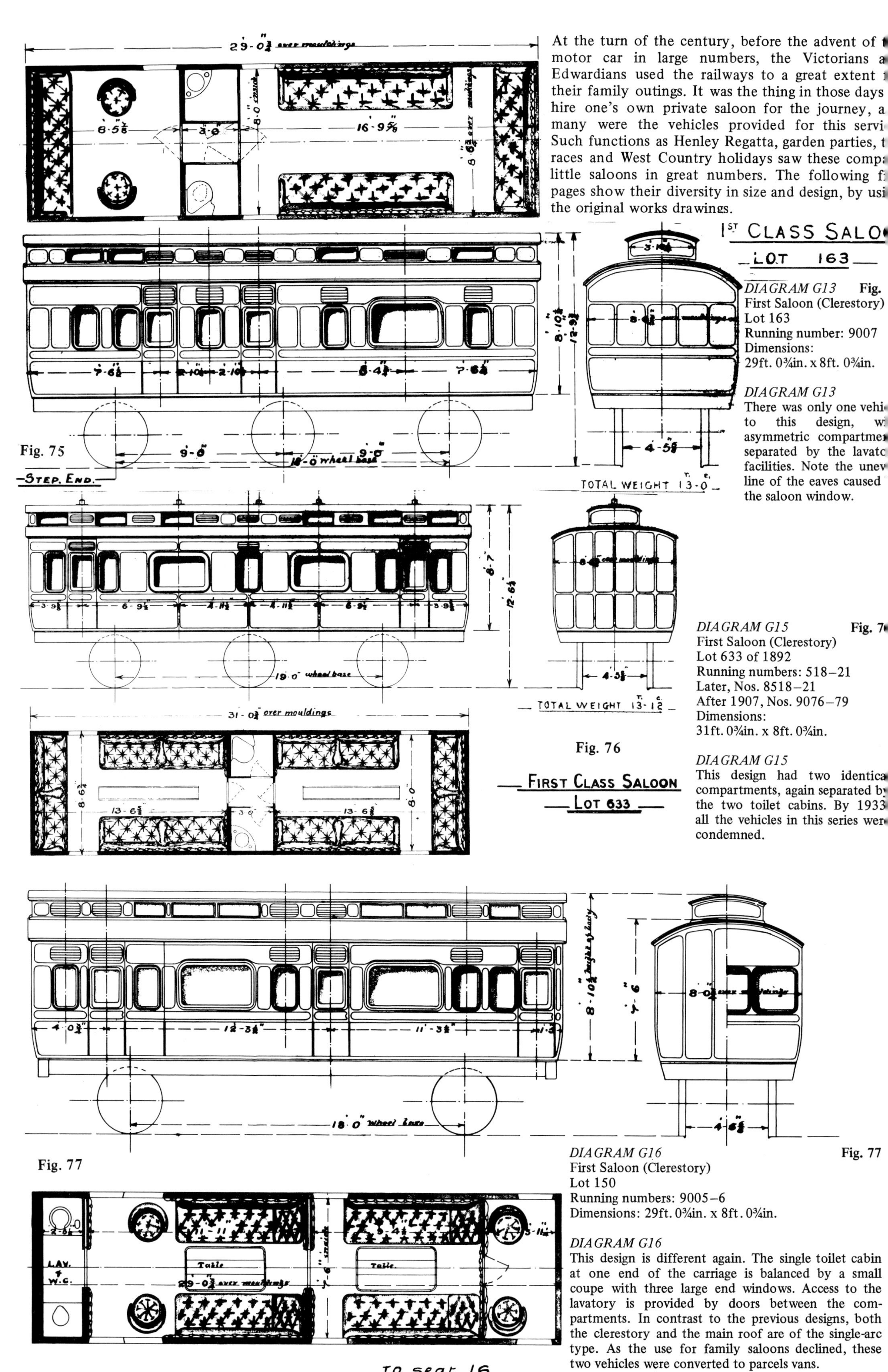


At the turn of the century, before the advent of t motor car in large numbers, the Victorians a Edwardians used the railways to a great extent f their family outings. It was the thing in those days hire one's own private saloon for the journey, a many were the vehicles provided for this servi Such functions as Henley Regatta, garden parties, t races and West Country holidays saw these compa little saloons in great numbers. The following fi pages show their diversity in size and design, by usi the original works drawings.

Fig. 75

*DIAGRAM G13* **Fig.**
First Saloon (Clerestory)
Lot 163
Running number: 9007
Dimensions:
29ft. 0¾in. x 8ft. 0¾in.

*DIAGRAM G13*
There was only one vehi to this design, wi asymmetric compartme separated by the lavato facilities. Note the unev line of the eaves caused the saloon window.

Fig. 76

*DIAGRAM G15* **Fig. 7**
First Saloon (Clerestory)
Lot 633 of 1892
Running numbers: 518–21
Later, Nos. 8518–21
After 1907, Nos. 9076–79
Dimensions:
31ft. 0¾in. x 8ft. 0¾in.

*DIAGRAM G15*
This design had two identica compartments, again separated by the two toilet cabins. By 1933 all the vehicles in this series were condemned.

Fig. 77

*DIAGRAM G16* **Fig. 77**
First Saloon (Clerestory)
Lot 150
Running numbers: 9005–6
Dimensions: 29ft. 0¾in. x 8ft. 0¾in.

*DIAGRAM G16*
This design is different again. The single toilet cabin at one end of the carriage is balanced by a small coupe with three large end windows. Access to the lavatory is provided by doors between the compartments. In contrast to the previous designs, both the clerestory and the main roof are of the single-arc type. As the use for family saloons declined, these two vehicles were converted to parcels vans.

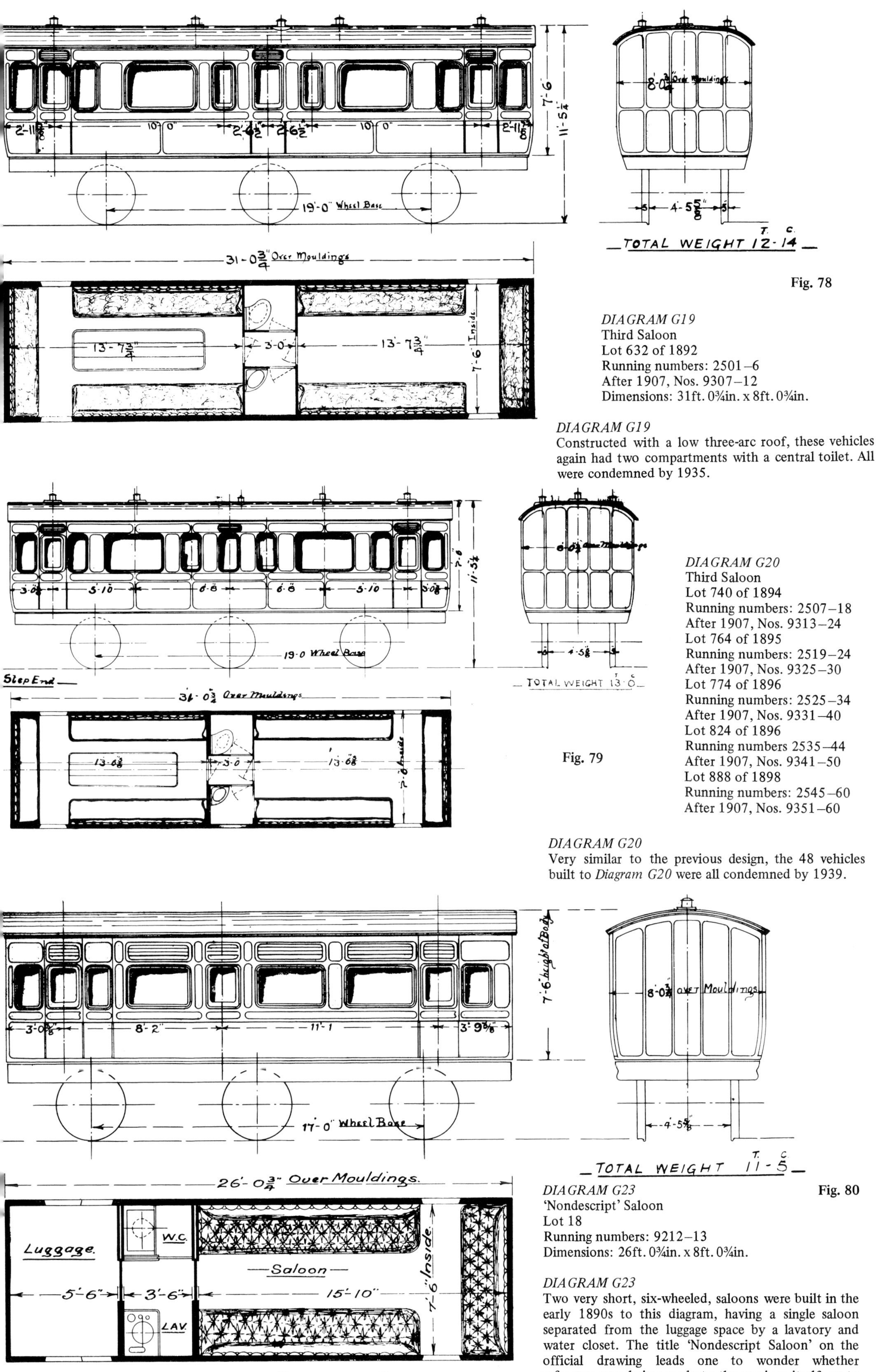


Fig. 78

*DIAGRAM G19*
Third Saloon
Lot 632 of 1892
Running numbers: 2501–6
After 1907, Nos. 9307–12
Dimensions: 31ft. 0¾in. x 8ft. 0¾in.

*DIAGRAM G19*
Constructed with a low three-arc roof, these vehicles again had two compartments with a central toilet. All were condemned by 1935.

*DIAGRAM G20*
Third Saloon
Lot 740 of 1894
Running numbers: 2507–18
After 1907, Nos. 9313–24
Lot 764 of 1895
Running numbers: 2519–24
After 1907, Nos. 9325–30
Lot 774 of 1896
Running numbers: 2525–34
After 1907, Nos. 9331–40
Lot 824 of 1896
Running numbers 2535–44
After 1907, Nos. 9341–50
Lot 888 of 1898
Running numbers: 2545–60
After 1907, Nos. 9351–60

Fig. 79

*DIAGRAM G20*
Very similar to the previous design, the 48 vehicles built to *Diagram G20* were all condemned by 1939.

*DIAGRAM G23*
'Nondescript' Saloon
Lot 18
Running numbers: 9212–13
Dimensions: 26ft. 0¾in. x 8ft. 0¾in.

Fig. 80

*DIAGRAM G23*
Two very short, six-wheeled, saloons were built in the early 1890s to this diagram, having a single saloon separated from the luggage space by a lavatory and water closet. The title 'Nondescript Saloon' on the official drawing leads one to wonder whether reference was being made to the carriage itself, or to the passengers it was expected to carry! Both vehicles were condemned in 1930.

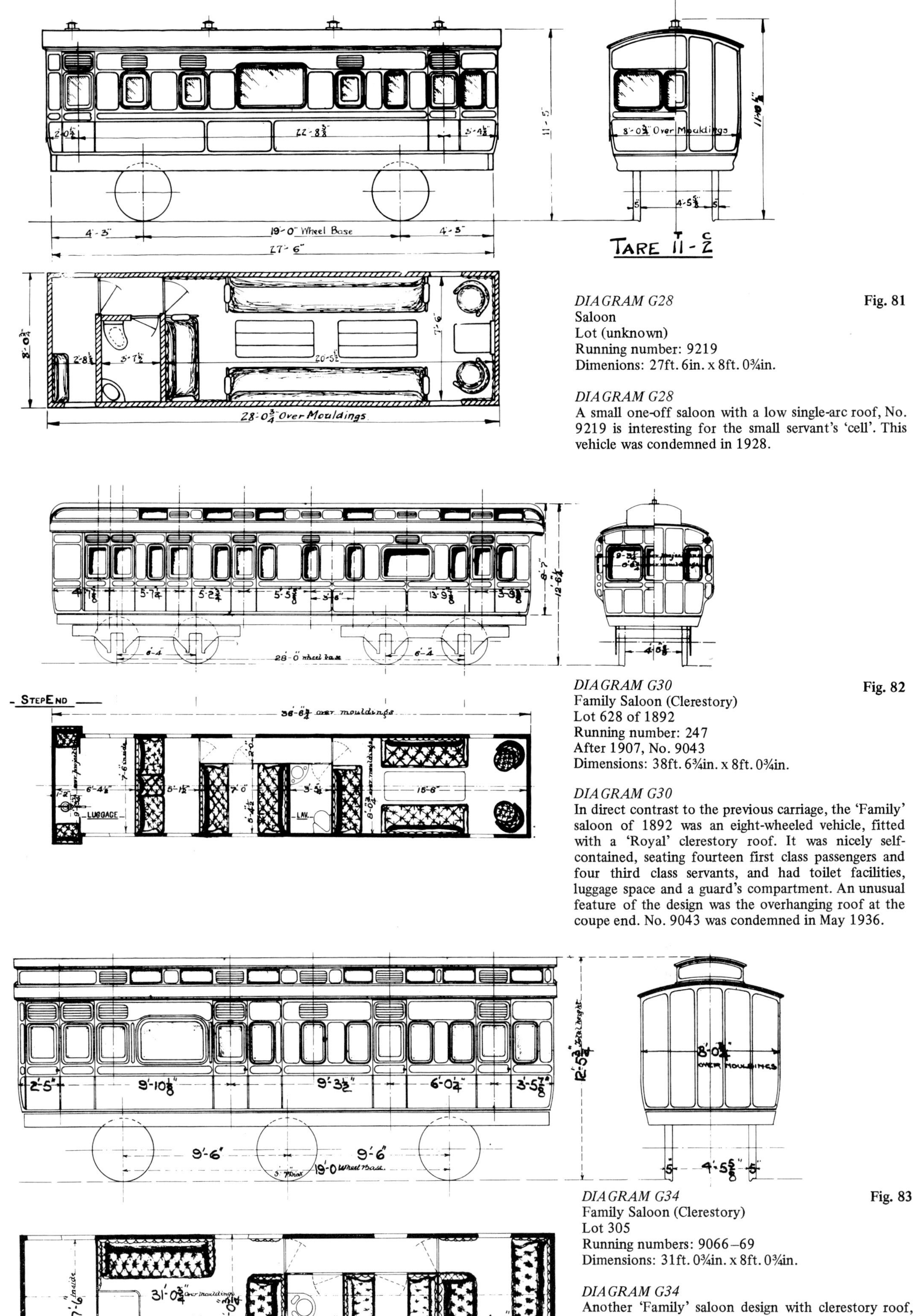


*DIAGRAM G28* **Fig. 81**
Saloon
Lot (unknown)
Running number: 9219
Dimenions: 27ft. 6in. x 8ft. 0¾in.

*DIAGRAM G28*
A small one-off saloon with a low single-arc roof, No. 9219 is interesting for the small servant's 'cell'. This vehicle was condemned in 1928.

*DIAGRAM G30* **Fig. 82**
Family Saloon (Clerestory)
Lot 628 of 1892
Running number: 247
After 1907, No. 9043
Dimensions: 38ft. 6¾in. x 8ft. 0¾in.

*DIAGRAM G30*
In direct contrast to the previous carriage, the 'Family' saloon of 1892 was an eight-wheeled vehicle, fitted with a 'Royal' clerestory roof. It was nicely self-contained, seating fourteen first class passengers and four third class servants, and had toilet facilities, luggage space and a guard's compartment. An unusual feature of the design was the overhanging roof at the coupe end. No. 9043 was condemned in May 1936.

*DIAGRAM G34* **Fig. 83**
Family Saloon (Clerestory)
Lot 305
Running numbers: 9066–69
Dimensions: 31ft. 0¾in. x 8ft. 0¾in.

*DIAGRAM G34*
Another 'Family' saloon design with clerestory roof, but running on six wheels, was *Diagram G34*. This plan had a small corridor on one side linking all the compartments. The external appearance of the design was characterized by the large saloon window and the off-centre ventilator for the toilet compartment. These carriages ended their days as parcels vans.

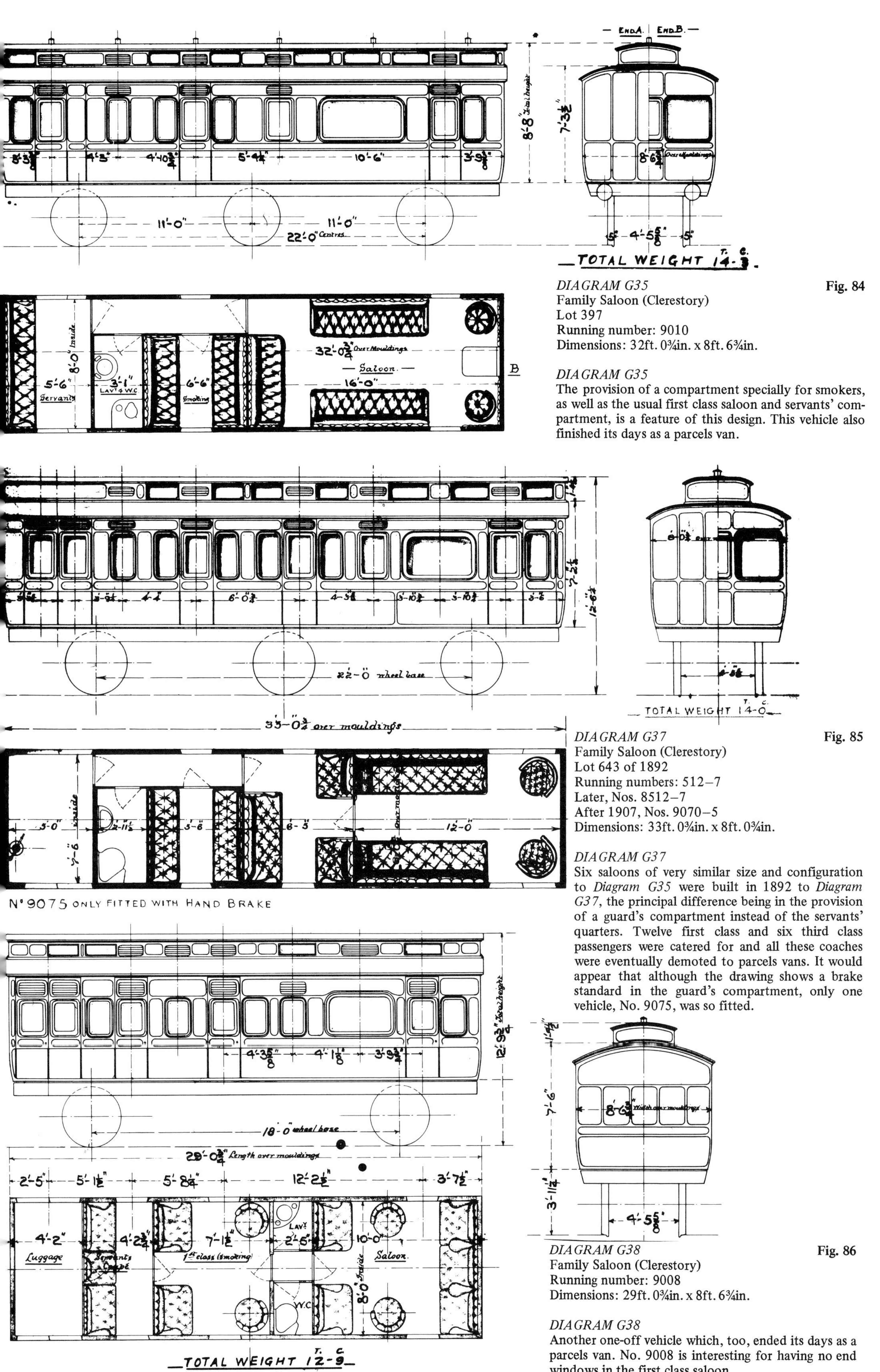


*DIAGRAM G35* **Fig. 84**

Family Saloon (Clerestory)
Lot 397
Running number: 9010
Dimensions: 32ft. 0¾in. x 8ft. 6¾in.

*DIAGRAM G35*

The provision of a compartment specially for smokers, as well as the usual first class saloon and servants' compartment, is a feature of this design. This vehicle also finished its days as a parcels van.

*DIAGRAM G37* **Fig. 85**

Family Saloon (Clerestory)
Lot 643 of 1892
Running numbers: 512–7
Later, Nos. 8512–7
After 1907, Nos. 9070–5
Dimensions: 33ft. 0¾in. x 8ft. 0¾in.

*DIAGRAM G37*

Six saloons of very similar size and configuration to *Diagram G35* were built in 1892 to *Diagram G37*, the principal difference being in the provision of a guard's compartment instead of the servants' quarters. Twelve first class and six third class passengers were catered for and all these coaches were eventually demoted to parcels vans. It would appear that although the drawing shows a brake standard in the guard's compartment, only one vehicle, No. 9075, was so fitted.

*DIAGRAM G38* **Fig. 86**

Family Saloon (Clerestory)
Running number: 9008
Dimensions: 29ft. 0¾in. x 8ft. 6¾in.

*DIAGRAM G38*

Another one-off vehicle which, too, ended its days as a parcels van. No. 9008 is interesting for having no end windows in the first class saloon.

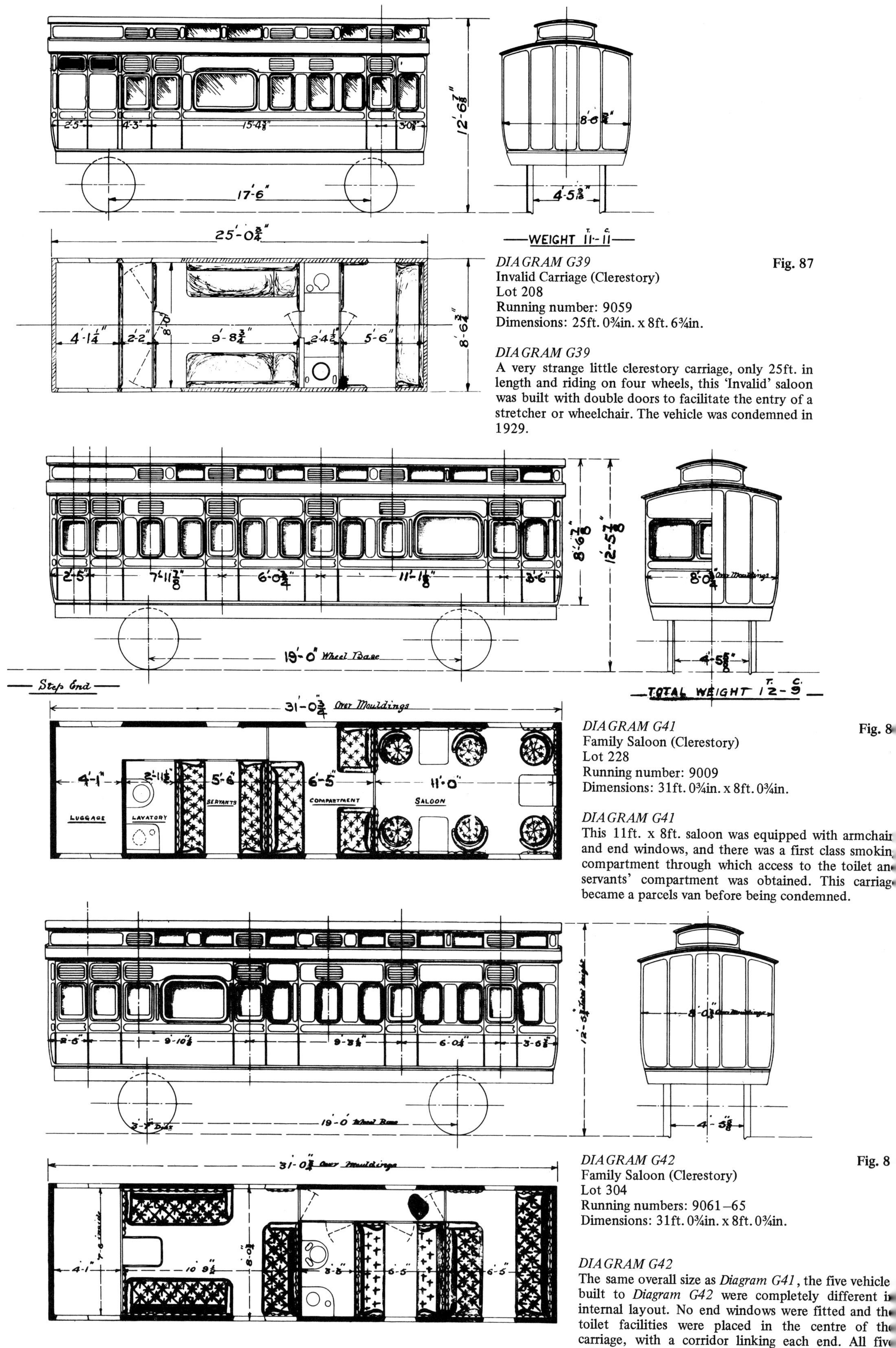


*DIAGRAM G39* **Fig. 87**
Invalid Carriage (Clerestory)
Lot 208
Running number: 9059
Dimensions: 25ft. 0¾in. x 8ft. 6¾in.

*DIAGRAM G39*

A very strange little clerestory carriage, only 25ft. in length and riding on four wheels, this 'Invalid' saloon was built with double doors to facilitate the entry of a stretcher or wheelchair. The vehicle was condemned in 1929.

*DIAGRAM G41* **Fig. 8**
Family Saloon (Clerestory)
Lot 228
Running number: 9009
Dimensions: 31ft. 0¾in. x 8ft. 0¾in.

*DIAGRAM G41*

This 11ft. x 8ft. saloon was equipped with armchair and end windows, and there was a first class smokin compartment through which access to the toilet an servants' compartment was obtained. This carriag became a parcels van before being condemned.

*DIAGRAM G42* **Fig. 8**
Family Saloon (Clerestory)
Lot 304
Running numbers: 9061–65
Dimensions: 31ft. 0¾in. x 8ft. 0¾in.

*DIAGRAM G42*

The same overall size as *Diagram G41*, the five vehicle built to *Diagram G42* were completely different i internal layout. No end windows were fitted and th toilet facilities were placed in the centre of th carriage, with a corridor linking each end. All fiv vehicles were eventually stripped to serve as parcel vans.

Fig. 90

*DIAGRAM G33*

After the short foray into the four and six-wheeled saloons, **Fig. 90** shows one of the *Diagram G33* series of first class bogie saloons, as built in 1900. This is No. 225 in the original livery of the period. **Fig. 91** shows the same vehicle in the 1910 period, after re-numbering. Changes, apart from the livery, are the removal of the protection bars from the droplights in the guard's compartment, the substitution of hammered glass for the etched panes in the toilet compartments and the provision of a ventilating section in one of these windows. The vehicle has also been fitted with the Westinghouse brake, presumably to allow it to work on to 'foreign' lines where this system of braking was used.

Fig. 91

*DIAGRAM G33*
**Figs. 92 & 93** show alternate ends of No. 9024 in 1947. The livery at this time is still the wartime all-over brown with straw lettering. Notice that, at this late stage in its life, the carriage has been fitted with full electric light and the associated dynamo and battery, and regulator boxes.

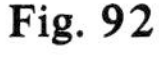
**Fig. 92**

**Fig. 93**

*DIAGRAM G33*
First Saloon (Clerestory)
Lot 950 of 1900
Running numbers: 223–6
Later, Nos. 8223–6
After 1907, Nos. 9027–30

Lot 1046 of 1904
Running numbers: 219–20
Later, Nos. 8219–20
After 1907, Nos. 9023–24
Dimensions: 47ft. 6¾in. x 8ft. 6¾in.

Lot 1027 of 1903
Running numbers: 221–2
Later, Nos. 8221–2
After 1907, Nos. 9025–6

Lot 1051 of 1904
Running numbers: 217–8
Later, Nos. 8217–8
After 1907, Nos. 9021–2

94

*DIAGRAM G45*

In the late 1920s several of the *Diagram G33* series were revamped as Invalid saloons and given the revised *Diagram 45.* **Fig. 94** shows No. 9021 at Old Oak Common after conversion in 1928. The larger picture **(Fig. 95)** shows the suspended settee and folding table in the restyled saloon of No. 9025. The photograph dates from 1921 when the coach was given first class classification. The complicated arrangement of springs and turnbuckles, seen beneath the foot of the settee, was designed to smooth out any jolts, or tendency to swing, induced by a less than perfect permanent way!

Fig. 95

IMPERIAL DIRECT WEST INDIA MAIL SERVICE JAMAICA VIA AVONMOUTH
303

Four handsome saloons were built to this design in 1901. **Fig. 96** *(above)* illustrates No. 303 fitted with roof boards for the Jamaica Service via Avonmouth, a promotion which only lasted for a short period. The corridor side is nearest the camera.

Lot 980 of 1901
Running numbers: 300–3
Later, Nos. 8300–3
After 1907, Nos. 9046–9
Dimensions: 52ft. 0¾in. x 8ft. 6¾in.

**Fig. 97**

This page illustrates the difference between *Diagram G33 & G47*. In **Fig. 97** the compartment side of No. 9046 to *Diagram G47* is seen in the 1925 livery, and in **Fig. 98** the corridor side of No. 9025 of the *Diagram G33* series can be seen at Old Oak Common, in 1912.

**Fig. 98**

Fig. 99

*DIAGRAM G53*
The saloon shown on this page started life as a restaurant car in 1900. One of two built to *Diagram H2* under Lot 929 they were originally numbered 236–237. They later became Nos. 8236–7 and, after 1907, they were given the numbers 9516–17. Eventually, after World War I, No. 9517 was refitted as a saloon with a dining room. It became No. 9097 and was given *Diagram G53*. **Fig. 99** shows the exterior of the carriage and **Fig. 100** shows the first class dining room, looking through from the lavatory end.

*DIAGRAM G53*
First Saloon (Clerestory)
Lot (unknown)
Running number: 9097
Dimensions: 56ft. 0¾in. x 8ft. 6¾in.

These two photographs *(opposite)* show, very well, the difference between the normal first class saloon decor and the opulence of the 'Special' classification. The upper picture **(Fig. 101)** shows the main saloon in vehicle No. 9055, a toplight saloon built to *Diagram G43*, and the lower illustration **(Fig. 102)** shows the coupe end of No. 9100. This latter vehicle was a hybrid created by the mounting of a 54ft. x 9ft. elliptical type body on the underframe of the old 'Queen's Saloon' in 1912. The vehicle was given the title 'Official Saloon' and *Diagram Q,* and no lot number was issued for the conversion. Initially, the vehicle was used by the Chief Mechanical Engineer, George Jackson Churchward.

Fig. 100

Fig. 103

Fig. 104

*DIAGRAM G43*
First Saloon (Toplight)
Lot 1209 of 1912
Running number: 9055
Dimensions: 57ft. x 9ft.

*DIAGRAM G43*
**Fig. 103** shows No. 9055 as built in 1912 and painted in the crimson lake livery of that period. Note that no indication of class appears on the waist panels of the doors. The interior of the saloon is shown on the previous page **(Fig. 101)**.

Fig. 105

*DIAGRAM G55*
Third Saloon (Multibar Toplight)
Lot 1305 of 1921
Running numbers: 9372–4
Dimensions: 57ft. x 8ft. 11¼in.

*DIAGRAM G55*
**Figs. 104 & 105** show both sides of No. 9373, in 1951. Note that the toplights have been sheeted over and that the underframe is of the angle-trussed type.

Fig. 106

*DIAGRAM G56*
Saloon
Lot 1250 of 1923
Running numbers: 9369–71
Dimensions: 56ft. 11¼in. x 8ft. 11¼in.

*DIAGRAM G56*
Note, again, the angle-trussed underframe and that the bogies are of the 1914 pattern.

*DIAGRAM G59*
First Saloon
Lot 1431 of 1930
Running numbers: 9004–5
Dimensions: 61ft. 4½in. x 9ft. 0in.

*DIAGRAM G59*
In contrast to the previous design were the two vehicles to *Diagram G59*, which had the same basic outlines as the 'Cornish Riviera' stock. **Fig. 107** shows No. 9055 in 1951 after being modernized. The bow-ended configuration can be seen, as can the end windows of the coupe. (See also *GW Coaches, Part II, page 164*).

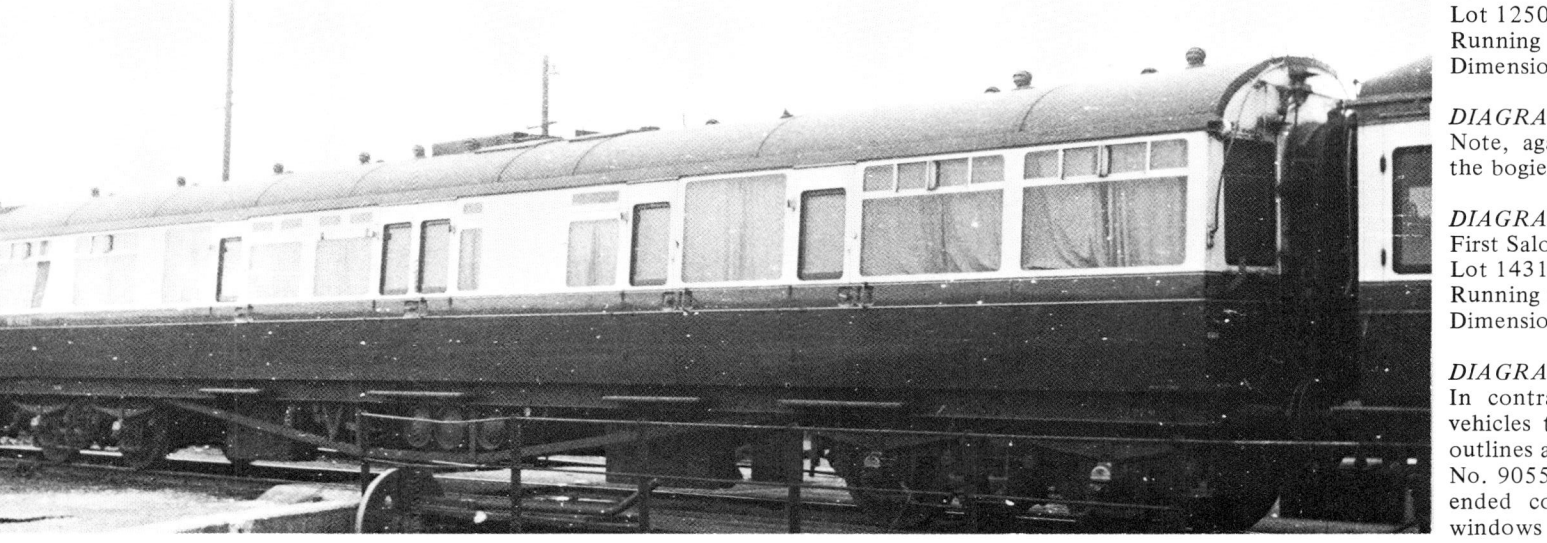

Fig. 107

Fig. 108

Two official pictures of the *Diagram G59* saloons. **Fig. 108** illustrates No. 9004 as it appeared at the beginning of World War II and is photographed from the corridor side of the carriage. **Fig. 109** shows No. 9005 from the reverse side, and was photographed in 1947. A feature, which only becomes obvious when two photographs are put together, is that the handrails and roof steps appear to have been fitted to opposite ends of the two coaches. The *Diagram G59* saloons were completely self-contained, being equipped with a kitchen, pantry and guard's compartment, and were intended for private hire on occasions such as Newbury Races or Henley Regatta. Until 1961, both vehicles ran on 7ft. 6in. bogies, but in that year No. 9005 was one of the first vehicles to be fitted with B R B4 type bogies.

Fig. 109

Fig. 110

The interior fittings of the two bow-ended saloons were indeed luxurious, as can be seen from the next three illustrations. On the left **(Fig. 110)** is the dining saloon with its separate armchairs, and on the right **(Fig. 111)** is the lounge saloon with settees and a large multiwave radio fixed to the bulkhead. The view in the opposite direction **(Fig. 112)**, looking out through the end of the coupe, shows that, although fitted with gangways, the communicating door was glazed so that a complete end view was obtained, providing no blank door was placed on the gangway bellows.

Fig. 112

Fig. 111

Fig. 113

Two final pictures of the special saloons as they appeared in the 1950s. In the upper photograph **(Fig. 113)** No. 9004 is seen with the corridor side nearer the camera, and in the lower view **(Fig. 114)** No. 9005 has been photographed from the kitchen side, as can be detected by the frosted glass lights. In the 1960s, No. 9005 became the General Manager's Saloon and No. 9004 was sent to the North Eastern Region for service to the Chief Civil Engineer. Note that these carriages have the full livery on both ends.

Fig. 114

Fig. 115

*DIAGRAMS G60 & G61*
The 'Super Saloons' were a series of special vehicles which were originally constructed in 1931/2 to take the place of the short-lived 'Pullman' service for the 'Ocean Liner' and 'Torquay Pullman' expresses of 1929. As a result of this, they were familiarly known as 'Pullman's' or 'Cunard' stock. Their width of 9ft. 7in. was to the extreme of the loading gauge and the recessed doors were necessary to allow steps for access and to ensure that, if a door should open during a journey, little damage would be done. When built, they were all given 'Royal' names, No. 9111 being *King George* and No. 9112, of course, *Queen Mary*. Full details are given in the companion to this volume, *GW Coaches, Part II*. These magnificent carriages were only used for special or Royal occasions and, therefore, lasted much longer than ordinary service stock. In fact, three are preserved by the Great Western Society at Didcot and another two by the Dart Valley Railway at Buckfastleigh. **Figs. 115 & 116** show Nos. 9111 and 9112 in British Railways' days, painted in chocolate and cream and with a single waist lining (see also *GW Coaches, Part II, pages 174–178*).

*DIAGRAMS G60 & G61*
'Super Saloons'
Lot 1471 of 1932
Running numbers: 9111–2 *(Diagram G60)*
Running numbers: 9113–8 *(Diagram G61)*
Dimensions: 61 ft. 4½in. x 9ft. 7in.

Fig. 116

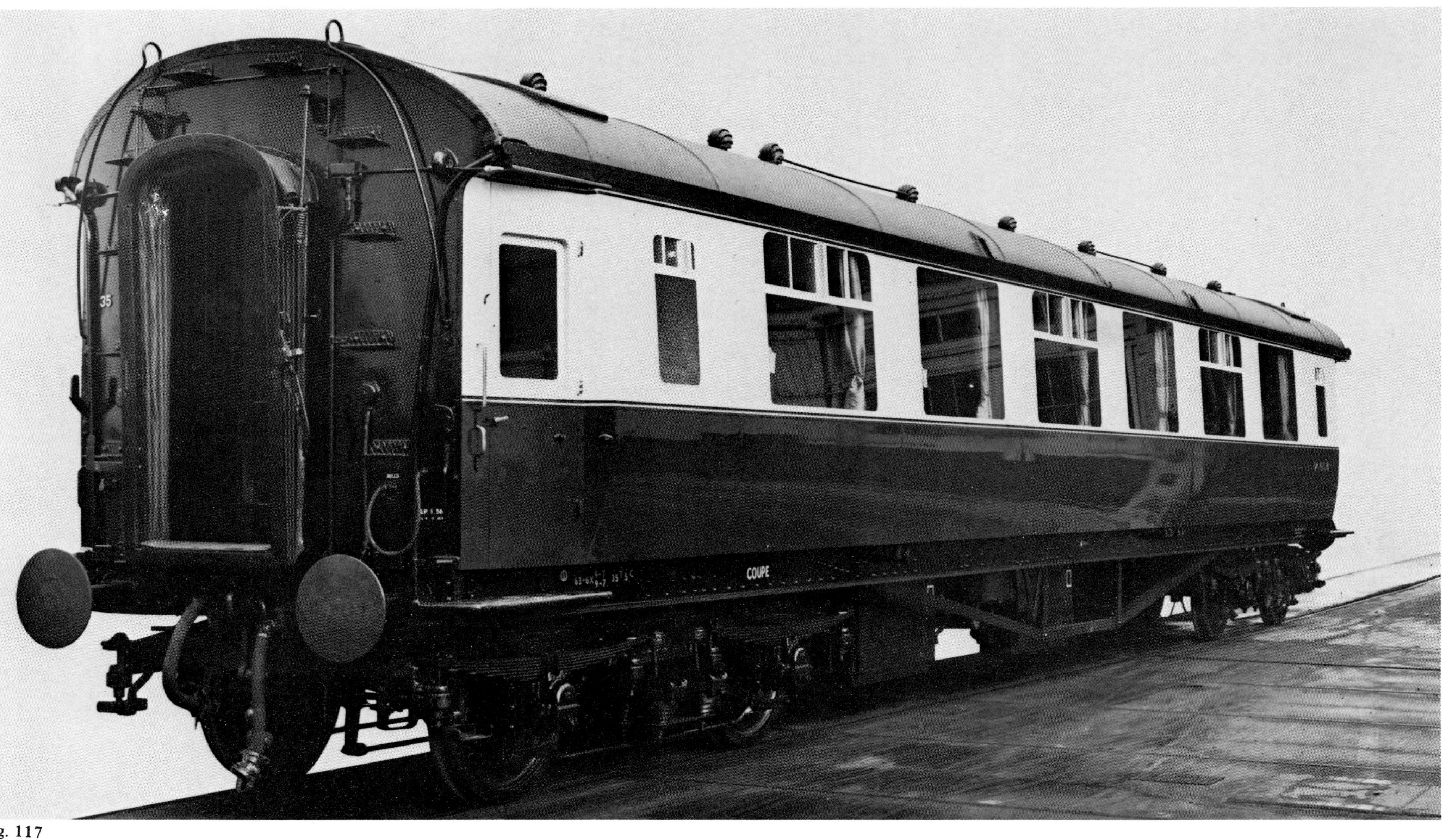


**Fig. 117**

*DIAGRAM G60*

**Fig. 117**

This perspective view of the old *King George* saloon No. 9111 shows well the full-bodied lines of these vehicles, and the cut-away flat doors and bow-ends to advantage. The lavatory side is seen nearest the camera and worthy of note is the extra flexible cable for the operation of the instruction bells.

Fig. 118

Two photographs, illustrating the corridor side of No. 9114 (ex-*Duke of York*) in British Railways' days. **Fig. 118** shows the carriage in 1951 painted in the livery of strawberry and cream. In 1954 No. 9114 was shopped at Swindon and appeared again in the chocolate and cream livery as shown in the large official view in **Fig. 119**. Although two separate diagrams were allotted to the 'Super Saloons', the only difference between the two seems to have been in the details of the interior trim and furnishings. The furnishing of the two vehices, to *Diagram G60*, was contracted to Messrs Trollope & Sons whilst the remaining six vehicles, to *Diagram G61*, were finished by Swindon in the standard GWR fashion. The result of this was that the *Diagram G60* vehicles were panelled with walnut between the windows and on the coupe ends, whereas the *Diagram G61* carriages had large scenic photographs in these positions.

Fig. 119

Fig. 120

In 1935, Nos. 9117 and 9118 were drastically altered to provide dining facilities. This meant having a kitchen at one end which used up most of the space which had previously been taken by the large coupe compartment. **Fig. 120** shows No. 9117 in 1952 at Old Oak Common, still retaining the double waist lining, and No. 9116 is shown for comparison in **Fig. 121**.

*DIAGRAM G62*
First Saloon
Lot 1626 of 1940
Running numbers: 9001–2
Dimensions: 60ft. 11¾in. x 8ft. 11in.

Fig. 121

*DIAGRAM G62*
Two special duty vehicles were built to this design for VIP use in 1940. In the first picture, **(Fig. 122)** No. 9001 is seen inside the stock shed at Old Oak Common in 1950 (see also *GW Coaches, Part II, page 246*).

Fig. 122

**Figs. 123 & 124** *(below)* are official photographs of No. 9001 taken at Swindon in 1954. Although the coaches were 70ft. long, their width was kept down to 8ft. 11in. to enable them to work through on to other companies' lines. This made them more versatile than the *Diagram G60 & G61* vehicles. Note also that the stock had a tare weight of 42 tons and was therefore mounted on heavy duty six-wheeled bogies.

W 9001

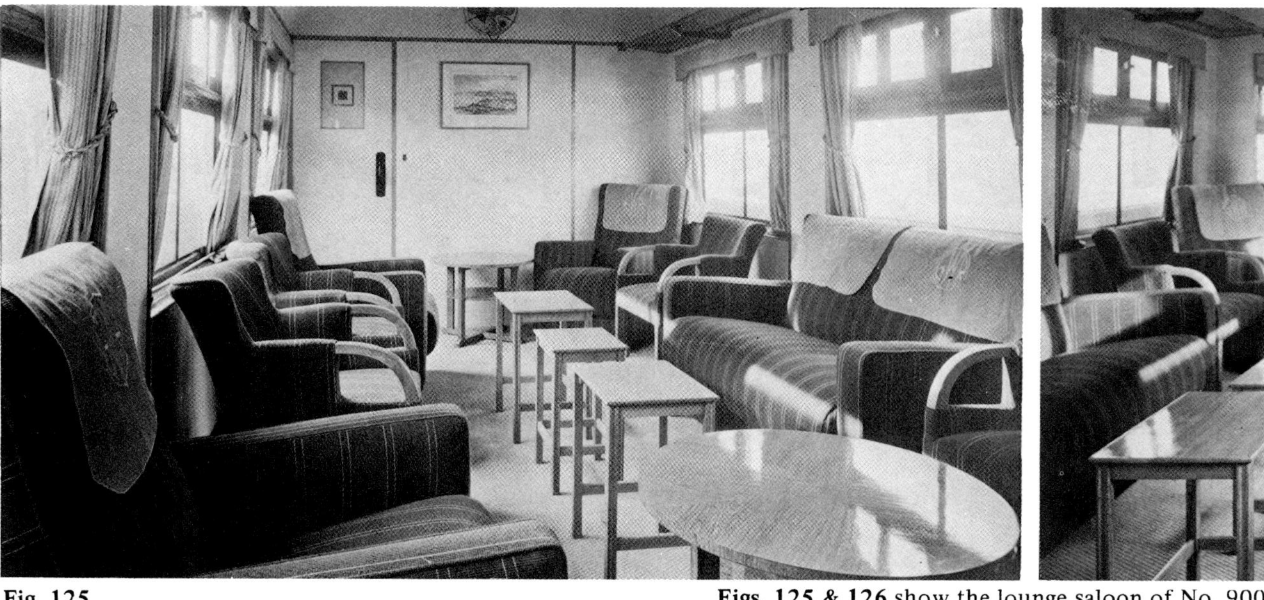

Fig. 125

Fig. 126

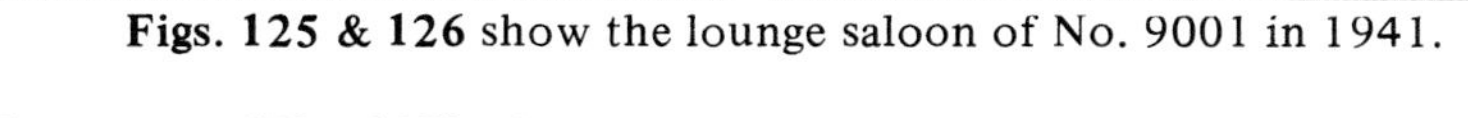

**Figs. 125 & 126** show the lounge saloon of No. 9001 in 1941.

In the illustration, **(Fig. 127)**, the usual arrangement of double seats on one side of the gangway, and singles on the other side, can be seen in the dining saloon of No. 9002. The picture **(Fig. 128)** depicts the lounge of the same vehicle with its prominent radio and typical period decor.

Fig. 127

Fig. 128

Fig. 129

All these 'special' saloons were fitted with electric lighting but they retained gas equipment for cooking. **Fig. 129** shows the ovens, rings and plate-warming racks in the kitchen of No. 9002. **Fig. 130** shows the interior of the toilet compartment.

*DIAGRAMS G64 & G65*
Special Saloons
Lot 1673 of 1945
Running numbers: 9006 *(Diagram G64)*
Running numbers: 9007 *(Diagram G65)*
Dimensions: 60ft. 11¼in. x 8ft. 11in.

Fig. 130

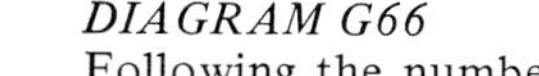

Fig. 131

*DIAGRAMS G64 & G65*
Lot 1675 was the last order for saloons given by the old Great Western Railway and was for two vehicles of similar dimensions but differing in internal layout. Details of the interiors are shown in the photographs that follow. No. 9006 is seen in **Fig. 131** and No. 9007 in **Fig. 132** (see also *GW Coaches, Part II, page 258*).

*DIAGRAM G66*
Following the numbering sequence of the saloon diagrams, the final diagram allocated to a Great Western-built saloon was *Diagram G66* which was given to No. 9005 when it was outshopped in 1961 with B4 bogies. **Fig. 133** shows the coach in this condition.

Fig. 132

Fig. 133

**Fig. 134**

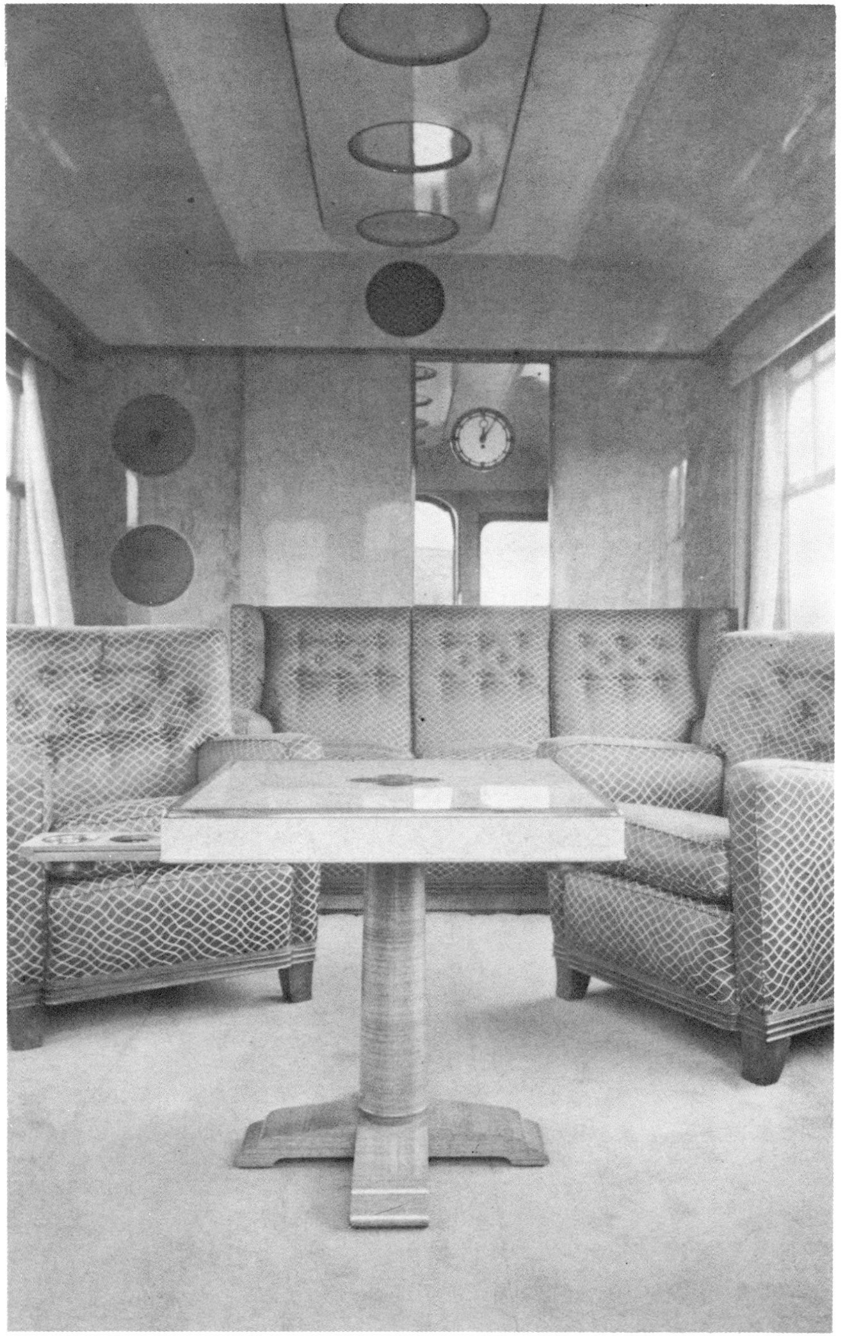

Nos. 9006 and 9007 were unusual in being mounted on underframes which were taken from war-damaged stock, and they commonly worked together as a VIP set. No. 9006 was equipped with a kitchen, dining room, two bedrooms a bathroom and two lounges. **Fig. 134** shows the view towards the coupe end of one of the lounges. The elaborate panelling and the table, apparently veneered in oak and maple, are worthy of note, as is the speedometer above the gangway door. **Fig. 135** shows the view towards the centre of the carriage. No. 9007 also had a lounge, together with two large bedrooms and a guard's compartment, with a radio.

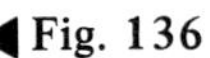

Fig. 136

**Fig. 136** shows the spacious corridor in No. 9006 which linked the lounge with the two small bedrooms. The doors on the left are respectively, the toilet, bedroom 1 and bedroom 2. The dining room, which seated eight people, is shown in **Fig. 137** and the corridor door, with its three unusual circular lights, is on the right-hand side. The distinctive clock can be seen, mounted in the mirror, as in **Fig. 134**. Examination of the clocks will reveal the order in which the photographs were taken.

Fig. 137

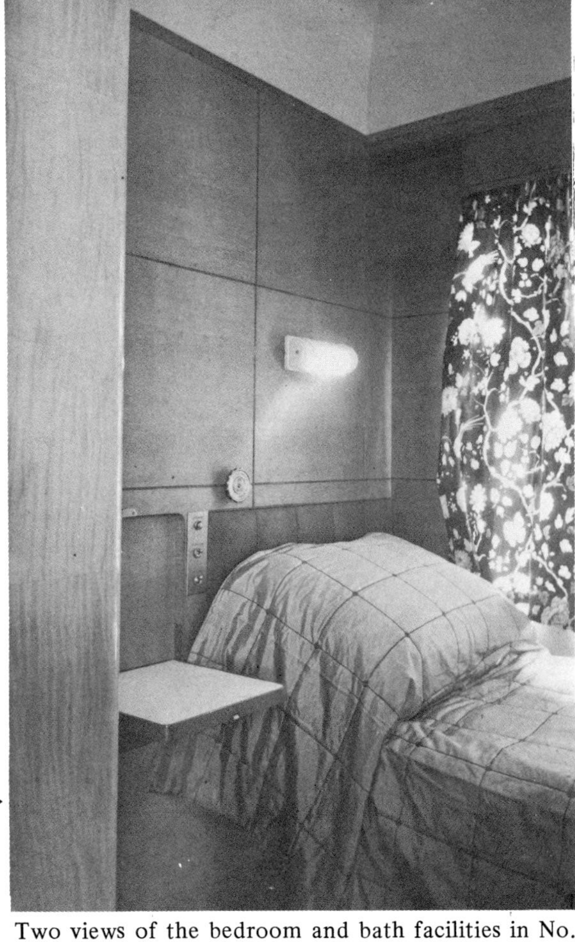

Fig. 138

Two views of the bedroom and bath facilities in No. 9006. **Fig. 138** shows one of the two single bedrooms with its chintz curtains and fold-down bedside table. The tiny bathroom is seen, in all its stark simplicity, in **Fig. 139**. There are waterproof curtains to be drawn over the ventilators and, in emergency, this panel could be used as an escape hatch.

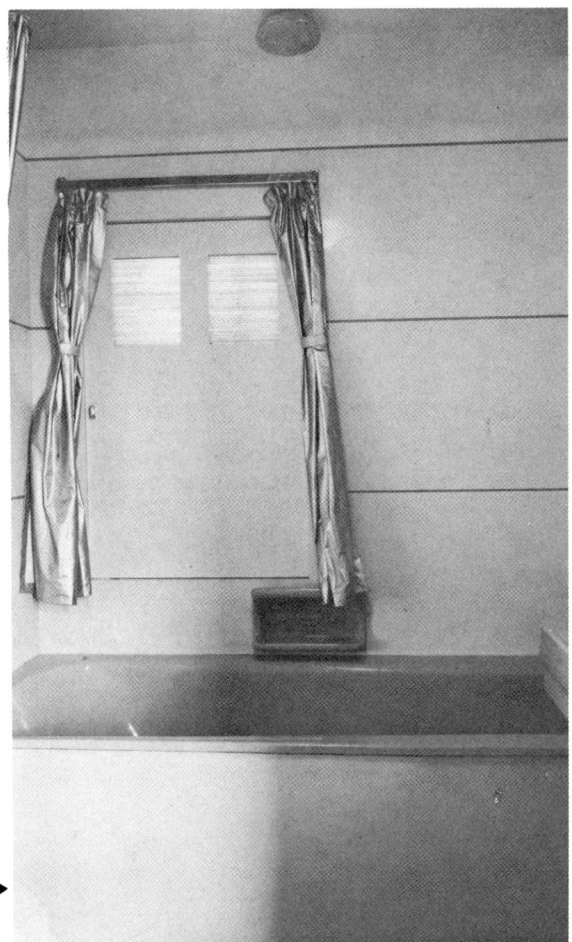

Fig. 139

Fig. 140

**Fig. 140** shows a three-quarter view of No. 9006 portraying the kitchen end and corridor side, in the 1950s, when both this carriage and No. 9007, had been fitted with air-conditioning and portable steps, for use in the Western Region Royal Train. At this period, the carriages were still painted in the chocolate and cream livery, with a double waist lining. Note that the end nearest the camera, being the non-coupe end, is painted black.

**Fig. 141**

**Fig. 141** is taken from the opposite corner of No. 9006 and shows that the coupe end has received the full livery. In 1955, both Nos. 9006 and 9007 were furnished internally and painted in the dark claret with grey roofs Royal livery in order that they could be used in the Royal Train. **Figs. 142 & 143** show the carriages in this livery.

**Fig. 142**

**Fig. 143**

ɪhe late introduction of dining cars on the Great Western ailway stemmed from a number of factors. The first was an ıfavourable report on the operation of such vehicles which as submitted by the Traffic Department in 1891. In essence, is report showed that the LNWR and GNR were operating ning cars at only a very small margin over operating costs at a slight loss. If the costs of the construction of the hicles were also set against receipts, a loss was inevitably own. The second factor was that the services on which the rs would be best employed, to Wales and the West of ıgland, passed through Swindon where all trains were quired to stop in order that passengers could use the otorious' refreshment room. Until the operators could be ought out, or the contract imposing the condition could be scinded, any facilities provided on the train would be superıous. In addition to these factors, at the time when dining rs were being considered, the carriage works were heavily committed to the conversion of broad gauge stock to the standard gauge.

*AGRAM H2*
rst Diners (Clerestory)
ɔt 801 of 1896
ınning numbers: 250–2
ter, Nos. 8250–2
ter 1907, Nos. 9501–3
ɔt 843 of 1897
ınning number: 235
ter, No. 8235
ter 1907, No. 9504
ɔt 929 of 1900
ınning numbers: 236–7
ter, Nos. 8236–7
ter 1907, Nos. 9516–7 (No. 9517 renumbered 9097 before 1920).
mensions: 56ft. 0¾in. x 8ft. 6¾in.

*DIAGRAM H2*

The three vehicles ordered on Lot 801 were, therefore, the first dining cars to be built for the Great Western Railway. Each vehicle seated sixteen first class passengers, in accommodation that was rather more richly finished than was normal, and was equipped with a kitchen/pantry and two lavatories, as the occupants were expected to remain in the dining car for the whole journey. The first use of the carriages was in the 'South Wales Corridor' set of 1896, with one vehicle being allocated. A second carriage was allocated to a West of England express, but only as far as Bristol, and the third vehicle was spare. No. 235 was probably built to allow the facility to be extended to other routes, as were the pair built to Lot 929. In the early 1900s, the 1896 and 1900-built carriages were rebuilt as composites and the lavatories were removed. This increased seating capacity for all classes, to twenty nine. World War I saw Nos. 9501 and 9502 marshalled into an ambulance train to provide meals and refreshments. The building of new restaurant cars from 1929–31 made these pioneer vehicles redundant and all but Nos. 9502 and 9516 were withdrawn. The two survivors were given a face-lift and re-emerged in 1932 as 'Cafe Cars', a GWR euphemism for 'Buffet Car'. In 1936 they were withdrawn but may have been given a stay of execution employed in two exhibition trains. **Fig. 144** shows No. 252 of the original batch, as built, with the class and title of the coach in large letters on a cream waist panel (see also *GW Coaches, Part I, pages 82 & 18 and GW Coaches, Part II, page 3*).

**Fig. 144**

*IAGRAM H7*

his was a series of four vehicles built as ɔmposites, originally three classes. **Fig. 145** ıows No. 1580, as built, carrying the roof oard for the 'South Wales Corridor'. In **Fig. 46**, No. 9520 is seen at York in 1932 with a ɔof board reading 'Oxford, Banbury, Leicester, ottingham, Sheffield, York & Newcastle' (see lso *GW Coaches, Part I, pages 200–202*).

*AGRAM H7* Composite Diner (Clerestory)
Lot 1010 of 1903
Running numbers: 580–1
Later, Nos. 1580–1
After 1907, Nos. 9518–9
Dimensions: 56ft. 0¾in. x 8ft. 6¾in.
Lot 1011 of 1903
Running numbers: 578–9
Later, Nos. 1578–9
After 1907, Nos. 9520–1

Fig. 148

*DIAGRAM H8*

No. 575 was the first of Churchward's new 'Dreadnought' stock to enter service and marked a radical departure from the traditional clerestory style for express stock. To begin with, the new restaurant cars were marshalled with the most recent clerestory sets, initially in a new service which ran non-stop from Paddington to Plymouth and then on to Penzance. This train very soon became known as the 'Cornish Riviera Limited', a prestige service, having the longest non-stop run in the world. The unusual dining cars were soon joined by a complimentary rake of stock. As built, the 'Dreadnought' diners were equipped with a central kitchen and two saloons, one of which was for first class only and the other for both second and third class. From 1936–8, Nos. 9509–9515 were modernized with flush steel panelling above the waist and larger windows. **Figs. 147 & 148** show No. 9511 in this condition in the stock shed at Old Oak Common in 1950, **Fig. 148** giving a view into the first class saloon. No. 9511 was unusual in that soon after being built, it was fitted with 'American' six-wheeled bogies, as can be seen. No. 9512 is seen in **Fig. 149** at Old Oak Common bearing the strawberry and cream livery. All these carriages were condemned by 1959 (see also *GW Coaches, Part I, page 221*).

*DIAGRAM H8*
Composite Diner (Dreadnought)
Lot 1056 of 1904
Running number: 575
Later, Nos. 1575
After 1907, No. 9515
Lot 1060 of 1904
Running numbers: 572–4
Later, Nos. 1572–4
After 1907, Nos. 9512–14
Lot 1076 of 1905
Running numbers: 569–71
Later, Nos. 1569–71
After 1907, Nos. 9509–11
Dimensions: 68ft. 0¾in. x 9ft. 6¾in.

Fig. 149

Fig. 151

*DIAGRAM H11*
Originally running on 9ft. 'American' type bogies, they were later given six-wheeled bogies. **Fig. 150** shows No. 9508 after reconditioning, in 1939/40, with six-wheeled bogies, and bearing the chocolate and cream livery with a dark grey roof.

*DIAGRAM H12*
This was a one-off conversion of a 'Concertina' 70ft. third, with two compartments being fitted out as a buffet.

*DIAGRAMS H13 & H14*
The only difference between the two designs was that vehicles to *Diagram H13* had bench type seats whereas those in *Diagram H14* were individual. Both designs would seat 42 first class passengers. **Fig. 151** depicts No. 9529 as reconditioned in 1931 and **Fig. 152** shows No. 9527 after reconditioning and the fitting of flush steel panelling to the saloon section in 1936 (see also *GW Coaches, Part II, page 37*).

*DIAGRAM H11*
Composite Diner (Dreadnought)
Lot 1086 of 1905
Running numbers: 567–8
Later, Nos. 1567–8
After 1907, Nos. 9507–8
Lot 1093 of 1905
Running numbers: 565–6
Later, Nos. 1565–6
After 1907, Nos. 9505–6
Dimensions: 70ft. 0in. x 9ft. 6¾in.

*DIAGRAMS H13 & H14*
First Diner (Concertina)
Lot 1114 of 1906 *(Diagram H13)*
Running numbers: 401–4
Later, Nos. 8401–4
After 1907, Nos. 9522–25
Lot 1115 of 1906 *(Diagram H14)*
Running numbers: 405–6
Later, Nos. 8405–6
After 1907, Nos. 9526–27
Lot 1118 of 1906 *(Diagram H13)*
Running numbers: 407–12
Later, Nos. 8407–12
After 1907, Nos. 9528–33
Dimensions: 70ft. 0in. x 9ft. 0in.

Fig. 152

*DIAGRAM H15*
**Fig. 153** shows No. 9540, as built, and illustrates well the imposing aspect of these 70ft. carriages when they were first turned out in the fully-lined livery. The 9ft. 'American' bogies, with which these vehicles were originally fitted, can also be seen. The roof board shows that, in spite of the initial reluctance to introduce dining cars, they soon found their way into services all over the system. **Fig. 154** is another view of the carriages as constructed, this time showing No. 9544 with roof boards for the 'South Wales Express'. The lettering on the board is cream on a brown background. **Fig. 155** is a second view of the same coach, after reconditioning and the fitting of large windows and ordinary plate bogies, in 1930 (see also *GW Coaches, Part II, pages 47–49*).

*DIAGRAM H15*
Dining Car (to seat 42)
Lot 1131 of 1907
Running numbers: 9534–45
Dimenions: 70ft. 0in. x 9ft. 0in.

▼ **Fig. 155**

Fig. 156

**Fig. 156**, taken at Old Oak Common in 1947, is of No. 9543 and shows the carriage after the small droplights had been replaced by larger windows with sliding ventilators. The carriage is still running on the six wheel bogies that were fitted in 1938. Note the frosted glass in the kitchen windows.

◀ Fig. 157

Fig. 158

**Figs. 157 & 158** show both sides of Nc. 9542 still running on 9ft. plate bogies in 1952. The flush steel panelling of the saloon er.d can again be seen.

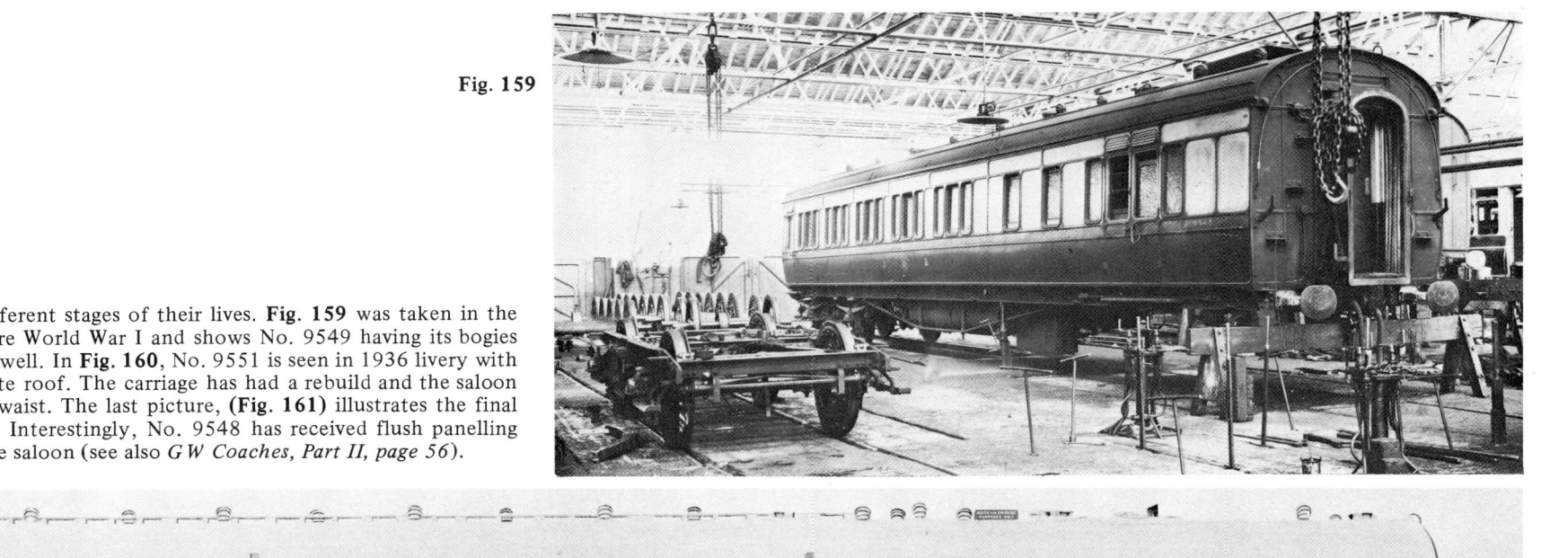

*DIAGRAM H16*
Dining car (to seat 30)
Lot 1140 of 1908
Running numbers: 9546–51
Dimensions: 57ft. 0in. x 9ft. 0in.

*DIAGRAM H16*
Three pictures of this design at different stages of their lives. **Fig. 159** was taken in the carriage shop at Swindon just before World War I and shows No. 9549 having its bogies changed, using the special transfer well. In **Fig. 160**, No. 9551 is seen in 1936 livery with the 'roundel' monogram and a white roof. The carriage has had a rebuild and the saloon has been flush-panelled above the waist. The last picture, **(Fig. 161)** illustrates the final style of painting under the GWR. Interestingly, No. 9548 has received flush panelling on the kitchen section, as well as the saloon (see also *G W Coaches, Part II, page 56*).

**Fig. 159**

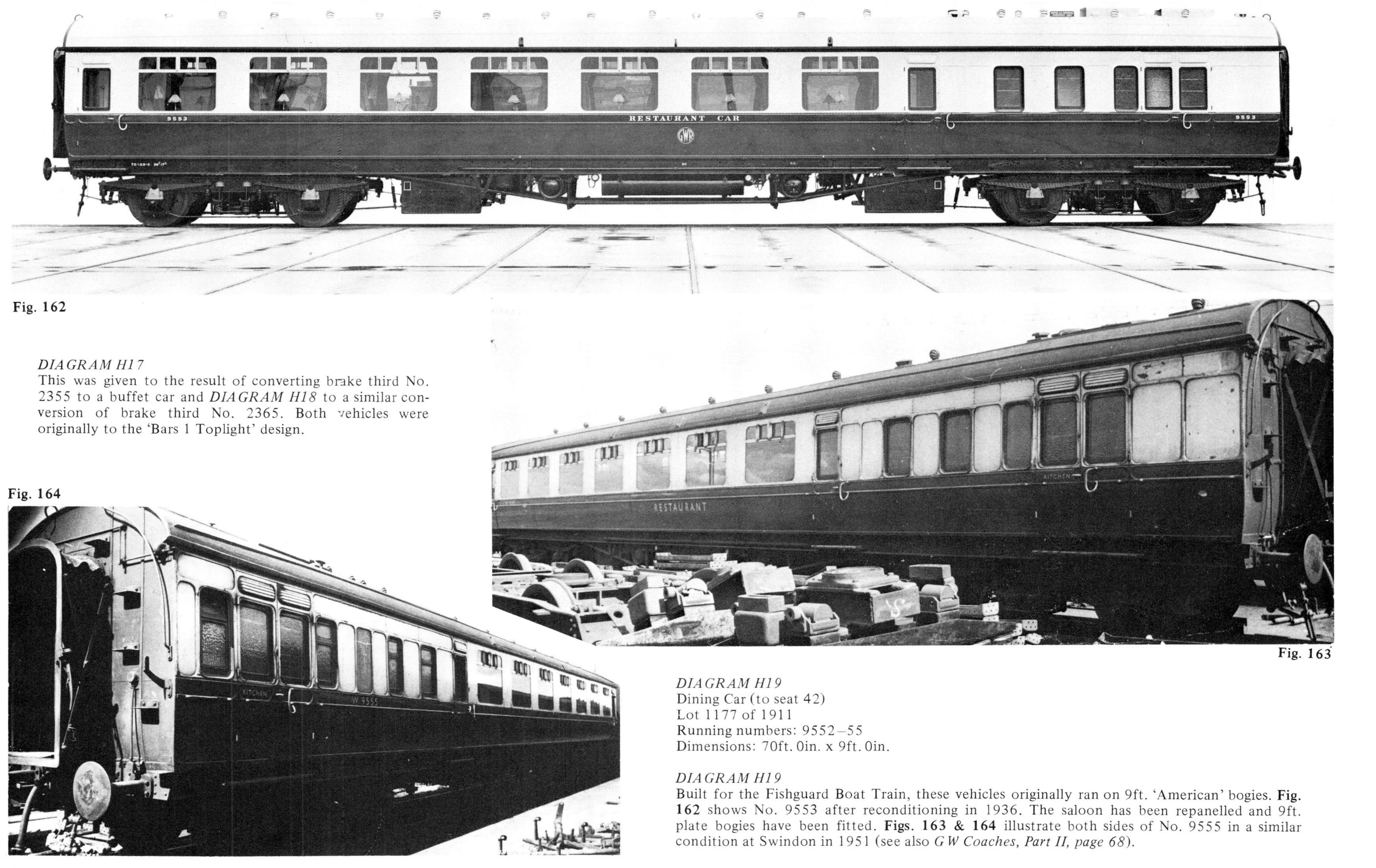


Fig. 162

*DIAGRAM H17*
This was given to the result of converting brake third No. 2355 to a buffet car and *DIAGRAM H18* to a similar conversion of brake third No. 2365. Both vehicles were originally to the 'Bars 1 Toplight' design.

Fig. 164

Fig. 163

*DIAGRAM H19*
Dining Car (to seat 42)
Lot 1177 of 1911
Running numbers: 9552–55
Dimensions: 70ft. 0in. x 9ft. 0in.

*DIAGRAM H19*
Built for the Fishguard Boat Train, these vehicles originally ran on 9ft. 'American' bogies. **Fig. 162** shows No. 9553 after reconditioning in 1936. The saloon has been repanelled and 9ft. plate bogies have been fitted. **Figs. 163 & 164** illustrate both sides of No. 9555 in a similar condition at Swindon in 1951 (see also *G W Coaches, Part II, page 68*).

Fig. 165

*DIAGRAM H20*
Kitchen First Brake (Toplight)
Lot 1189 of 1911
Running number: 8303
Dimensions: 70ft. 0in. x 9ft. 0in.

*DIAGRAM H20*
Only one vehicle was built to this design and it was allocated to the Plymouth Boat Trains. Both sides of the coach can be seen in **Figs. 165 & 166**, taken at Old Oak Common in 1950. No. 8303 was condemned in 1955.

*DIAGRAM H21*
This was another diagram given to the conversion of brake thirds to buffet cars. In this case, Nos. 3732 and 3734 were converted.

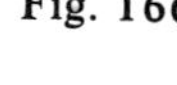

Fig. 166

*DIAGRAM H22*
Dining Car (to seat 42)
Lot 1219 of 1913
Running number: 9556
Dimensions: 70ft. 0in. x 9ft. 0in.

*DIAGRAM H22*
Another one-off vehicle, No. 9556, is shown in **Fig. 167** as built, and bearing the crimson lake livery. Note that six-wheeled 'American' bogies were fitted to the carriage from the start.

Fig. 168

In common with many other restaurant cars, No. 9556 was reconditioned and given flush steel panelling. **Figs. 168 & 169** show the compartment and corridor sides respectively, in 1952, after this had taken place. The bogies have also been replaced by the six-wheeled plate type. This vehicle was condemned in August 1961.

*DIAGRAM H23*
This was allocated to an ambulance buffet car which was converted from a clerestory diner.

Fig. 169

*DIAGRAM H24*
**Fig. 170** shows No. 9560 in 1938, bearing the 'roundel' livery with the white roof and sliding windows.

Fig. 170

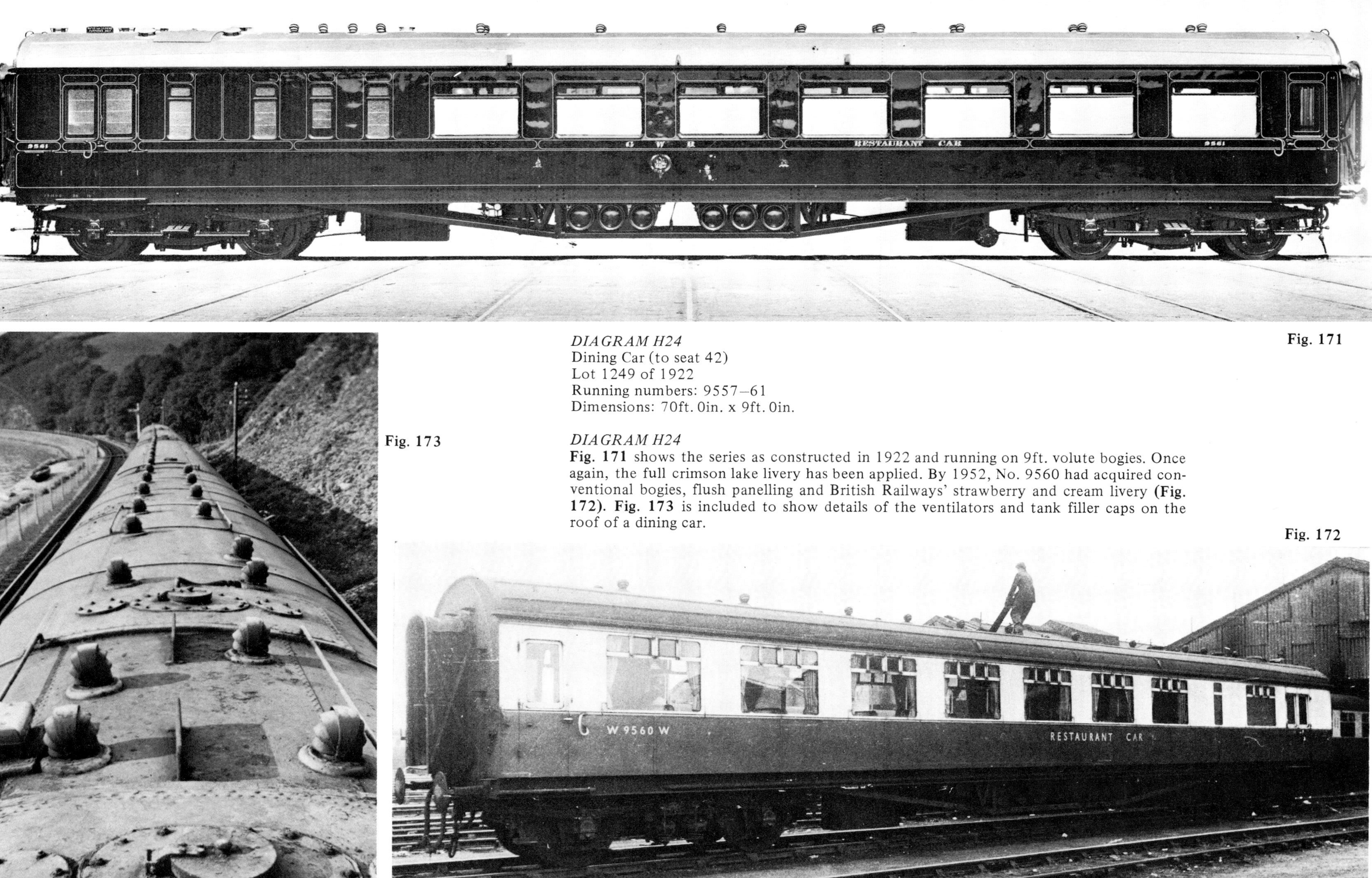


Fig. 171

*DIAGRAM H24*
Dining Car (to seat 42)
Lot 1249 of 1922
Running numbers: 9557–61
Dimensions: 70ft. 0in. x 9ft. 0in.

Fig. 173

*DIAGRAM H24*
**Fig. 171** shows the series as constructed in 1922 and running on 9ft. volute bogies. Once again, the full crimson lake livery has been applied. By 1952, No. 9560 had acquired conventional bogies, flush panelling and British Railways' strawberry and cream livery **(Fig. 172)**. **Fig. 173** is included to show details of the ventilators and tank filler caps on the roof of a dining car.

Fig. 172

*DIAGRAM H25*
Composite Dining Car (to seat 30)
Lot 1330 of 1924
Running numbers: 9563–67
Dimensions: 57ft. 0in. x 8ft. 6in.

**Fig. 175**

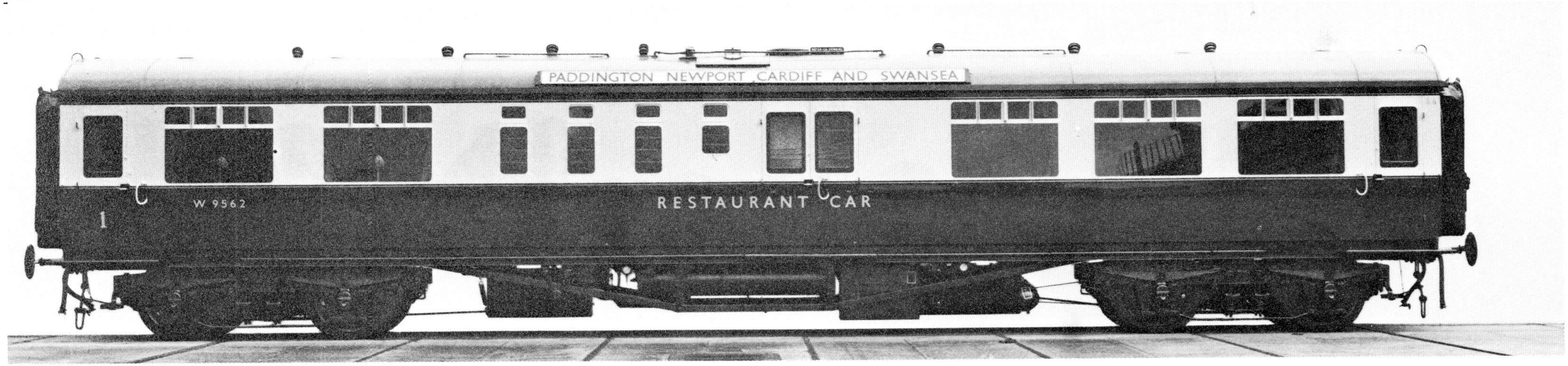

**Fig. 176**

*DIAGRAM H25*
Designed for cross-country services, these vehicles were shorter and narrower than the express dining cars, and ran on 7ft. plate bogies. There was seating for twelve first class and eighteen third class passengers. **Fig. 174** shows No. 9567 in 1950 with the single word 'Restaurant' on the kitchen panel. The same side of No. 9562 is seen in 1949, **(Fig. 175)**, with the full title 'Restaurant Car'. For comparison, the corridor side of No. 9564 is shown in the post-war GWR livery with the title in the waist panel **(Fig. 176)**.

**Fig. 177**

*DIAGRAM H26*
These coaches were amongst the first to appear after the reversion to a chocolate and cream, fully lined, livery. **Figs. 177 & 178** show No. 9568 in all its glory, lined in spite of its flush panelling! Originally these vehicles were fitted with 'buckeye' couplings, as can be seen at the left of **Fig. 178**. No. 9568 was the 'model' for the official photographs of this system and the resulting pictures can be seen in **Figs. 179 & 180**.

*DIAGRAM H26*
Composite Dining Car
Lot 1331 of 1923
Running numbers: 9568–71
Dimensions: 71ft. 4½in. x 9ft. 0in.

**Fig. 178**

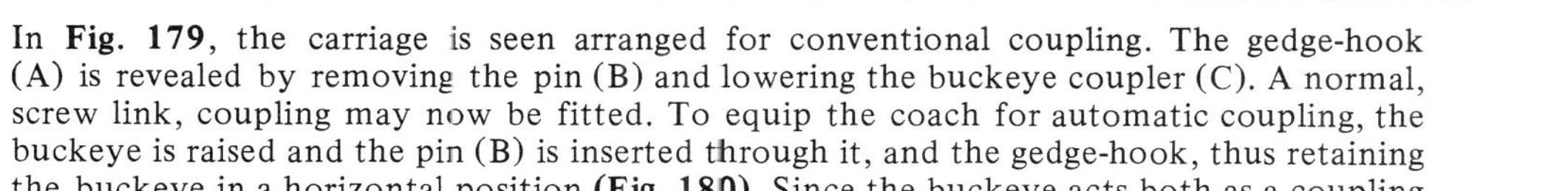


In **Fig. 179**, the carriage is seen arranged for conventional coupling. The gedge-hook (A) is revealed by removing the pin (B) and lowering the buckeye coupler (C). A normal, screw link, coupling may now be fitted. To equip the coach for automatic coupling, the buckeye is raised and the pin (B) is inserted through it, and the gedge-hook, thus retaining the buckeye in a horizontal position **(Fig. 180)**. Since the buckeye acts both as a coupling and a buffer, the conventional buffers are not required. These, therefore, are hinged and when the pins (D) are removed, the buffers may be lowered to a position where they will not interfere with the movement of the carriage. Notice also the chain (E), which allows the shunter to operate the buckeye from beside the coach.

Fig. 181

Fig. 182

*DIAGRAM H26*

The *Diagram H26* design was originally built for the 'South Wales Express', but they swiftly found their way on to other services, as can be seen from the roof board on No. 9572 in **Fig. 181**. In 1948, these carriages were rebuilt with sliding window vents. No. 9568 is shown in this state in the official photograph in **Fig. 183** and No. 9571 is seen in the stock shed at Old Oak Common, in 1950, **(Fig. 182)**. Note again the variation in title on these two carriages.

Fig. 183

Fig. 184

*DIAGRAM H27*
A total of six vehicles was built under Lot 1331, to three diagrams. *Diagram H26* has already been described and *Diagram H27* is illustrated on this page. There was accommodation for eighteen first class and thirty two third class passengers. In contrast to *Diagram H26*, the vehicles to *Diagrams H27 & H28* were flat-ended. **Fig. 184** shows No. 9572 as outshopped in 1946 carrying the last GWR livery, and **Figs. 185 & 186** show the vehicle in British Railways' days, the latter showing detail of the roof.

Fig. 185

Fig. 186

*DIAGRAMS H27 & H28*
Composite Dining Car (to seat 50)
Lot 1331 of 1923
Running number: 9572 *(Diagram H27)*
Running number: 9573 *(Diagram H28)*
Dimensions: 70ft. 0in. x 9ft. 0in.

*DIAGRAM H28*
This vehicle differed from No. 9572 *(Diagram H27)* only in the arrangement of the first class. **Figs. 187 & 188** show the corridor side in 1936 and 1952 respectively. Both Nos. 9572 and 9573 ran on six-wheeled plate bogies.

*DIAGRAM H29*
Another bow-ended vehicle mounted on six-wheeled bogies, No. 9574 could seat eighteen first class and thirty two third class diners. **Fig. 189** was taken in 1946 and shows the kitchen side of the carriage.

**Fig. 188** ▶

*DIAGRAM H29*
Composite Dining Car (to seat 50)
Lot 1334 of 1924
Running number: 9574
Dimensions: 71ft. 4½in. x 9ft. 0in.

**Fig. 189**

Fig. 191

Fig. 192 ▶

The carriages shown on this page are something of an enigma. Their numbering follows on from *Diagram H29* but No. 9574 is supposed to have been the only vehicle built on this lot. Externally, too, the bodies are similar, although Nos. 9575 and 9576 are shown mounted on four-wheeled bogies. **Fig. 190** dates from 1940, **Fig. 191** is post-war, but pre-1948, and **Fig. 192** is dated 1951.

*DIAGRAMS H30, H31 & H32*
Articulated Express Stock

First Diner *(Diagram H30)*
Lot 1357 of 1925
Running numbers: 10002/10/18/26/34/42
Later, Nos. 9645–48
Dimensions: 50ft. 6¾in. x 9ft. 0in.

Kitchen Car *(Diagram H31)*
Lot 1358 of 1925
Running numbers: 10003/11/19/27/35/43
Later, Nos. 9657–62
Dimensions: 46ft. 3in. x 9ft. 0in.

**Fig. 194** ▶

Third Diner *(Diagram H32)*
Lot 1359 of 1925
Running numbers: 10004/12/20/28/36/44
Later, Nos. 9649–52
Dimenions: 50ft. 6¾in. x 9ft. 0in.

**Fig. 193** is the official photograph of one of the sets, taken at the last shopping in 1934. Between 1936 and 1937, the sets were divided and the coaches were numbered to run separately. **Fig. 194** shows Kitchen Car No. 9657 carrying the first British Railways' livery and in **Fig. 195**, No. 9650 is seen, mounted on six-wheeled bogies, in the 1950 strawberry and cream livery (see also *GW Coaches, Part II, pages 129–131*).

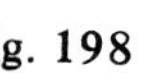

**Figs. 196 & 197** show No. 9648, one of the first diners, in 1949 and 1952 respectively. **Fig. 198** is the official photograph of the sets as built in 1925. Note the self-explanatory roof board.

Fig. 196

Fig. 197

Fig. 198

Fig. 199

Fig. 200

*DIAGRAM H33*
Composite Diner (to seat 36)
Lot 1349 of 1925
Running numbers: 9578–81
Dimensions: 58ft. 4½in. x 9ft. 0in.

*DIAGRAM H33*
These bow-ended dining cars were designed for cross-country services and could seat twelve first and twenty four third class passengers. **Fig. 199** shows the kitchen side of No. 9578 after reconditioning in 1939, and **Fig. 201** shows the opposite side of No. 9579 in the same condition. It is interesting to compare **Fig. 201** with **Fig. 200** which shows No. 9580 after it had been rebuilt in 1952 as a buffet dining car. Principal differences are the blanking off of the centre double doors and the higher sills of the nearer windows. This is the result of the installation of a stand-up buffet counter. Roof boards on No. 9580 read 'Paddington, Bristol and Weston-super-Mare' and on No. 9579 'Paddington, Birmingham and Wolverhampton'.

*DIAGRAM H34*
This was given to three ex-Cambrian Railways tea cars. Cambrian numbers were 325, 333 and 334 and they became Nos. 6332–34. All were condemned by September 1951 (see also *GW Coaches, Part II, page 124*).

Fig. 201

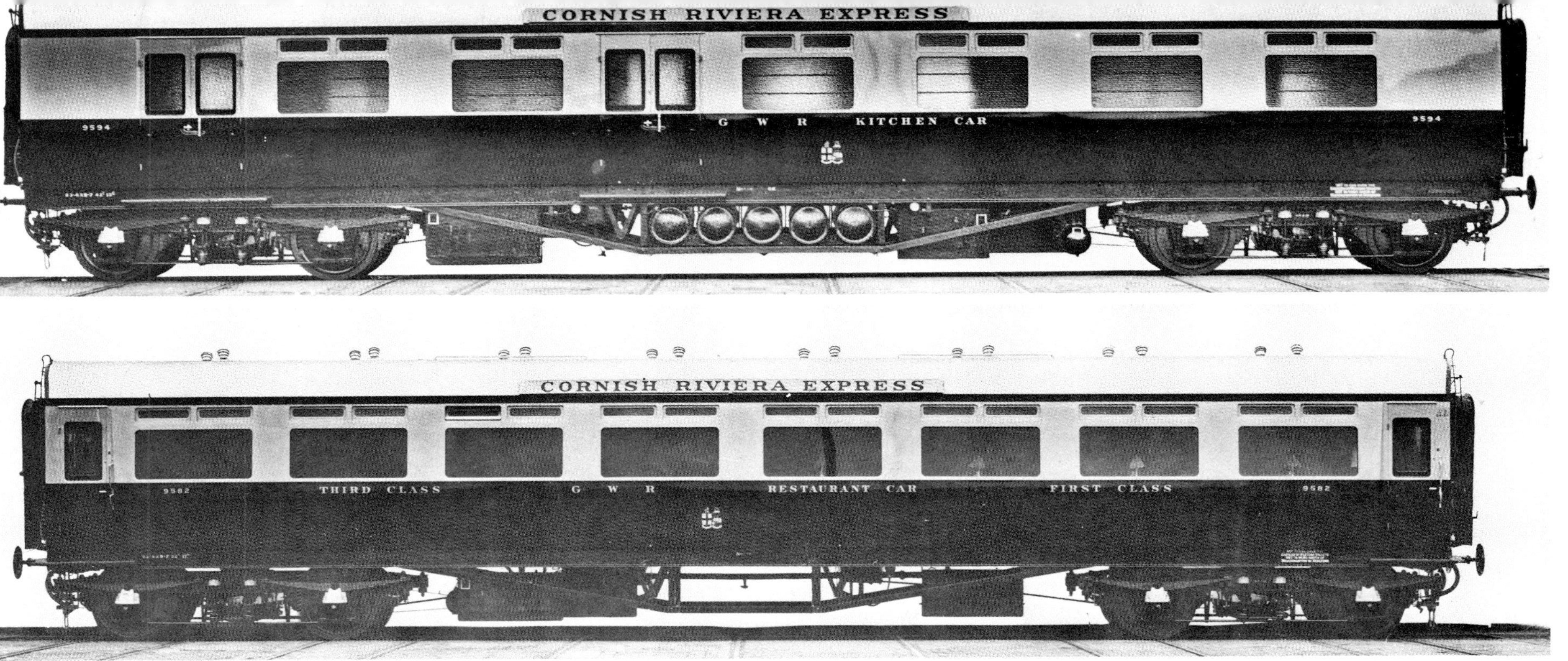


Fig. 203

**Figs. 202, 203 & 204** show the three 1929-built dining cars for the 'Cornish Riviera Express'. No. 9594 is to *Diagram H35*, No. 9528 to *Diagram H36* and No. 9588 to *Diagram H37*. The intention was that three car 'sets', comprising a composite saloon, a kitchen car and a third saloon, would be run.

Fig. 204

**Fig. 205**

*DIAGRAM H35*
Kitchen Car
Lot 1420 of 1929
Running numbers: 9594–9600
Dimensions: 61ft. 4½in. x 9ft. 7in.

*DIAGRAM H35*
**Fig. 205** shows No. 9598 in British Railways 1949 livery, mounted on 9ft. plate bogies (see also *GW Coaches, Part II, page 155*).

*DIAGRAM H37*
Third Dining Saloon
Lot 1422 of 1929
Running numbers: 9588–93
Dimensions: 61ft. 4½in. x 9ft. 7in.

*DIAGRAM H37*
In **Fig. 207**, No. 9590 is seen in the strawberry and cream livery.

*DIAGRAM H36*
Composite Dining Saloon (to seat 55)
Lot 1421 of 1929
Running numbers: 9582–87
Dimensions: 61ft. 4½in. x 9ft. 7in.

**Fig. 206**

*DIAGRAM H36*
Seating was divided into twenty four first class and thirty one third class places. **Fig. 206** shows No. 9583 in the British Railway's 1951 livery (see also *GW Coaches, Part II, page 156*).

**Fig. 207**

*DIAGRAM H37*

**Fig. 208** illustrates No. 9589 of the *Diagram H37* series at Old Oak Common in 1950, and one of the sister vehicles, No. 9590, is seen at Swindon after an overhaul and refit in 1951 in **Fig. 209**. This latter carriage was eventually reclassified as a corridor third and ran in this guise until it was condemned in 1962.

Fig. 208

Fig. 209

9601
THIRD CLASS
G W R
RESTAURANT CAR
FIRST CLASS
9601
9607
THIRD CLASS
RESTAURANT CAR
GWR
FIRST CLASS
9607
9606
G.W.R
THIRD CLASS
RESTAURANT CAR
FIRST CLASS
G.W.R
9606

Composite Restaurant Car (to seat 43)
Lot 1451 of 1930
Running numbers: 9601–10
Dimensions: 61ft. 4½in. x 9ft. 0in.

This series of bow-ended vehicles *(shown on the opposite page)* was intended for cross-country services and were mounted on 9ft. plate bogies. They were all condemned by February 1962. **Figs. 210 & 211** show examples of the series in the 1931 and 1936 liveries respectively, and No. 9606 is seen in the last GWR livery, after reconditioning had resulted in the fitting of sliding window vents **(Fig. 212)** (see also *GW Coaches, Part II, page 170*).

**Fig. 213**

*DIAGRAM H38*
This superb official photograph **(Fig. 213)** shows No. 9607, in perspective, and the 1935 livery to advantage. This series departed from the usual in that the kitchen unit, instead of being placed centrally, was at one end of the carriage. Next to it was the small first class saloon and then the third class accommodation.

Fig. 215

*DIAGRAM H39*
First Restaurant Car (to seat 23)
Lot 1468 of 1932
Running numbers: 9611–20
Dimensions: 61ft. 4½in. x 9ft. 3in.

*DIAGRAM H39*
The series, as built, is illustrated by No. 9611 in **Fig. 214** and, after reconditioning and the fitting of sliding vents, by No. 9617 in **Fig. 215**. In British Railways' days, No. 9618 was demoted from first class and the vehicle is shown in **Fig. 216**. The *Diagram H39* series were built as part of a twin-set, the other half of which was a third class dining saloon to *Diagram H40*.

Fig. 217

*DIAGRAM H40*
Third Dining Saloon (to seat 63)
Lot 1469 of 1932
Running numbers: 9621–30
Dimensions: 61ft. 4½in. x 9ft. 3in.

Fig. 218

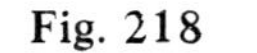

*DIAGRAM H40*
A point of interest in this series was the fitting of a single toilet at one end of the vehicle. The result was that only one access door was fitted to one side of the carriage, instead of the more normal two doors on the other side. This can be seen in **Fig. 217**, the official photograph of the carriages as built with hinged ventilators. **Fig. 218** illustrates the two-car set referred to earlier, and **Fig. 219** is a view of No. 9623, after the fitting of sliding ventilators and carrying British Railways' livery. This is taken from the opposite side to the view in **Fig. 217** and comparison of the two will clarify the point regarding the doors.

Fig. 219

*DIAGRAM H40*

Three more pictures of the third class dining saloon in British Railways' ownership. **Fig. 220** shows the corridor side of No. 9628 in 1952 and **Fig. 221** is of the lavatory side of No. 9626. Note that all the access doors are hinged on the left-hand side. In the final picture of No. 9639, **(Fig. 222)**, the rocf board reads 'Paddington, Newport, Cardiff and Swansea' and is written in white letters on a claret ground (see also *GW Coaches, Part II, page 179*).

**Fig. 220**

**Fig. 222**

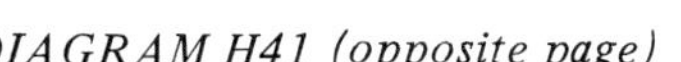

*DIAGRAM H41 (opposite page)*

Two vehicles were built to this design and were fitted with 9ft. pressed-steel bogies. The coaches were reconditioned in 1934 and condemned in November 1963. **Fig. 223** shows No. 9631 as built and bearing the later chocolate and cream livery, with double waist lining and the 'roundel' monogram. The cream background to the monogram is interesting as is the cream panel with the title 'Buffet Car'. This is a typical example of the GWR taking every opportunity to advertise. The lettering was about 9in. high and executed in gold. The small cast plates on the roof read 'Water for drinking purposes only'. **Fig. 224** is an official plan of the internal layout of these carriages.

**Fig. 221**

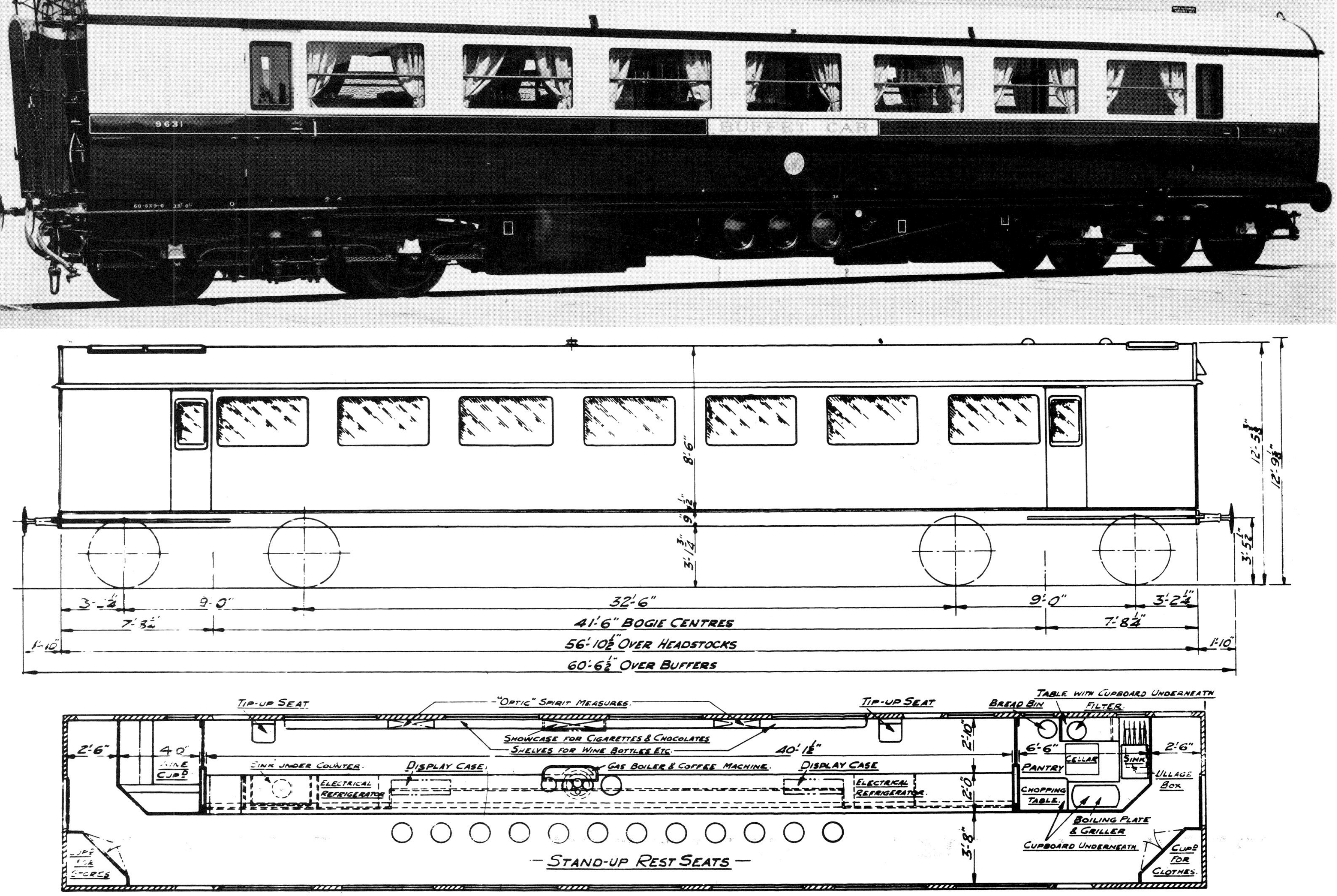
9631
BUFFET CAR
12'9⅝"
12'5⅝"
8'6"
9½"
3'1¾"
3'5½"
3'2¼"
9'0"
32'6"
9'0"
3'2¼"
7'8¼"
41'6" BOGIE CENTRES
7'8¼"
1'10"
56'10½" OVER HEADSTOCKS
1'10"
60'6½" OVER BUFFERS
TIP-UP SEAT
"OPTIC" SPIRIT MEASURES.
TIP-UP SEAT
BREAD BIN
TABLE WITH CUPBOARD UNDERNEATH
FILTER.
SHOWCASE FOR CIGARETTES & CHOCOLATES
SHELVES FOR WINE BOTTLES ETC.
2'6"
4'0"
CUPD
40'1½"
2'10"
6'6"
2'6"
SINK UNDER COUNTER.
DISPLAY CASE.
GAS BOILER & COFFEE MACHINE.
DISPLAY CASE
PANTRY
CELLAR
SINK
ELECTRICAL REFRIGERATOR
ELECTRICAL REFRIGERATOR.
2'0"
ULLAGE BOX
CHOPPING TABLE.
BOILING PLATE & GRILLER
3'8"
CUPBOARD UNDERNEATH
CUPD FOR CLOTHES.
– STAND-UP REST SEATS –

Fig. 225

*DIAGRAM H41 (above)*
Buffet Car
Lot 1518 of 1934
Running numbers: 9631–32
Dimensions: 57ft. 0in. x 9ft. 0in.

Fig. 226

*DIAGRAM H41*
**Fig. 225** is another official photograph of No. 9631, this time showing the carriage in full broadside view. **Fig. 226** shows the same vehicle, in the British Railways' strawberry and cream livery, and is of importance as it illustrates the opposite side of the coach to that seen in the other pictures. The second vehicle of the series is illustrated in **Fig. 227**, another official view, taken in 1939. Notice that sliding vents have been fitted and that the monogram has lost its cream background.

Fig. 227

Fig. 228

*DIAGRAM H42*
Kitchen Car (Excursion Stock)
Lot 1529 of 1935
Running numbers: 9633–34
Dimensions: 60ft. 0in. x 9ft. 0in.

*DIAGRAM H42*
No. 9633 is seen, as built, with the 'roundel' livery in **Fig. 228** (see also *GW Coaches, Part II, page 199*).

*DIAGRAM H43*
First Dining Car (Cententary)
Lot 1540 of 1935
Running numbers: 9635–36
Dimensions: 61ft. 4½in. x 9ft. 7in.

Fig. 229

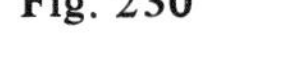

Fig. 230

*DIAGRAM H43*
Mounted on 9ft. pressed-steel bogies, the two vehicles to this design were fitted with sliding vent windwos in 1938, and had the seating changed
sliding vent windows

*DIAGRAM H43*
Mounted on 9ft. pressed-steel bogies, the two vehicles to this design were fitted with sliding vent windows in 1938, and had the seating changed from bench type to individual chairs in 1948. **Figs. 229 & 230** were taken in 1951 and show the kitchen and corridor sides, respectively, of this series. Both vehicles were condemned in 1962. The distinctive recessed doors of the 'Centenary' coaches are evident (see also *GW Coaches, Part 11, pages 214 & 215*).

◀**Fig. 231**

*DIAGRAM H44*
Third Dining Saloon (Centenary)
Lot 1541 of 1935
Running numbers: 9637–38
Dimensions: 61ft. 4½in. x 9ft. 7in.

*DIAGRAM H44*
**Fig. 231** is a 1950 view of No. 9638 bearing the strawberry and cream livery. The sliding vent windows were fitted in 1938 (see also *GW Coaches, Part II, pages 216 and 217*).

**Fig. 232** ▼

*DIAGRAMS H45 & H46*
These were allocated to conversions of two 'Super Saloons', built originally to *Diagram G61*. Kitchens were fitted in 1935 to *Princess Royal* and *Princess Elizabeth* and they became Nos. 9117 *(Diagram H45)* and 9118 *(Diagram H46)* respectively and were given the title 'Special First Class Dining Car'. **Figs. 232 & 233** show No. 9118 *Princess Elizabeth*.

Fig. 234

*DIAGRAM H47*
First Restaurant Car (with kitchen)
Lot 1532 of 1935
Running numbers: 9641–42
Dimensions: 60ft. 0in. x 9ft. 0in.

*DIAGRAM H47*
These first class dining cars were built as one half of a twin-car set, the other half of which were third class dining cars to *Diagram H48*, described next. The two vehicles to *Diagram H47* provided first class dining facilities for twenty three passengers and were mounted on 9ft. pressed-steel bogies. **Fig. 234** is the official photograph of No. 9642, as built and bearing the 'roundel' livery, in 1950, in **Fig. 235**.

Fig. 235

Fig. 236

*DIAGRAM H48*
Third Dining Saloon
Lot 1533 of 1935
Running numbers: 9639–40
Dimensions: 60ft. 0in. x 9ft. 0in.

*DIAGRAM H48*
The third class accommodation in the twin-car set provided places for sixty four diners, and the official Swindon view of the carriages, as built, can be seen in **Fig. 236**. The absence of ventilators on the windows of this carriage, and on the saloon of No. 9642 *(previous page)*, is explained by the louvres which can be seen at the left-hand end of No. 9640 **(Fig. 236)**. These louvres were the intake for the air-conditioning with which these twin-car sets were fitted. They can be seen more clearly in **Fig. 237**, which shows the coach in British Railways' days. The white-painted cabinet, seen between the queen posts in **Fig. 236**, is the container for the propane gas tanks (see also *GW Coaches, Part II, page 202*).

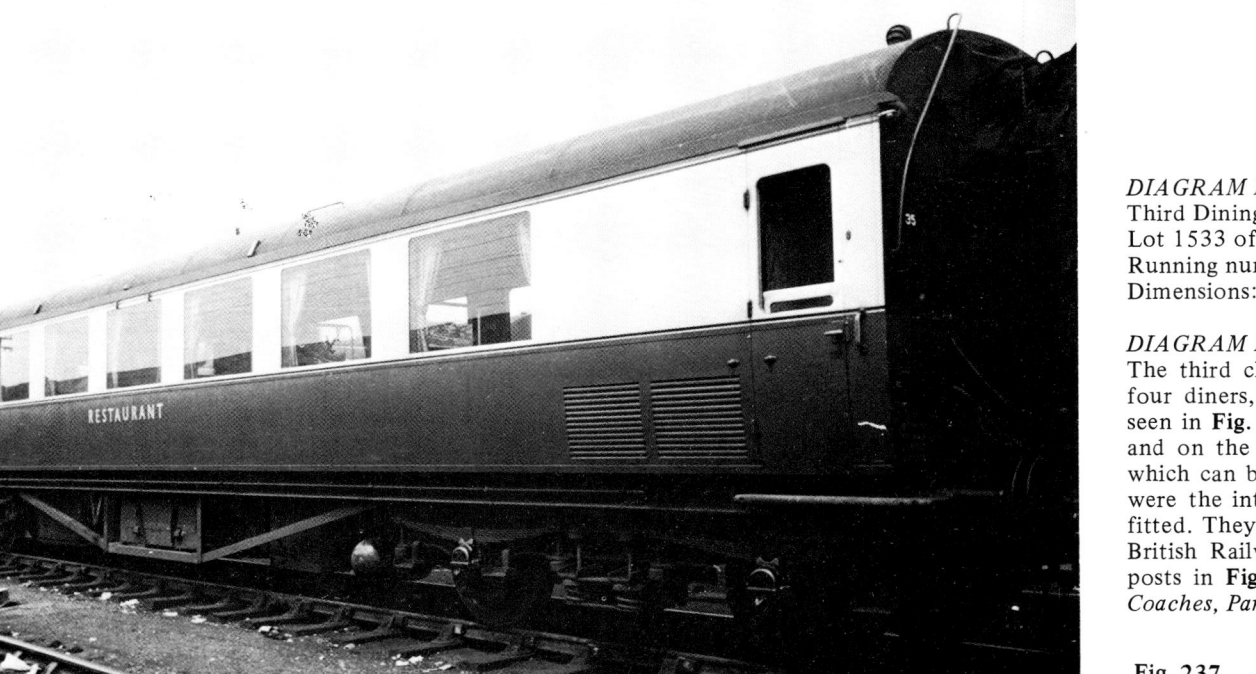

Fig. 237

Fig. 238

*DIAGRAMS H49, H50 & H51*

These were allocated to coaches converted from the articulated sets of 1925 *(see pages 76–77)*. The kitchen cars were given the new *Diagram H49* and photographs can be seen in **Figs. 217 & 218** *(page 85)*. *Diagram H50* was given to the first class dining saloons and the official photograph of the conversion is seen in **Fig. 238** (note the fitting of sliding vent windows).

**Figs. 219 & 220** *(page 86)* show these carriages at later dates. *Diagram H51* was the new diagram given to the third class saloons, and the official photograph of the conversion is **Fig. 239**. When first converted, the coaches ran on 7ft. plate bogies but, in 1938, the saloons were mostly fitted with six-wheeled bogies. The saloons ran until April 1962 and the kitchen cars ran until December of the same year.

Fig. 239

**Fig. 240**

*DIAGRAM H53*
This was given to two buffet thirds which were built on Lot 1556 in 1936. They were numbered 9643 and 9644 and had a buffet saloon and three third class compartments (see also *G W Coaches, Part II, page 221*).

**Fig. 241**

*DIAGRAM H54*
Kitchen Car (Excursion Stock)
Lot 1579 if 1937
Running numbers: 9663–68
Dimensions: 60ft. 0in. x 9ft. 0in.

*DIAGRAM H54*
These vehicles were mounted on 9ft. pressed-steel bogies and were condemned in December 1962. **Fig. 240** is the official Swindon photograph of No. 9663, as built, and shows the corridor side of the vehicle. The kitchen side is seen in **Fig. 241** when No. 9668 had received the strawberry and cream livery (see also *G W Coaches, Part II, page 229*).

**Fig. 242**

*DIAGRAM H55*
Buffet Car
Lot 1602 of 1938
Running numbers: 9676–80
Dimensions: 60ft. 11¼in. x 8ft. 11in.

*DIAGRAM H55*
This rather oblique view of No. 9676 **(Fig. 242)** shows the vehicle in 1962 and is interesting for the title 'Buffet Car', which can be seen carried in a cream panel.

Fig. 243

*DIAGRAM H56*
The kitchen side of No. 9669 is seen in **Fig. 244**, taken in 1949. Six-wheeled bogies were also fitted on this series.

Fig. 244

Fig. 245

*DIAGRAM H55*
Accommodation in this series was arranged as a counter area and a 20 seat saloon. **Fig. 243** illustrates No. 9677, in 1951, carrying a roof board for 'The Bristolian' and shows the six-wheeled bogies on which these coaches were mounted (see also *GW Coaches, Part II, page 240*).

*DIAGRAM H57*
Six-wheeled bogies were also fitted to this series and the corridor side of No. 9672 is seen in **Fig. 245.**

Fig. 246

*DIAGRAM H57*
Composite Restaurant Car
Lot 1601 of 1938
Running numbers: 9671–75
Dimensions: 60ft. 11¼in. x 8ft. 11in.

*DIAGRAM H57*
**Fig. 246** depicts No. 9674 at Swindon in 1955 with the kitchen side facing the camera The cabinets for the propane gas tanks are again evident between the queen posts. Another view of the corridor side is given in **Fig. 247**. No. 9672 is seen at Old Oak Common in 1953.

Fig. 247

Fig. 248

Fig. 249

*DIAGRAM H58*
This was allocated to the buffet restaurant car which resulted from the rebuilding of one of the *Diagram H33* series of composite diners. Only one vehicle was involved and it was given the new number 9580. **Figs. 248 & 249** are official photographs and were taken in 1952 at the time of conversion.

Fig. 250

The next few pages illustrate a number of vehicles that were built at Swindon after the Great Western Railway had ceased to exist. The new vehicles represent a continuation of existing design policy, and the others are conversions of coaches built earlier, under the GWR.

**Fig. 250**: Restaurant car No. E1961 of 1960, in British Railways' maroon livery.

**Fig. 251**: First class diner No. M310 of 1961 (Lot 30633) in maroon livery.

Fig. 251

Fig. 253

**Fig. 252**: Kitchen diner No. W305, built on Lot 30013, to British Railways' *Diagram 16*, in 1952.

**Fig. 253**: Cafeteria car No. 9660 of 1956. Originally built on Lot 1358 to *Diagram H49* in 1936.

**Fig. 254**: Buffet restaurant car No. 9644. Originally built on Lot 1556 to *Diagram H53* in 1936.

Fig. 254

◀Fig. 255

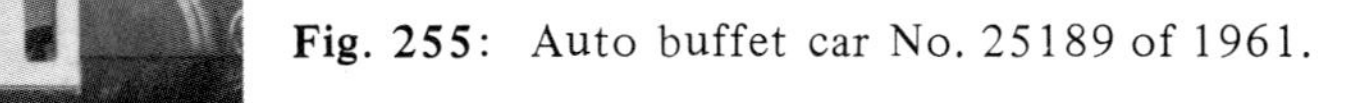

**Fig. 255**: Auto buffet car No. 25189 of 1961.

**Fig. 256**: Buffet car No. W1813, built on Lot 30520 in 1960.

**Fig. 257**: Restaurant car No. W1944, built in 1960 on Lot 30575.

Fig. 258

**Fig. 258**: Restaurant car No. W1902. British Railways' standard of 1957.

**Fig. 259**: Buffet restaurant car No. W1739. British Railways' standard of 1961.

Fig. 259

**Fig. 260**

**Fig. 261**

The 'Milford Boat Expresses', from Paddington to the Irish boats at Milford Haven, Pembrokeshire were the first long-distance trains, on the GWR, on which light refreshments could be obtained. The two views above were taken in carriages built specially for this service, in 1900. **Fig. 260** shows the interior of the buffet (second class) No. 242 to *Diagram H5* which also had a small kitchen. The offset gangway allowed for a double seat at one side and a single at the other, in the second class. In the first class, however, spacious single seats were provided either side of the central gangway, as can be seen in **Fig. 261**. This photograph shows the interior of No. 2941 *(Diagram H6)*. These coaches were not, strictly, dining saloons and service was provided by a member of the GWR Hotels and Refreshements Department, from the kitchen in an adjoining buffet (second class).

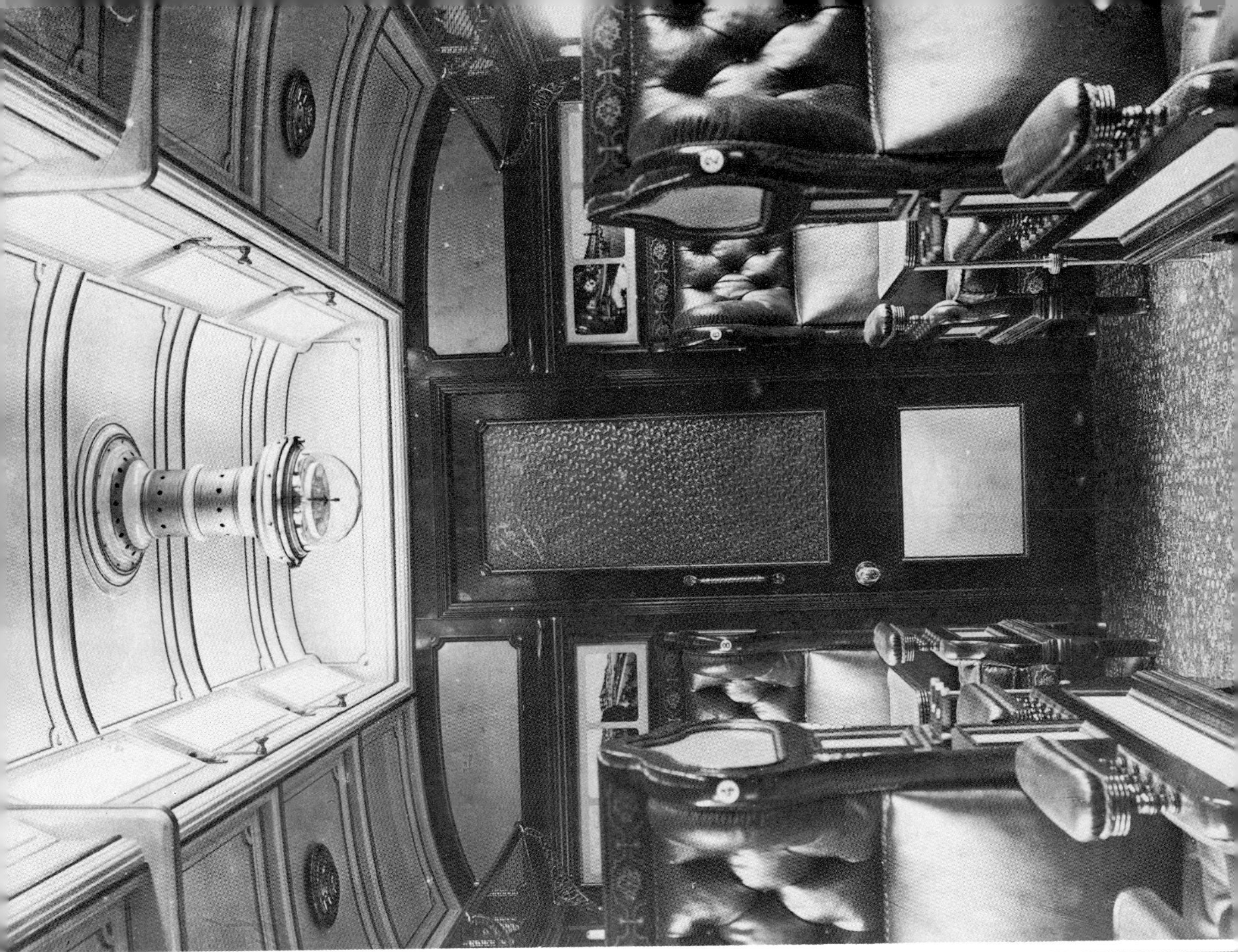

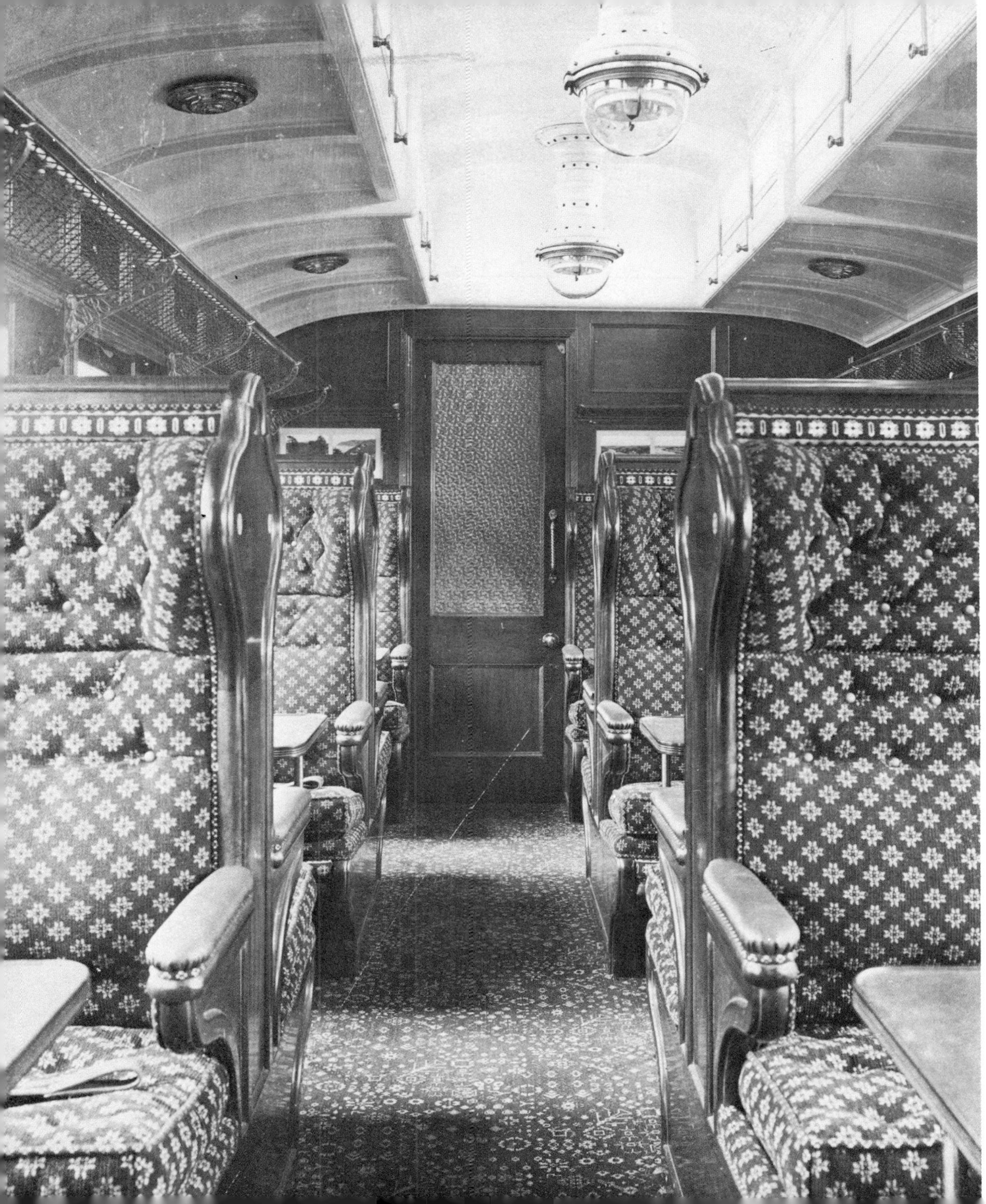

**Figs. 262 & 263 (opposite page)**: Two views of the first class accommodation in the clerestory composite dining cars which were built in 1902 to *Diagram H7*. Splendidly upholstered in dark green morocco leather, trimmed with green and gold braid, the compartment has a green patterned carpet and a prominent electric light fitting. The bell push to summon the attendant is situated above the table shown in **Fig. 262**, below the racks for the wine bottles. In both photographs the GWR monogram can be seen, worked into the supports of the luggage racks.

**Fig. 265**

The second class compartment of a coach to *Diagram H7* is seen, upholstered with the standard pattern material, in **Fig. 264 (left)**. The mouldings on the ceiling have been left undecorated and the standard of finish is generally much less plush than in the previous illustrations. Once again accommodation has been increased by offsetting the gangway.

**Fig. 265 (above)**: In contrast to this is the first class saloon of No. 405, a 70ft. 'concertina' coach, built to *Diagram H14* in 1906. Racks are provided between the windows to secure wine bottles, but one wonders how long the vases of flowers would remain upright as the coach snaked through a junction or station approach!

Fig. 267

The ‘concertina’ vehicles of 1906 *(Diagram H13)* were also very wide and allowed for the extra seat. The first class saloon of No. 402 is seen in **Fig. 267**. Note the very elaborate, electrically lit, chandelier.

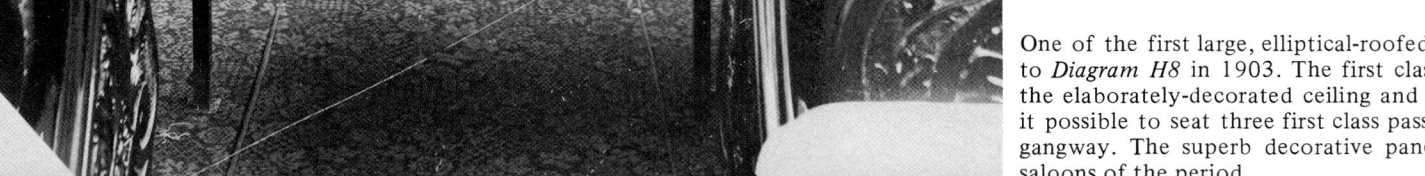

One of the first large, elliptical-roofed, dining cars was the ‘Dreadnought’ composite built to *Diagram H8* in 1903. The first class saloon is seen in **Fig. 266** and points to note are the elaborately-decorated ceiling and the fact that the great width of these vehicles made it possible to seat three first class passengers across the width of the coach, with an offset gangway. The superb decorative panel in the door seems to be a feature of the dining saloons of the period.

Fig. 268

**Figs. 268 & 269** illustrate the classless dining saloons of the 70ft. dining cars built to *Diagrams H22 & H24*. **Fig. 268** shows No. 9556 of *Diagram H22* series and **Fig. 269** shows No. 9561 to *Diagram H24*. The similarity between the two designs is striking when one considers that ten years and World War I separate their building dates. In the original photographs it is possible to see the embroidered border and initials GWR on the Irish linen antimacassars. The fairing in of the ventilation fan is a curious feature that is common to both coaches.

Fig. 269

**Fig. 271** portrays the third class saloon of the same vehicle which looks rather uncomfortable. The central gangway in this compartment allows for two seats either side. ▶

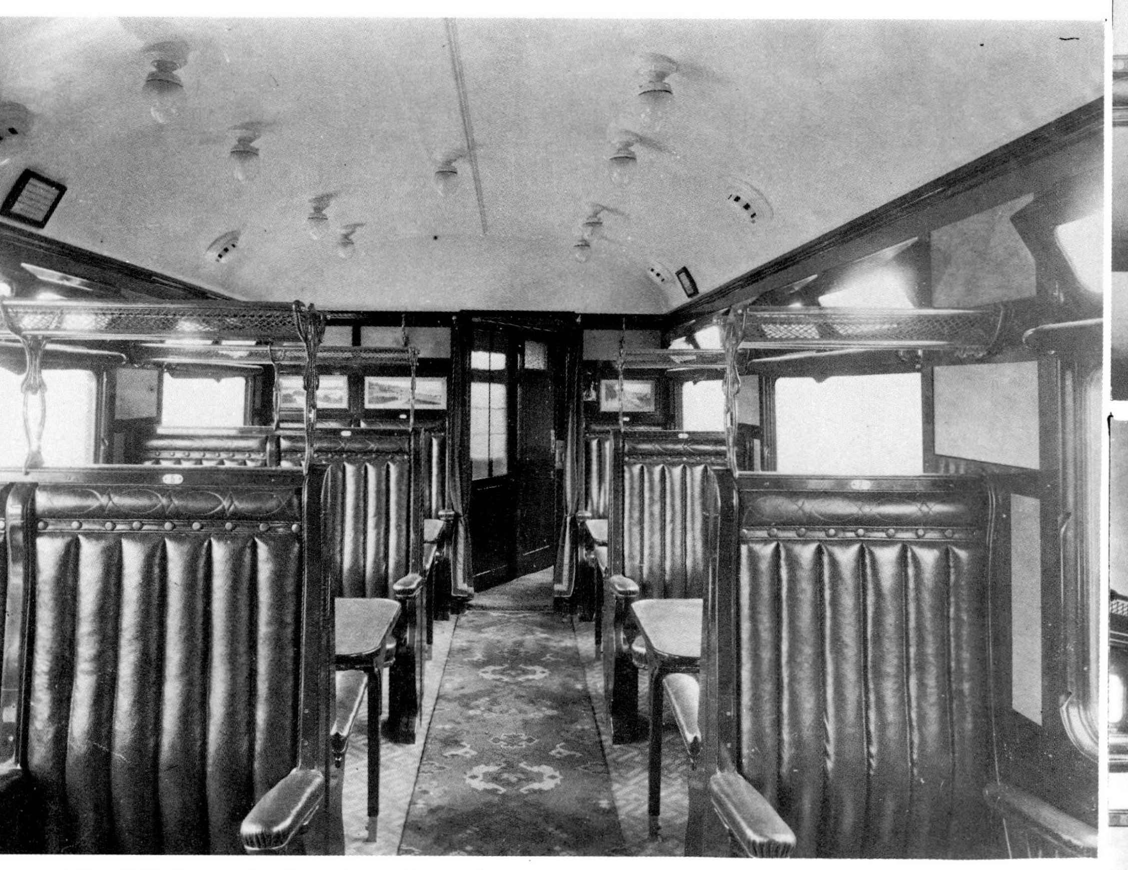

**Fig. 270** shows the first class saloon of No. 9568, one of the bow-ended composite diners built to *Diagram H26* in 1923.

**Fig. 272** portrays the interior of No. 9573 *(Diagram H28)* and shows the change from leather upholstery to chocolate-coloured cloth. The notice on the wall to the right asks passengers to assist the management by obtaining bills before paying for meals. ▶

Fig 273 Fig. 274

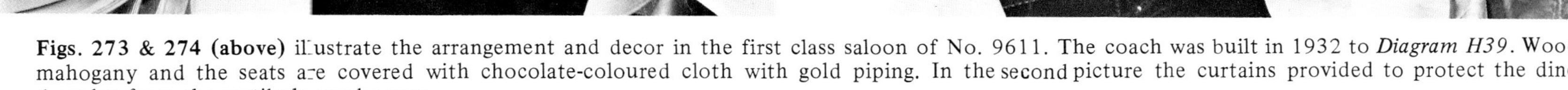

**Figs. 273 & 274 (above)** illustrate the arrangement and decor in the first class saloon of No. 9611. The coach was built in 1932 to *Diagram H39*. Woodwork is mahogany and the seats are covered with chocolate-coloured cloth with gold piping. In the second picture the curtains provided to protect the diners from draughts from the vestibule can be seen.

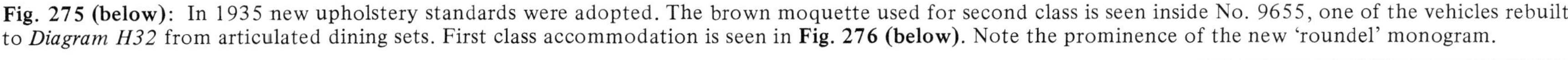

**Fig. 275 (below)**: In 1935 new upholstery standards were adopted. The brown moquette used for second class is seen inside No. 9655, one of the vehicles rebuilt to *Diagram H32* from articulated dining sets. First class accommodation is seen in **Fig. 276 (below)**. Note the prominence of the new 'roundel' monogram.

Fig. 275 Fig. 276

Fig. 277

The interiors of the 1934 built buffet cars *(Diagram H41)* can be seen in these two pictures. **Fig. 277** shows the customers' side of the counter, with the 'stand-up' stools. Note the prominent crest on the crockery and the linoleum, chequered in chocolate and cream. The attendant's side, with its coffee machine and refrigerator, is seen in **Fig. 278**.

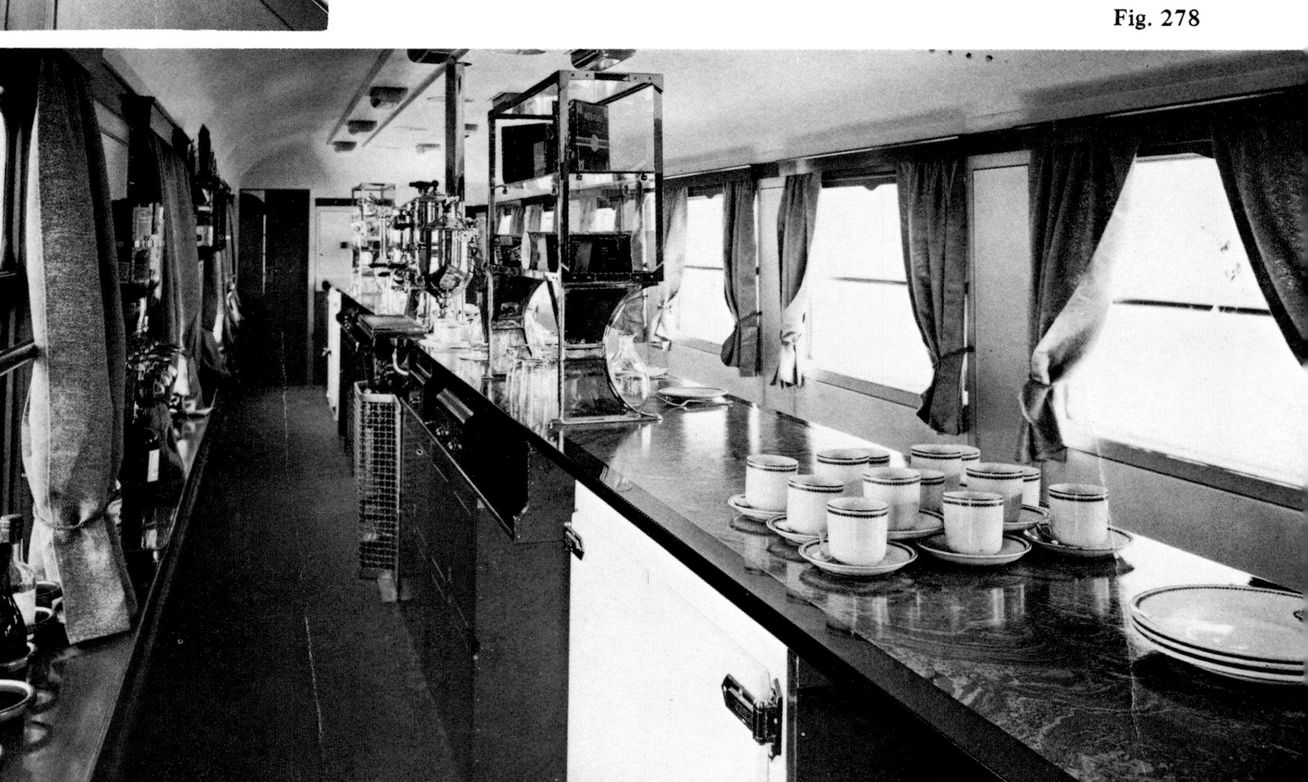

Fig. 278

The next two photographs give an illustration of the differences between first and third class accommodation in the refreshment cars. **Fig. 279** shows the rather plain third class saloon of a composite diner to *Diagram H38*. In the first class saloon of No. 9653 **(Fig. 280)**, the table-cloths and antimacassars are the most obvious acknowledgement of the class. Panelling in this coach, one of the 'Centenary' series to *Diagram H43*, was a light veneer, inlaid with a dark walnut strip. Upholstery was of a blue-green tartan moquette with curtains to match. The carpets were brown.

**Fig. 279**

**Fig. 280**

◀ **Fig. 281** shows another view of No. 9635. The veneer panelling and stripe can be clearly seen. An air of spaciousness is apparent in this and the previous picture, and this was carried over to the corridors of compartment stock, as can be seen in **Fig. 282**.

Fig. 282

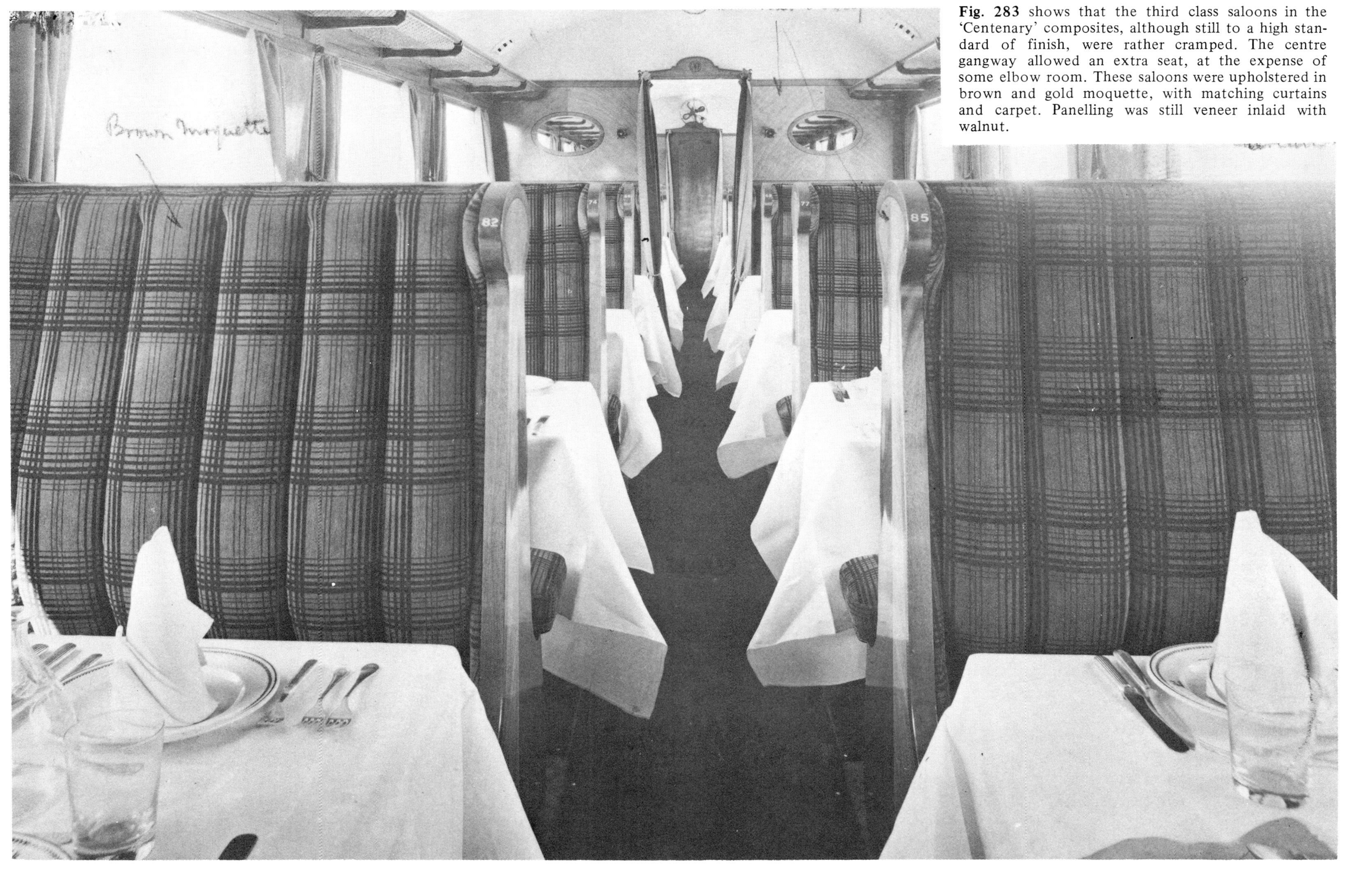


**Fig. 283** shows that the third class saloons in the 'Centenary' composites, although still to a high standard of finish, were rather cramped. The centre gangway allowed an extra seat, at the expense of some elbow room. These saloons were upholstered in brown and gold moquette, with matching curtains and carpet. Panelling was still veneer inlaid with walnut.

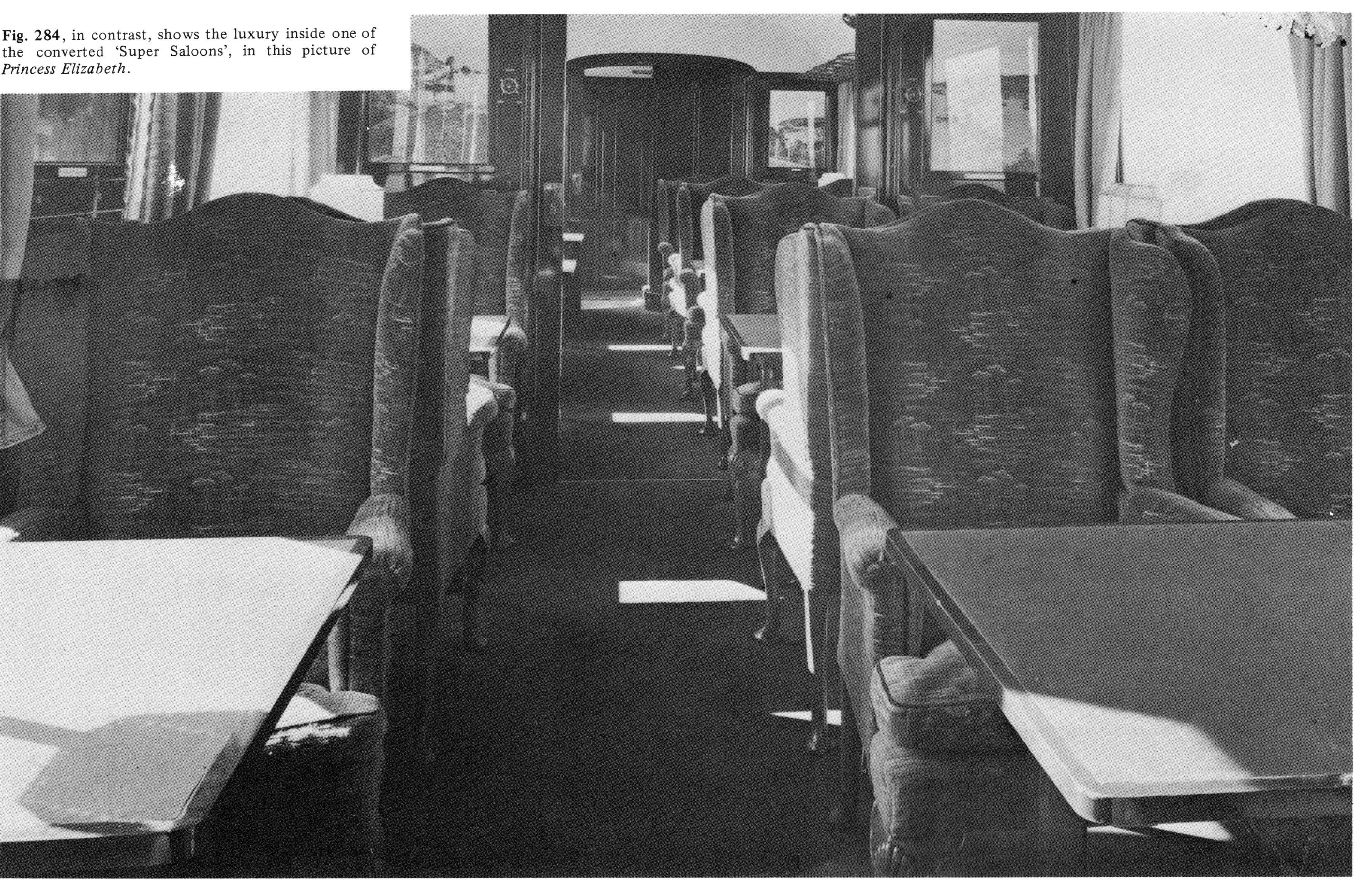

**Fig. 284**, in contrast, shows the luxury inside one of the converted 'Super Saloons', in this picture of *Princess Elizabeth*.

In the same year as the 'Centenary' coaches, two 60ft. first diners were built to *Diagram H47*. As one might expect, interior finish was very similar and **Fig. 285** shows the interior of No. 9641. ▶

◀
**Fig. 286** shows that the contemporary design for third class, *Diagram H48*, has equivalent similarities to the 'Centenary' stock.

Fig. 287

**Figs. 287 (above), 288 (below) & 289 (right):** In 1936 two third class buffet cars were constructed to *Diagram H53* and their interior is shown in these pictures. **Fig. 287** illustrates the attendant's side, and **Figs. 288 & 289** show

Fig. 288

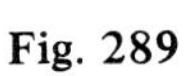

Fig. 289

Fig. 290

In the late 1930s, the GWR began to reconstruct many of the older dining cars to bring them up to the standards of contemporary new construction. **Fig. 290** shows the internal fittings of No. 9527, built to *Diagram H14* in 1906, after complete reconditioning in 1937. This view should be compared with **Fig. 267**.

**Fig. 291** shows that a similar transformation has taken place inside No. 9551, originally built as a 'top-light' diner in 1908. Note the prominent use of the 'roundel' monogram and that sliding vents have been fitted to the windows. No. 9551 was to be reconditioned again in 1947 by the contractors, Messrs Hamptons Ltd.

Fig. 291

The 1935 built dining cars to *Diagrams H47 & H48* were soon reconditioned and the appearance of No. 9639 of *Diagram H48* series, after this work had been done, is seen in **Fig. 292.**

**Fig. 293** illustrates the kitchen stove and sink units in *Diagram H49* series which resulted from the separating and reconditioning of the 3 car articulated sets of 1925. The photograph was taken inside No. 9662 in 1937.

**Fig. 292**

**Fig. 293**

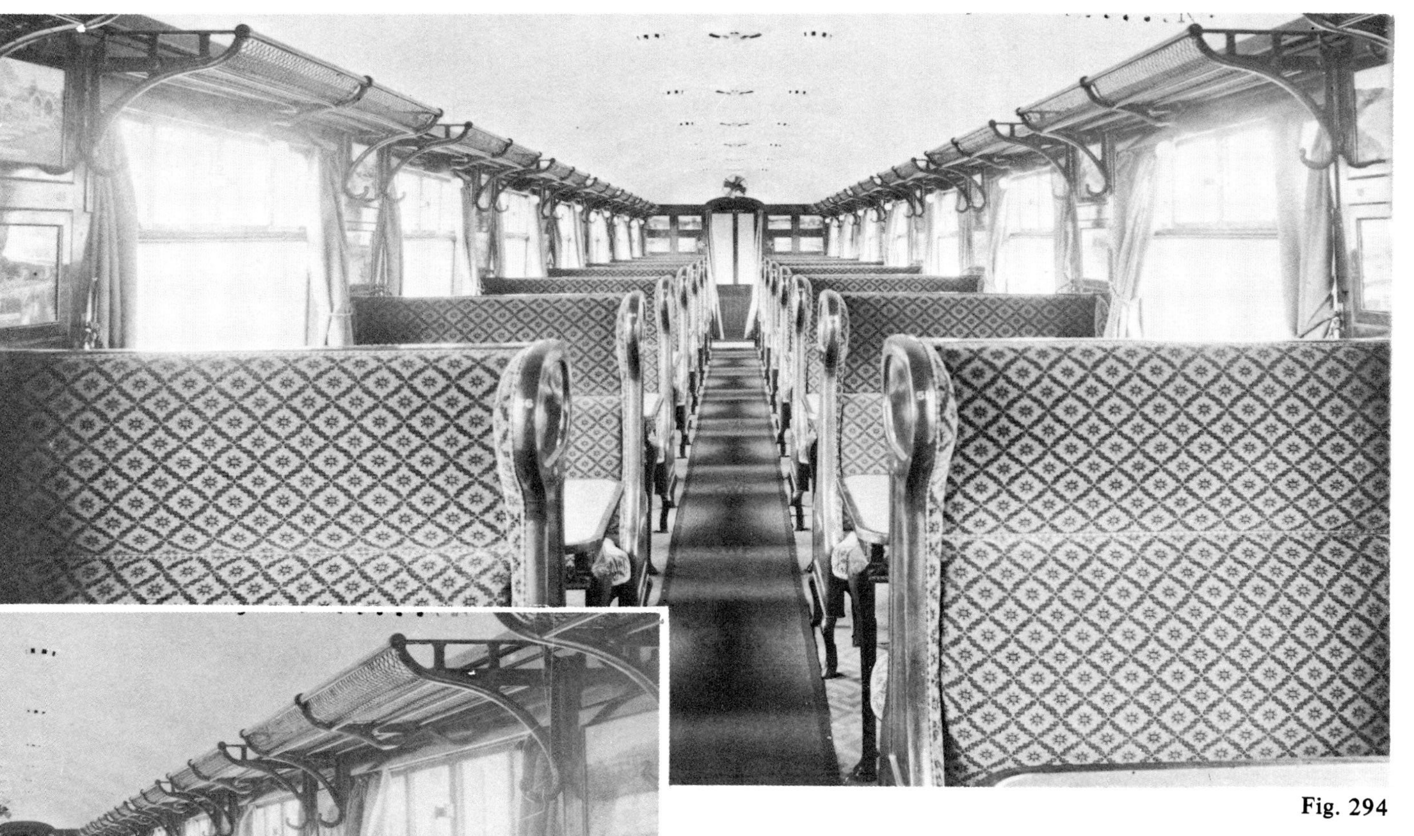

Fig. 294

Fig. 295

The other vehicles from the articulated sets were similarly reconditioned. **Fig. 294** illustrates the interior of No. 9652 *(Diagram H51)*, which has been given a rather old-fashioned third class upholstery and trim. The first class coaches *(Diagram H50)*, of which No. 9645 is an example, received an unusual, non-standard, gangway carpet, **(Fig. 295)**. The intertwined monogram is a curious departure from the policy of the time which seemed to be; 'if it belongs to the Company, put a 'roundel' on it'.

Fig. 296

A more conventional finish was given to the 'Cornish Riviera' composite diners when they were reconditioned in 1938. The third class saloon is seen in **Fig. 296** and the first class saloon in **Fig. 297**.

Fig. 297

The single vehicle to *Diagram H22*, No. 9556, was also reconditioned in 1938. The first class saloon is shown in **Fig. 298.** ▶

**Fig. 299** shows the interior of a reconditioned third class 'Centenary' diner, No. 9673. ▼

Fig. 300

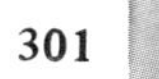

Five brand-new vehicles built in 1937 were the buffet/refreshment cars to *Diagram H55*. The interior arrangement is shown on this page, in **Fig. 300** the seating accommodation can be seen and in **Fig. 301** the counter, with its 'stand-up' stools is shown. Note that no carpets are provided and that the seats have particularly low backs to preserve the airiness of the coach.

Fig. 301

**Fig. 302** shows the interior of No. 9641 *(Diagram H48)*, after reconditioning, with the familiar walnut inlaid panelling and tartan moquette upholstery. This was one of the air-conditioned coaches, as evidenced by the absence of ventilators in the windows. ▶

◀ The leather-bound upholstery in the third class saloon of No. 9674, seen in **Fig. 303**, would seem to be a retrogressive step. In fact, the coach was one of five built in 1938 to *Diagram H57*. The similarity to contemporary LNER excursion stock is striking.

Fig. 304

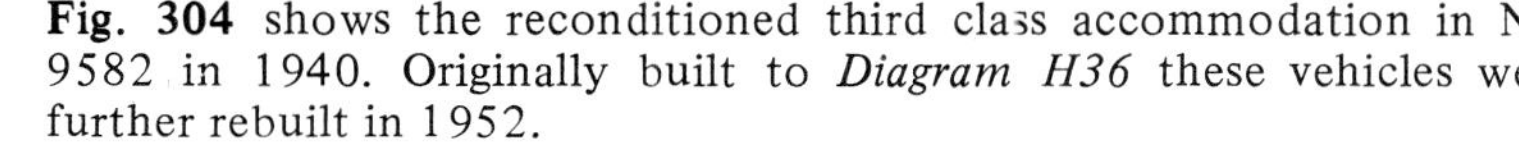

**Fig. 304** shows the reconditioned third class accommodation in No. 9582 in 1940. Originally built to *Diagram H36* these vehicles were further rebuilt in 1952.

**Fig. 305** shows No. 9564 which was reconditioned in 1942, probably after it and its sister vehicles had finished their duties in evacuation trains. The original building date was 1924 to *Diagram H25*. The apparatus hanging from the roof obviously has some special purpose, but quite what, is a mystery!

Fig. 305

The modernized interior of composite diner No. 9602 *(Diagram H38)* is seen in the next two pictures taken in 1939. **Fig. 306** illustrates the third class saloon and **Fig. 307** the first class, complete with its air-circulating fan.

**Fig. 306**

**Fig. 307**

Fig 308

Fig. 309

In 1946, *Diagram H38* series were reconditioned again, and this time the transformation was dramatic. **Fig. 308** illustrates the result in the third class saloon, and in spite of the airiness, the etched glass screens, whilst decorative, did little to relieve the starkness of the decor. The first class saloon **(Fig. 309)** in which the former bench seats have been replaced by individual chairs, is similarly rather stark.

Fig. 310

The etched screens and semi-concealed lighting were very much a part of post-war fashion and they were incorporated into several GWR vehicles. In 1947, Messrs Hamptons Ltd. reconditioned several vehicles, including No. 9548, which was originally built to *Diagram H16* in 1908, the first class accommodation of which is shown in **Fig. 310**.

**Fig. 311** illustrates another example of work carried out by Messrs Hamptons Ltd. In this picture the third class decor in No. 9637, one of the 'Centenary' series to *Diagram H44*, is seen. Sister carriage No. 9638 was similarly treated.

Fig. 311

**Fig. 312**

**Fig. 313**

In **Figs. 312 & 313** we see more examples of the work of Messrs Hamptons Ltd. In 1950 they redesigned No. 9609, one of *Diagram H38* series. It is interesting to compare these pictures with **Figs. 308 & 309** to observe the differences in detail between the work done in the factory at Swindon and that done by the contractors.

**Fig. 314** is the final picture in this section and illustrates the reconditioned interior of No. W9586 in 1951. This coach was built to *Diagram H36* in 1929, over twenty years earlier. The airy, stark, simplicity of this view is in marked contrast to the heavy, elaborate, luxury of the views in **Figs. 260 & 261**.

The earliest sleeping cars were broad gauge vehicles, for first class only, built in 1877 and given *Diagrams J1 and J2*. They were converted to narrow gauge in 1881.

*Diagram J3* was given to the first class sleeping cars which were built in 1890 and the subsequent *Diagram J4* was allocated to a series of composite sleeping cars built on Lots 669 and 672, in 1892, and on Lot 747 in 1895. *Diagrams J3 & J4* were characterized by their bay windows, and drawings may be found in *G W Coaches, Part I, pages 83 & 107.*

*Diagram J5* provided accommodation for eight first class passengers and an attendant, with facilities for light refreshments. Details of these coaches are given in *G W Coaches, Part I, pages 84, 127 & 128.*

In 1907, ten years after the building of the clerestory sleeping cars, came the first of the 'Dreadnought' series, built on Lot 1123 to *Diagram J6*. The official photograph and drawing of this series can be found in *G W Coaches, Part II, page 41.*

*Diagram J7* was allocated to four first class sleeping cars which were acquired from the LSWR.

**Fig. 315** is the first picture in this section and shows the interior of a typical sleeping car built between the wars. The photograph was taken inside No. 5140, one of *Diagram J10* series, and shows that there was not much room between the berths for third class passengers, although they appear to be sleeping soundly!

Fig. 316

Fig. 317

*DIAGRAM J8*
Composite Sleeping Car
Lot 1218 of 1914
Running numbers: 9090–1
Dimensions: 56ft. 11¾in. x 8ft. 11¾in.

*DIAGRAM J8*
These coaches were originally mounted on 7ft. 6in. plate bogies, then 9ft. plate type and finally, in 1939, on six-wheeled plate bogies. **Figs. 316 & 317** show the berth side of No. 9091 in the stock shed at Old Oak Common, in 1951. The roof boards read 'Paddington and Penzance' (see also *GW Coaches, Part II, page 78*).

Fig. 318

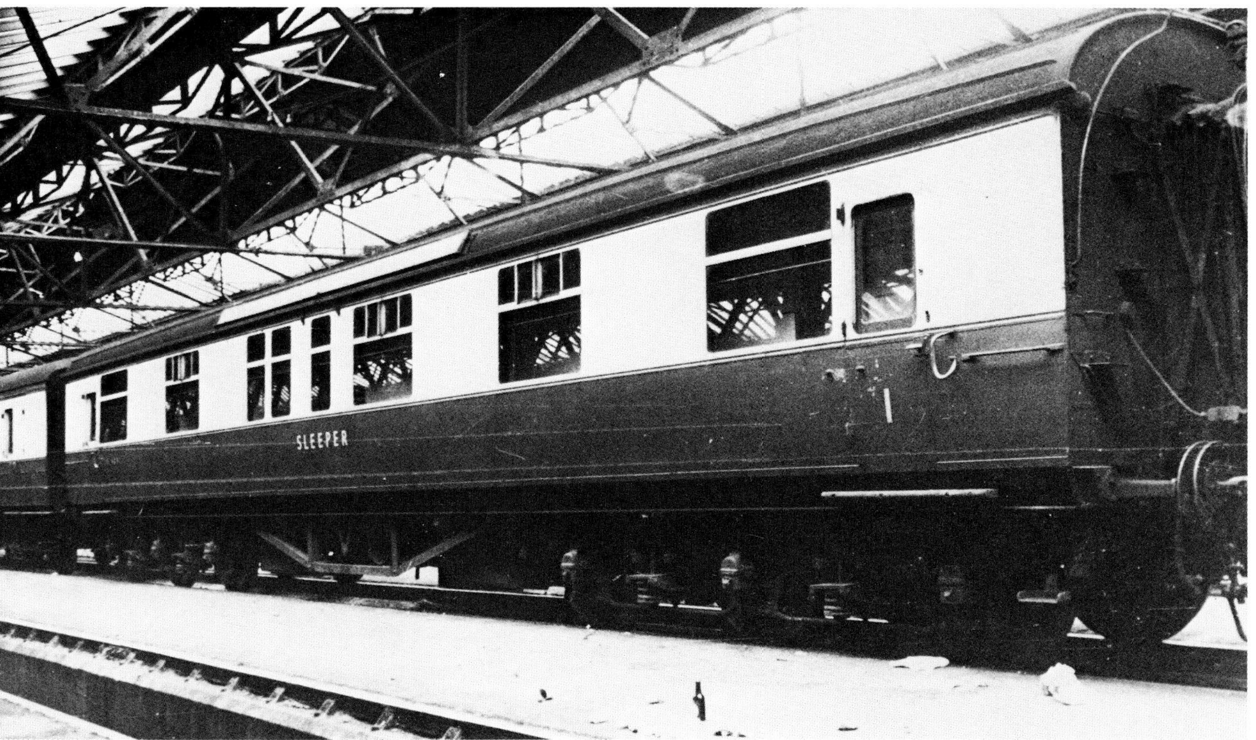


Two more pictures of No. 9091, the first, **Fig. 318**, shows the vehicle as outshopped in 1950 bearing the 'plum and spilt milk' livery. The view in **Fig. 319** was taken in 1951, again in the stock shed. It is worthy of note that only three of the windows have sliding vents, and these were fitted in 1939.

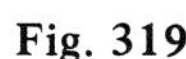

**Fig. 319**

**Fig. 320**

*DIAGRAM J9*
These coaches were mounted on three different types of bogie. Originally fitted with 7ft. 6in. plate type, they later received 9ft. plate type and finally 9ft. pressed-steel bogies. When built, accommodation was provided for four first class passengers in berths, and twenty four third class passengers seated. In 1929, the coaches were rebuilt and the third class accommodation was reduced to twelve places, now provided with berths.

**Fig. 320** shows the compartment side of No. 9093 as built and mounted on the 7ft. 6in. bogies. In **Fig. 321** the same side is seen, in 1950, and the rebuilding has resulted in sliding vent windows. **Fig. 322** shows the opposite side of No. 9093 in the stock shed, with the blinds drawn.

**Fig. 321**

*DIAGRAM J9*
Composite Sleeping Car
Lot 1251 of 1921
Running numbers: 7596 and 7600
Later, Nos. 9092–3

**Fig. 322**

Fig. 323

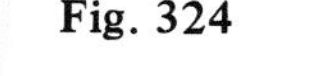

Fig. 324

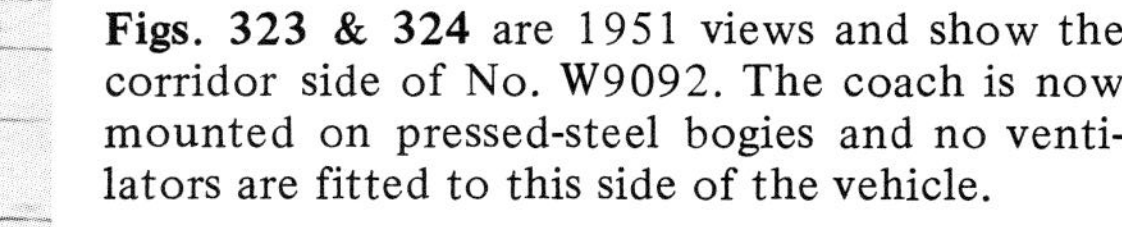

**Figs. 323 & 324** are 1951 views and show the corridor side of No. W9092. The coach is now mounted on pressed-steel bogies and no ventilators are fitted to this side of the vehicle.

**Fig. 325**

**Fig. 326**

*DIAGRAM J10 (J15)*
Third Sleeping Car
Lot 1395 of 1929
Running numbers: 5140–2
Dimensions: 58ft. 4½in. x 9ft. 0in.

*DIAGRAM J10 (J15)*
**Fig. 325** shows the corridor side of the series, as as built, and **Fig. 326** shows the compartment side of No. 9079, after conversion and re-numbering. Both photographs clearly show the 7ft. 6in. plate bogies fitted to this series. The conversion of No. 9079 made the vehicle a composite and resulted in the allocation of a new diagram *(J15)*. By the time the coach was in British Railways' service, sliding ventilators

*DIAGRAM J11*
This series of sleeping cars matched the extremely wide-bodied, contemporary, 'Cornish Riviera' stock. All the vehicles were condemned by 1961. Originally fitted with 7ft. 6in. plate bogies, the later series received the 9ft. plate type. **Figs. 328 & 329** show the compartment and corridor sides of the series, respectively. Accommodation was provided for twenty eight passengers (see also *GW Coaches, Part II, pages 147, 167 & 168).*

**Fig. 328**

**Fig. 329**

*DIAGRAM J11*
Third Sleeping Car
Lot 1419 of 1929
Running numbers: 9094–6
Lot 1440 of 1930
Running numbers: 9069–74
Dimensions: 61ft. 4½in. x 9ft. 7in.

**Fig. 330**

*DIAGRAM J12*
First Sleeping Car
Lot 1418 of 1930
Running numbers: 9080–1 and 9086–8
Lot 1439 of 1931
Running numbers: 9065–8
Dimensions: 61ft. 4½in. x 9ft. 7in.

*DIAGRAM J12*
The first class sleeping cars built to match the series just described, were given *Diagram J12* and had berths for ten passengers. An interesting difference between the two diagrams is the provision, from the outset, of six-wheeled plate bogies for the first class coaches. **Fig. 330** shows the corridor side of No. W9080 in 1949 and the roof boards read 'Paddington, Exeter, Plymouth and Penzance'. **Fig. 331** illustrates the compartment side of No. W9068, in 1951 (see also *GW Coaches, Part II, page 154*).

**Fig. 331**

*DIAGRAM J13 (bottom page)*
Composite Sleeping Car
Lot 1442 of 1931
Running number: 9075
Dimensions: 61ft. 4½in. x 9ft. 7in.

*DIAGRAM J13 (opposite page)*
Contemporary with the two previous designs, was this solitary composite vehicle to *Diagram J13*. Berths were provided for six first class and twelve third class passengers and the coach was mounted on 9ft. plate bogies. **Fig. 332** is the official view of the compartment side, and a perspective view is given in **Fig. 333** (see also *GW Coaches, Part II, page 169*).

W 9075 W
SLEEPING CAR

Fig. 334

*DIAGRAM J14*
Although they retained the recessed doors of the wide-bodied stock, the flat-ended coaches of *Diagram J14* series had neither their length nor their width. **Fig. 334** is the official view of No. 9076, as built, taken from the corridor side. For comparison, **Fig. 335** shows the berth side of No. W9077, in 1952.

Fig. 335

Fig. 336

*DIAGRAM J14*

**Fig. 336** is a perspective view of No. W9077 and clearly shows the 9ft. pressed-steel bogies on which this series was mounted.

*DIAGRAM J15*

**Fig. 337** is included here to maintain the order of diagram numbers, although it really belongs with *Diagram J10*. The vehicle is No. W9079 which was given *Diagram J15* on conversion to a composite in 1935. In 1942, the vehicle was refitted as a first class sleeping car for use by the military in the wartime 'Olive' train. The coach was finally refurbished in 1948 by Messrs Hamptons Ltd.

Fig. 337

Fig. 338

*DIAGRAM J16*
This diagram was allocated to No. 9093, on conversion from one of *Diagram J9* series for use in the 'Olive' train that was the mobile SHAEF headquarters in 1942. This coach was also refitted by Messrs Hamptons Ltd. in 1948. **Figs. 338 & 339** were taken in the stock shed at Old Oak Common in 1951.

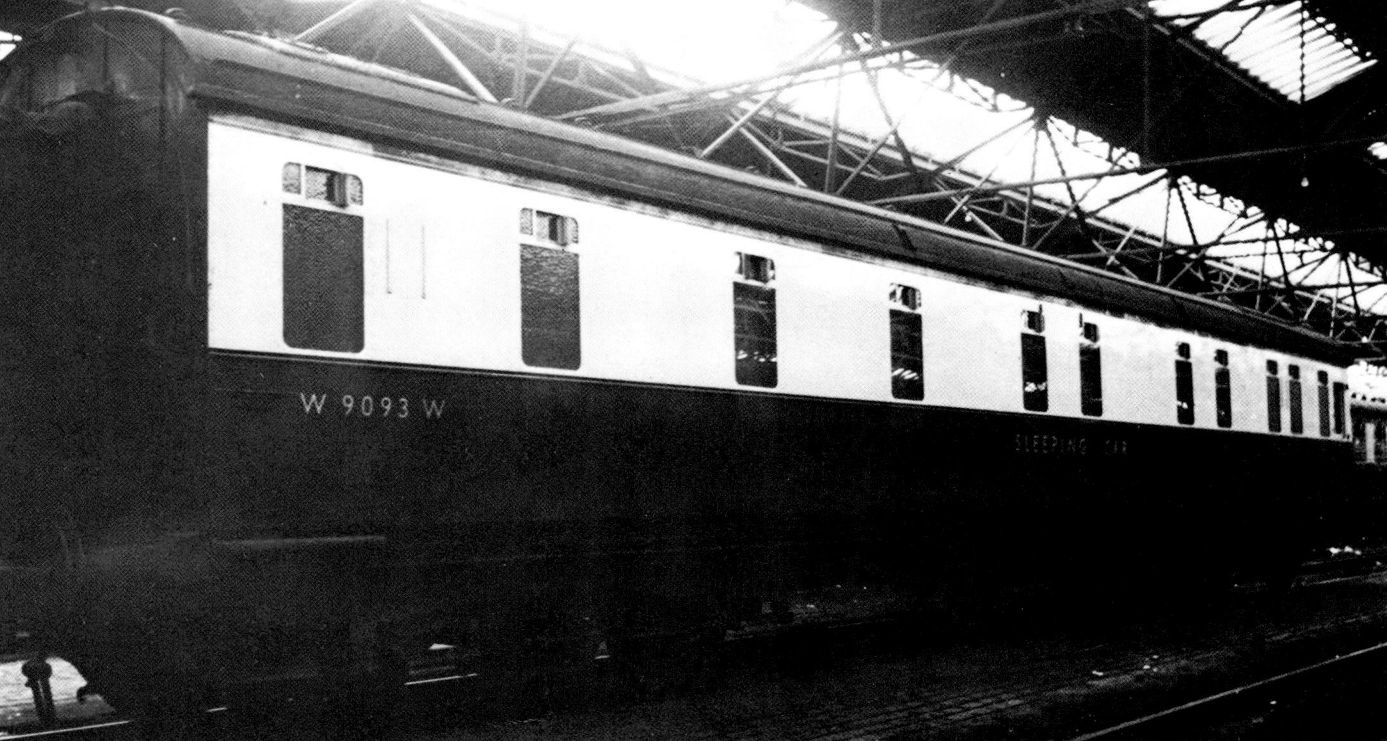


Fig. 339

*DIAGRAM J17 (opposite page)*
Built originally to *Diagram J12* in 1930, No. 9086 was extensively damaged in an air raid during the war, and was subsequently rebuilt to the new *Diagram J17* in 1945. **Figs. 340 & 341** show the coach at Swindon in 1950, and, judging by the snow on the roof and ground, were taken during the winter.

SLEEPING CAR
W 9086 W
SLEEPING CAR
W 9086 W
43
TWIN
SLFP

Fig. 342

*DIAGRAM J18*
Built to sleep ten passengers, these Hawksworth coaches had a very distinctive domed roof and ran on six-wheeled bogies. **Fig. 342** gives a high level view of No. W9082 at Penzance in 1952. In **Fig. 343**, No. W9082 is seen in the 'plum and spilt milk' livery and titled 'sleeper', whereas in **Fig. 344**, No. W9085 carries the same livery with the title 'Sleeping Car'.

Fig. 343

Fig. 345

*DIAGRAM J19*
This diagram was allocated to vehicles converted from *Diagram J14* in 1952. **Fig. 345** shows No. W9077 after conversion.

*DIAGRAM J20*
This diagram was allocated to Nos. W9070–2, converted in 1951 from *J11*.

Fig. 346

Two more photographs of British Railways' conversions. No. W9091 was originally built to *Diagram J8*, **(Fig. 346)**, and No. W9092 was once one of *Diagram J9* series. In **Fig. 347** it is seen after re-building in 1954. Six years later the coach was condemned.

Fig. 347

**Fig. 348** shows No. W9080 which was also reconditioned in 1954. Originally built to *Diagram J12* in 1930, this coach was condemned in 1960.

A British Railways sleeping car (SLSTP) 63ft. 5in. x 9ft. 0in. **Figs. 349 & 350** show No. W2572 as outshopped by Swindon in 1958. The livery is maroon with two straw and one black line on the waist.

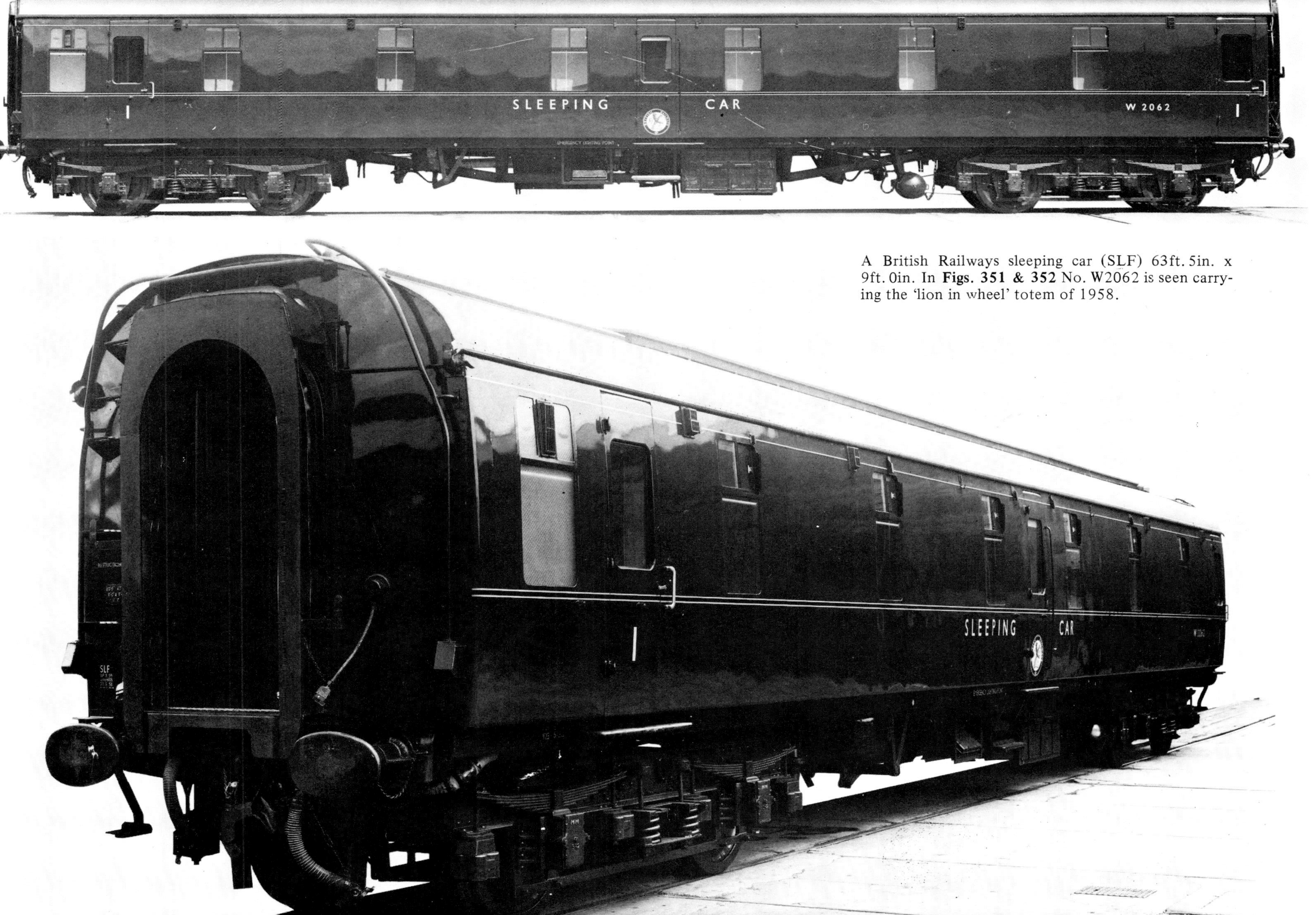


A British Railways sleeping car (SLF) 63ft. 5in. x 9ft. 0in. In **Figs. 351 & 352** No. W2062 is seen carrying the 'lion in wheel' totem of 1958.

A British Railways sleeping car (SLC). **Fig. 353** shows No. W2438 at Swindon in 1961, mounted on modern bogies.

Throughout the development of the carriages of the GWR, the passenger brake vans have, as one might expect, followed the design of contemporary passenger vehicles. In the early days, they were usually four or six-wheeled vans, sometimes with guard's accommodation, designed to blend into the line of the train and to provide stowage for the passengers' luggage. Details of the early examples are given in *G W Coaches, Parts I & II.*

*DIAGRAM K17*
Passenger Brake Van (Clerestory)
Lot 1043 of 1903
Running numbers: 1125–8
Dimensions: 54ft. 0¾in. x 8ft. 6¾in.

*DIAGRAM K17*
**Figs. 354 & 355** show what must have been one of the last clerestory vehicles in service, also one of the last running on Dean bogies. No. 1125 was condemned in March 1954 and is seen in these pictures at Old Oak Common in the all-over brown livery, and branded '10.10p.m. Postal Paddington to Penzance', in 1950. The vehicle has the recessed sliding doors and the offset gangway, typical of vans which were used in postal trains (see also *G W Coaches, Part I, page 213*).

**Fig. 354**

**Fig. 355**

*DIAGRAM K18*
Passenger Brake Van
Lot 1204 of 1912
Running numbers: 247–9
Dimensions: 57ft. 0in. x 9ft. 0in.

Fig. 356

Fig. 357

*DIAGRAMS K18 & K19*
The only difference between these two diagrams was that the former series were wooden panelled with raised mouldings and the latter were flush panelled in steel. **Fig. 356** shows No. 250 of *Diagram K19* series at Old Oak Common in 1951. No. 252 is seen at Penzance in **Fig. 357** and No. 254 is seen at Slough, in 1952, in **Fig. 358**. Note that all these vehicles are still running on 9ft. 'American' bogies, as originally fitted.

*DIAGRAM K19*
Passenger Brake Van
Lot 1241 of 1914
Running numbere: 250–4
Dimensions: 57ft. 0in. x 9ft. 0in.

Fig. 358

▲ **Fig. 359** is the official view of No. 250 as built in 1914 and carrying the crimson lake livery with painted panelling.

Fig. 360

*DIAGRAM K22*
Passenger Brake Van (Toplight)
Lot 1253 of 1915 – Running numbers: 255–6
Lot 1281 of 1922 – Running numbers: 257–66
Lot 1288 of 1921 – Running number: 267
Lot 1301 of 1922 – Running numbers: 1129–53
Dimensions: 56ft. 11¼in. x 8ft. 11¼in.

*DIAGRAM K22*
All these vehicles were condemned by December 1962. **Fig. 360** shows No. 1139, branded 'Parcels Train Brake Van', in 1950 and carrying the British Railways' strawberry and cream livery. The corridor side of the van is seen again in **Fig. 361** which shows No. 258 in 1949 carrying the double waist line livery (see also *GW Coaches, Part II, page 92*).

Fig. 351

*DIAGRAM K22*

Three more pictures of *Diagram K22* series which illustrate the non-corridor side of these vehicles. **Fig. 362** shows No. 1150 at Old Oak Common in 1949, **Fig. 363** shows No. 256 at Paddington in 1950 and **Fig. 364** shows No. 1130 marshalled into the middle of a rake of three similar vehicles.

**Fig. 362**

**Fig. 363**

**Fig. 364**

*DIAGRAM K34*
Passenger Brake Van (Toplight)
Lot 1344 of 1925
Running numbers: 1156–64
Lot 1345 of 1925
Running numbers: 1166–8
Dimensions: 57ft. 0in. x 9ft. 0in.

**Fig. 365**

*DIAGRAMS K24 to K33*
These were allocated to 40ft. low-roofed passenger brake vans which were converted to stores vans, meat vans and sleet cutters, etc.

**Fig. 366**

**Fig. 367**

**Fig. 365** shows the corridor side of No. 1164 in the 1947 GWR livery.

**Figs. 366 & 367** show the two sides of No. 1157, the former being the non-corridor side. The coach is branded for a particular service ('Paddington and Oxford') and also carries the title 'Parcels Train Brake Van'. The bogies on these coaches were the 1914 type 9ft. plate bogies.

Fig. 368

*DIAGRAM K35*
In common with the previous diagram, these coaches were rebuilds of wartime ambulance stock that had finally been returned to the GWR. In the two vehicles to *Diagram K35* the guard's compartment was placed almost centrally, one luggage compartment was 22ft. 4in. long and the other was 27ft. 9in. A side corridor was fitted and the vehicles were mounted on the 1914 bogies. **Figs. 368 & 369** show the two sides of No. 1154.

*DIAGRAM K35*
Passenger Brake Van (Toplight)
Lot 1344 of 1925
Running numbers: 1154–5
Dimensions: 57ft. 0in. x 9ft. 0in.

Fig. 369

*DIAGRAM K34*
The twelve vehicles to *Diagram K34* were produced by the rebuilding of stock that had been used in wartime ambulance trains. Internally they had one small and one large parcels compartment, together with a large guard's compartment. A full-length side corridor was provided and the ends had normal centre gangways. All the series were condemned in December 1962.

*DIAGRAM K36*
This was a similar conversion of ambulance stock on Lot 1344, and running numbers were 1157–63. The luggage compartments were 28ft. 1¾in. and 22ft. 0½in. long and the guard's compartment was placed between them. **Fig. 370** shows No. 1158 in GWR brown livery, branded 'Parcels Train Brake Van' and 'Paddington and Reading' (see also *GW Coaches, Part II, page 121*).

Fig. 371

*DIAGRAM K37*
This was the final brake van produced by rebuilding ambulance stock, and was allocated to a single vehicle, No. 1165, which was converted on Lot 1345.

*DIAGRAM H38*
Passenger Brake Van (Bow-ended)
Lot 1346 of 1926
Running numbers: 1169–74
Dimensions: 58ft. 4½in. x 8ft. 11¼in.

Fig. 372

*DIAGRAM K38*
These bow-ended vans were intended for the 'Ocean Mails' services. **Fig. 371** shows No. W1169 in British Railways all-over brown livery and branded 'Paddington and Penzance'. The gangways were centrally placed (see also *GW Coaches, Part II, page 122*).

Fig. 373

*DIAGRAM K39*
This was allocated to a one-off vehicle which was built in 1926 to replace No. 255 which had been completely burnt out. The coach was 57ft. x 9ft. and had flat ends, and it was condemned in March 1957.

*DIAGRAM K40*
Passenger Brake Van (Bow-ended)
Lot 1413 of 1930 – Running numbers: 1175–84
Lot 1462 of 1931 – Running numbers: 3–6/11/13/19/27–8/31–7/39/41/43/51/53/55–7
Lot 1481 of 1933 – Running numbers: 71–85
Dimensions: 61ft. 4½in. x 9ft. 0in.

*DIAGRAM K40*
Mounted on 7ft. plate bogies, these vehicles were designed for use on cross-country services. **Fig. 372** shows No. W53 painted in brown and branded 'Paddington & Penzance, Paddington & Chester'. In **Fig. 373** No. W33 is seen branded 'Return to Paddington' (see also *GW Coaches, Part II, page 153*).

Fig. 374

*DIAGRAM K41*

This series was intended for general service and was fitted with 9ft. pressed-steel bogies and an internal side corridor, although the gangways were centrally placed. **Fig. 374** shows No. W195 at Reading in 1949 branded 'Paddington & Penzance' and 'Paddington & Chester'.

**Figs. 375 & 376** show, respectively, the corridor and non-corridor sides of No. 147, branded for the Swindon and Carmarthen service, and were photographed at Swindon when the coach was outshopped in the last GWR livery (see also *G W Coaches, Part II, page 202*).

Fig. 375

*DIAGRAM K41*
Passenger Brake Van
Lot 1495 of 1934 – Running numbers: 101–110
Lot 1512 of 1934 – Running numbers: 111–120
Lot 1535 of 1935 – Running numbers: 181–200
Lot 1562 of 1936 – Running numbers: 138–157
Dimensions: 61ft. 4½in. x 9ft. 0in.

Fig. 376

Fig. 378

Fig. 379

*DIAGRAM K42*
Passenger Brake Van
Lot 1604 of 1937 – Running numbers: 158–167
Lot 1652 of 1940 – Running numbers: 121–130
Lot 1665 of 1945 – Running numbers: 91–100, and 268–277
Dimensions: 57ft. 0in. x 8ft. 11in.

These vans too were designed for general service and were mounted on 9ft. pressed-steel bogies. **Fig. 377** shows No. 166 as built in 1937 in the all-over brown livery and with 'roundel'. The brand, which reads 'To work 8.55p.m. Paddington to Cardiff' and the '1.48p.m. Cardiff to Paddington' is unusually specific. **Fig. 378** is a similar view of No. 124, taken in 1940, but no workings are specified for this coach. The final official photograph of the series, **Fig. 379**, shows No. 95 in the final GWR chocolate and cream livery, in 1948 (see also *GW Coaches, Part II, page 257*).

**Fig. 380** depicts the corridor side of No. W164 in British Railways strawberry and cream livery, and branded 'Return to Paddington'.

**Fig. 381** shows the non-corridor side of No. W130 branded 'Return to Swindon'.

*DIAGRAM K43*

This diagram was allocated to the three small four-wheeled brake vans, Nos. 135–7, on the Vale of Rheidol Railway.

Fig. 382

Fig. 383

*DIAGRAM K44*
Passenger Brake Van
Lot 1667 of 1941
Running numbers: 61–70
Dimensions: 59ft. 10in. x 8ft. 11in.

*DIAGRAM K44*
**Fig. 382** shows No. 69, as built in 1941, painted in the all-over brown livery with a dark grey roof and black underframe. The coach is branded 'Parcels Train Brake Van'. No. W66 is seen in the strawberry and cream livery in **Fig. 383**.

Fig. 384

*DIAGRAM K45*
**Fig. 384** is the official Swindon photograph of the series, as built, and depicts No. W311. The distinctive domed roof of the Hawksworth design and the 9ft. pressed-steel bogies are clearly illustrated. **Figs. 385 & 386** were taken at Old Oak Common, in 1951, and show the two sides of the coaches. In **Fig. 386**, No. W324 is on the carriage turntable.

Fig. 385

Fig. 386

*DIAGRAM K45*
Passenger Brake Van
Lot 1722 of 1949
Running numbers: 290–9
Lot 1740 of 1950
Running numbers: 300–24
Dimensions: 64ft. 0in. x 8ft. 11in.

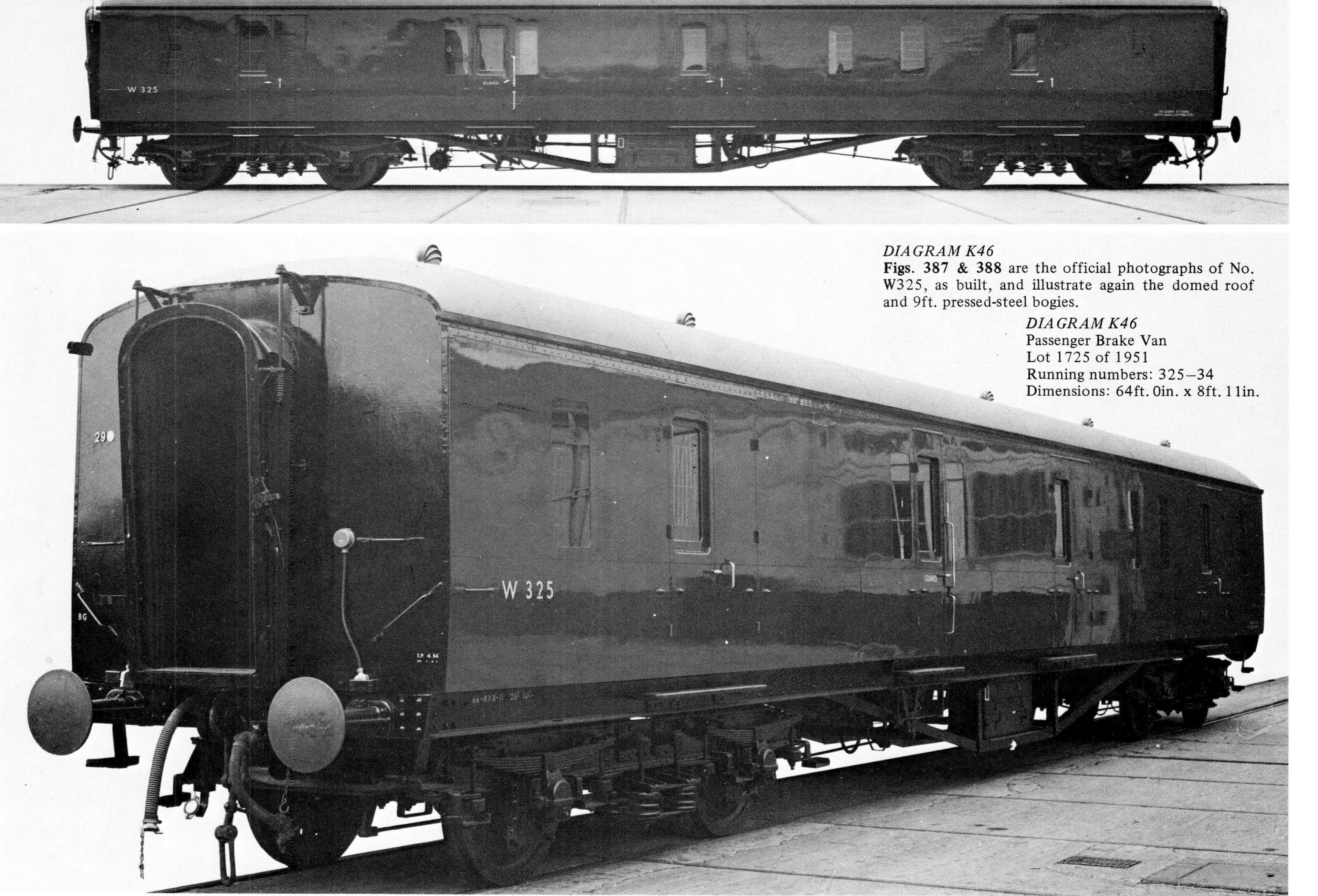


*DIAGRAM K46*

**Figs. 387 & 388** are the official photographs of No. W325, as built, and illustrate again the domed roof and 9ft. pressed-steel bogies.

*DIAGRAM K46*
Passenger Brake Van
Lot 1725 of 1951
Running numbers: 325–34
Dimensions: 64ft. 0in. x 8ft. 11in.

Fig. 389

The next two pages illustrate British Railways-designed passenger brakes built at Swindon. On this page **Figs. 389 & 390** are official pictures of No. W80675, built in 1954 and classified as Type N. The livery is maroon with a grey roof.

Fig. 390

**Figs. 391 & 392** show Nos. W80705 and 81015 which were classified as Type BG. This series was built in 1955.

Fig. 393

The final pictures in this section show two elderly, but long-lived, parcels vans. **Fig. 393** shows an old clerestory coach, built originally to *Diagram C10* in 1897, after conversion to a parcels van in 1940. There were eight such vehicles, Nos. 2925, 2931, 3005, 3067, 3131, 1305 and 1767. The converted coaches were given *Diagram M28*.

Fig. 394

**Fig. 394** shows the vehicle as it was in War Department ownership. There are several interesting features which suggest that it was used as a goods rather than a passenger brake while in War Department service. The first of these is the fitting of GWR self-contained goods buffers. These were shorter than the buffers used on coaching stock and would be needed for use with 3 link couplings. The second feature is the fitting of sanding apparatus. The pipes can be seen behind the footboards at the near end of the coach, which would be needed to assist with the braking of trains of loose-coupled, unfitted, wagons. The final point to note is the additional grab handle fitted by the door to the guard's compartment. This would provide for a shunter or guard standing on the ground beside the train. The official photograph of the series as built can be seen in **Fig. 99** in *GW Coaches, Part I, page 104*).

The second vehicle had an even more interesting history. Built in 1892 as a passenger brake van to *Diagram V5* on Lot 599 and given the number 2, the vehicle ran in GWR stock until 1917 when it was sold to the War Department for overseas service. In 1919 it was returned to the GWR, the guard's look-outs were removed, which brought the vehicle into *Diagram V4*, and it was returned to service with the number 1041.

The carriage of mails by the railways was an inevitable result of their ability to offer rapid transport between centres of population. The GWR built special carriages for this traffic from an early date, initially four and six-wheeled, in keeping with contemporary coaching stock, and used these only for sorting. In 1859, however, mail was set down and picked up by a moving train at Yatton on the Bristol and Exeter line. In 1866, the necessary apparatus for this operation was installed at a number of other stations on the main line to the West Country. Details of the early coaches are given below and photographs of some of them may be found in *GW Coaches, Part 1, pages 25–7, 99 & 213.*

*DIAGRAM L2*
Clerestory Stowage Van
Lot 303
Running numbers: 843–44
Dimenions: 46ft. 6¾in. x 8ft. 6in.
Codemned October 1932

*DIAGRAM L3*
Clerestory Van (with net)
Lot 465 – Running number: 841
Lot 598 – Running number: 838
Dimensions: 48ft. 6¾in. x 8ft. 6¾in.
Condemned April 1934

*DIAGRAM L4*
Clerestory Stowage Van
Lot 465
Running number: 842
Dimensions: 48ft. 6¾in. x 8ft. 6¾in.
Condemned September 1934

*DIAGRAM L5*
Low-roof Stowage Van
Lot 469
Running number: 916
Non-corridor. Became a passenger brake.

*DIAGRAM L6*
Clerestory Stowage Van
Lot 518
Running number: 845
Dimensions: 46ft. 6¾in. x 8ft. 6¾in.
Condemned March 1934

*DIAGRAM L8*
Clerestory Stowage Van
Lot 579
Running number: 859
Dimensions: 46ft. 6¾in. x 8ft. 6¾in.
Condemned February 1935

*DIAGRAMS L10 & L11*
Clerestory Stowage Van
Lot 607 of 1892
Running numbers: 862–3 *(Diagram L10)*
Running numbers: 864–5 *(Diagram L11)*
Dimensions: 40ft. 0¾in. x 8ft. 6¾in.
Mounted on Dean 6ft. 4in. bogies
The vans to *Diagram L10* had three sliding doors on one side and two on the other, those to *Diagram L11* had three doors on one side and only one on the other.

*DIAGRAM L12*
Clerestory Sorting Van
Lot 735 of 1894
Running number: 2083
Dimensions: 48ft. 6¾in. x 8ft. 6¾in.
This van also had three doors on one side and one on the other.

*DIAGRAM L9*
Clerestory Sorting Van
Lot 604 – Running numbers: 860–1
Lot 746 – Running number: 846
Condemned September 1934

*DIAGRAMS L13 & L14*
Sorting Van (Elliptical Roof)
Lot 1094 *(Diagram L13)*
Lot 1095 *(Diagram L14)*
Running numbers: 834–6 *(Diagram L13)*
Running numbers: 830–2 *(Diagram L14)*
Dimensions: 70ft. 0in. x 8ft. 6¾in.

**Fig. 396**

*AGRAMS L13 & L14*
e vans to *Diagram L13* had a pair of hinged doors on one side and two sliding doors on the ıer, with a net bay. *Diagram L14* vans had two sliding doors on each side. **Figs. 395 & 396** ɔw side and end views of No. W835, one of the vans to *Diagram L13*, photographed in 1949 Old Oak Common. **Fig. 397** shows No. 832 in early condition. Note the large GR monogram the centre of the vehicle and the apparatus on the side of the van for setting down and king up mailbags whilst the train is in motion. The low clerestory was originally fitted to se vehicles.

**Fig. 397**

Fig. 398

**Fig. 398** shows No. W835, one of the vans to *Diagram L13*, in British Railways crimson lake livery, and is viewed from the side with the single pair of hinged doors. In **Fig. 399**, No. 841 *(Diagram L14)* is seen after shopping at Swindon in 1937. This official photograph shows the two, recessed, sliding doors and the special 'late posting box' that could be used by travellers, at the cost of an extra halfpenny stamp! The lettering 'Royal Mail' was in gold, shaded in red.

Fig. 399

**Fig. 400 (opposite page)** is a full page illustration showing the interior of No. 831, one of the vans built to *Diagram L13*. The view is looking along the length of the vehicle with the sliding doors on the right-hand side and the hinged doors beyond the fourth sorter's stool. The letter racks can be seen in front of the sorters' position, and on the right-hand wall are the hooks for holding open mailbags. In the lower right-hand corner of the picture, a GWR pattern fire extinguisher can be seen below the box for late post. The pipes in the roof were for the steam heating supply.

**Fig. 401 (above)** is the companion photograph to **Fig. 400** and shows the view in the opposite direction along the vehicle. The net bay, in this case not used, is seen in the left foreground. The heavy curtains which can be seen in this and the previous photograph were fitted to combat the draughts which nearly always ensued with sliding doors. Normal letters could be sorted whilst the post office workers were seated. Small parcels and larger packets were dealt with standing up, hence the padded trays in the centre of the

*DIAGRAM L16*
Clerestory Postal Van
Rebuild from Lot 465
Running number: 840
Dimensions: 48ft. 6¾in. x 8ft. 6¾in.

*DIAGRAM L15*
These vehicles were rebuilds of earlier Lots 392 (No. 850) and 405 (Nos. 852 and 853). They had three sliding doors each side and two net bays. **Fig. 402** depicts No. 852 in the stock shed at Old Oak Common in 1932.

*DIAGRAM L18*
Travelling Post Office
Lot 1430 of 1929
Running numbers: 806–8
Dimensions: 57ft. 0in. x 8ft. 6in.

*DIAGRAM L15*
Clerestory Sorting Van
Lot 1096 of 1905
Running numbers: 850, 852 and 853
Dimensions: 46ft. 6¾in. x 8ft. 6¾in.

*DIAGRAM L18*
Originally mounted on 7ft. plate bogies these bogie vehicles were fitted with pickup apparatus. **Fig. 403** shows No. 807 in British Railways' days and the late posting box can be seen between the words Royal and Mail (see also *GW Coaches, Part II, pages 162 & 163*).

*DIAGRAM L19*
Sorting Van
Lot 1484 of 1932
Running numbers: 848–9
Dimensions: 57ft. 0in. x 9ft. 0in.
No pickup apparatus

*DIAGRAM L17*
Ex-Cambrian No. 293 (became GWR No. 811 in 1925)
Dimensions: 42ft. 0in. x 8ft. 6in.
This was a low-roofed vehicle.

**Fig. 403**

ROYAL MAIL
W 793 W

*DIAGRAM L20*
Sorting Van
Lot 1500 of 1933
Running number: 796
Dimensions: 57ft. 0in. x 8ft. 6in.
(see also *GW Coaches Part II, pages 184 & 190*).

*DIAGRAM L21*
Post Office Collector Van
Lot 1499 of 1933
Running numbers: 793–5
Dimensions: 57ft. 0in. x 9ft. 0in.

*DIAGRAM L21*
**Fig. 404** shows the apparatus side of No. 794 in the 1951 British Railways maroon livery. The lights fitted to the outside of the TPOs can be seen beside the doors, and in this case they are electrically lit, which must have been an improvement over the oil lamps seen on No. 852 in **Fig. 402** (see also *GW Coaches, Part II, pages 188 & 189*).

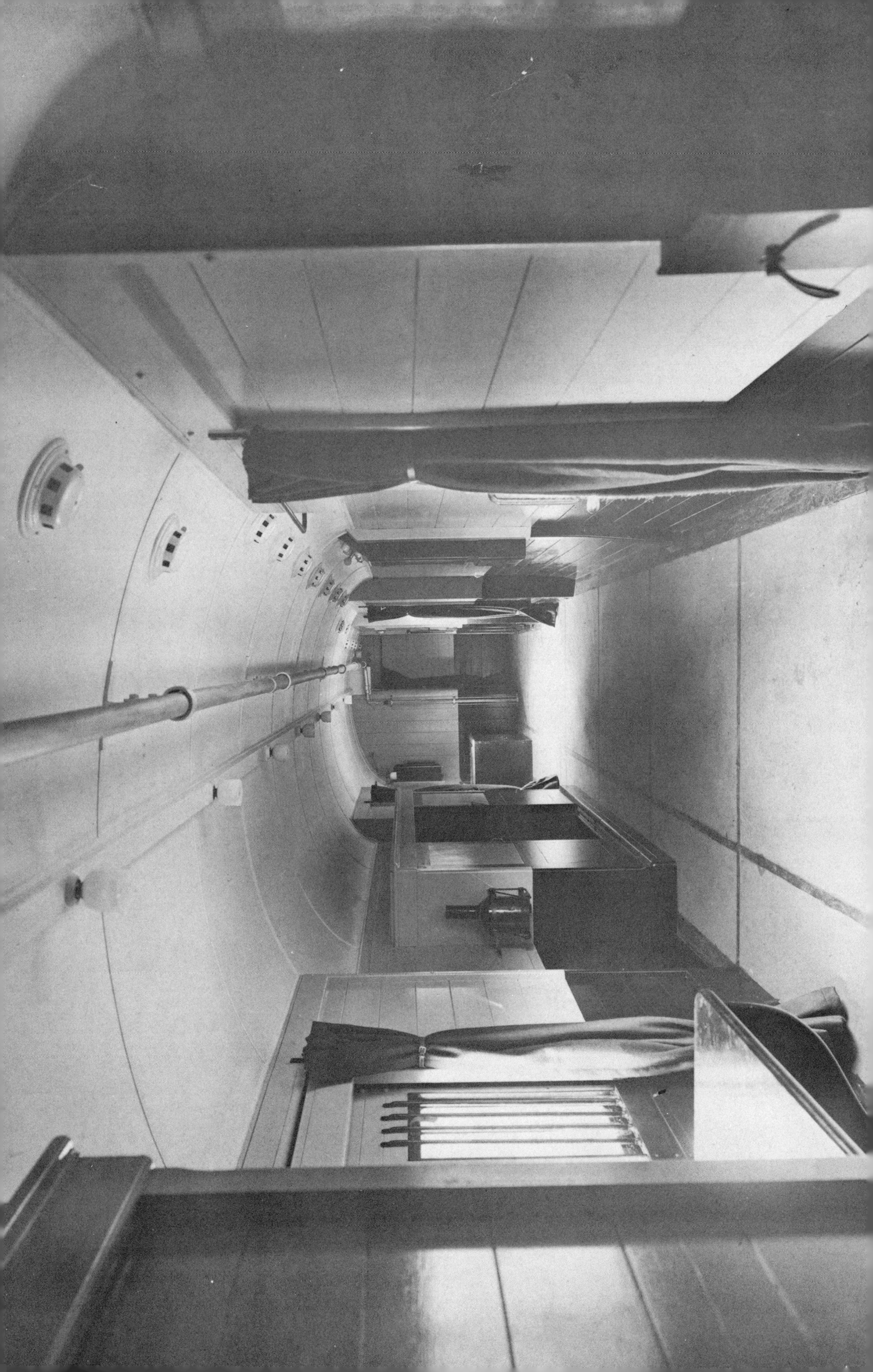

*DIAGRAM L21*
**Fig. 405 (opposite page)** gives an excellent view of the interior of No. 795 and shows that, although fitted with apparatus for picking up and setting down mailbags, these coaches were not fitted with sorting racks. Provision was made for the comforts of the staff, although of a meagre nature. A large wardrobe can be seen to the left of centre and a toilet is situated at the far end of the vehicle. A water heater and sink were installed, as was an electric oven for limited cooking facilities. The steam heating pipe runs along the roof of the vehicle and the usual heavy curtains are provided to reduce draughts. It is noticeable that no seating is provided.

**Fig. 406**

**Fig. 407**

*DIAGRAM L22*
Post Office Delivery Van
Lot 1501 of 1933
Running numbers: 797–800
Lot 1502 of 1934
Running numbers: 801–3
Dimensions: 50ft. 0in. x 8ft. 6in.

*DIAGRAM L22*
The first series of vehicles built to *Diagram L22* were built with pickup apparatus, but the second series were not so equipped. **Fig. 406** shows the letter rack side of No. 799 and the livery is British Railways maroon. Notice the offset placing of the lettering 'Royal Mail'. **Fig. 407** shows the apparatus side of No. 797, again in British Railways maroon livery (see also *GW Coaches, Part II, page 191*).

once that the traditional layout has changed little over the years. Letter racks are on the right with the newspaper and light packets table in the centre. The sliding doors, with their heavy curtains, can be seen to the left, and in the left lower part of the picture, the lever for operating the net is shown in the closed position.

*DIAGRAM L23*
Post Office Stowage Van
Lot 1503 of 1933
Running numbers: 812–4
Dimensions: 50ft. 0in. x 8ft. 6in.
*DIAGRAM L23*
These vehicles were built with guards' compartments and fitted with pickup nets on both sides. **Fig. 409** clearly shows the offset position of one set when it is compared with **Fig. 410**. No apparatus is fitted for setting down on the side with the offset net.

Fig. 411

*DIAGRAM L23*
In 1940, No. 814 was destroyed in an air raid and a replacement was built on Lot 1666. This replacement vehicle is seen in **Fig. 411**.

*DIAGRAM L24*
Post Office Stowage Van
Lot 1504 of 1933
Running numbers: 815–7
Dimensions: 46ft. 6in. x 8ft. 6in.

*DIAGRAM L24*
No apparatus was fitted to this series, although provision was made for fitting, if necessary. This can be seen in **Fig. 412**, depicting No. 816 at Old Oak Common in 1948 (see also *GW Coaches, Part II, page 192*).

Fig. 412

*DIAGRAM L24*
**Fig. 413 (opposite page)** shows the interior of No. 815, one of *Diagram L24* series, and illustrates how small the internal variations were, in spite of the different diagrams. This view should be compared with that of **Fig. 406**.

Fig. 414

*DIAGRAM L23*
Two further views of No. 814 of *Diagram L23* series. **Fig. 414** shows the vehicle with the doors open and the net extended, and was taken at Old Oak Common stock shed in 1952. In **Fig. 415**, the coach is seen after passing through Swindon Works in 1954.

Fig. 415

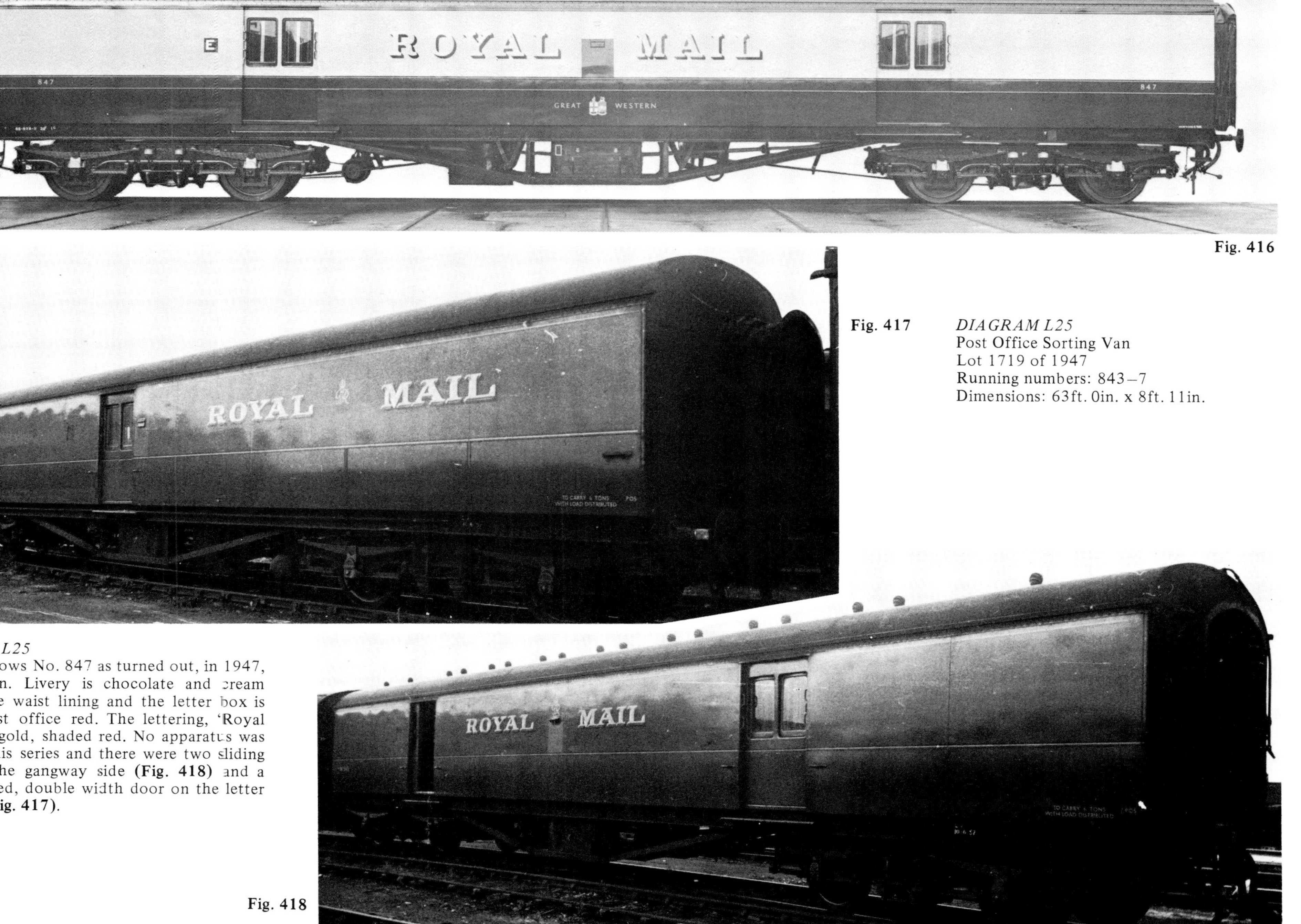


Fig. 416

Fig. 417

*DIAGRAM L25*
Post Office Sorting Van
Lot 1719 of 1947
Running numbers: 843–7
Dimensions: 63ft. 0in. x 8ft. 11in.

*DIAGRAM L25*
**Fig. 416** shows No. 847 as turned out, in 1947, by Swindon. Livery is chocolate and cream with double waist lining and the letter box is painted post office red. The lettering, 'Royal Mail' is in gold, shaded red. No apparatus was fitted to this series and there were two sliding doors on the gangway side **(Fig. 418)** and a single, hinged, double width door on the letter rack side **(Fig. 417)**.

Fig. 418

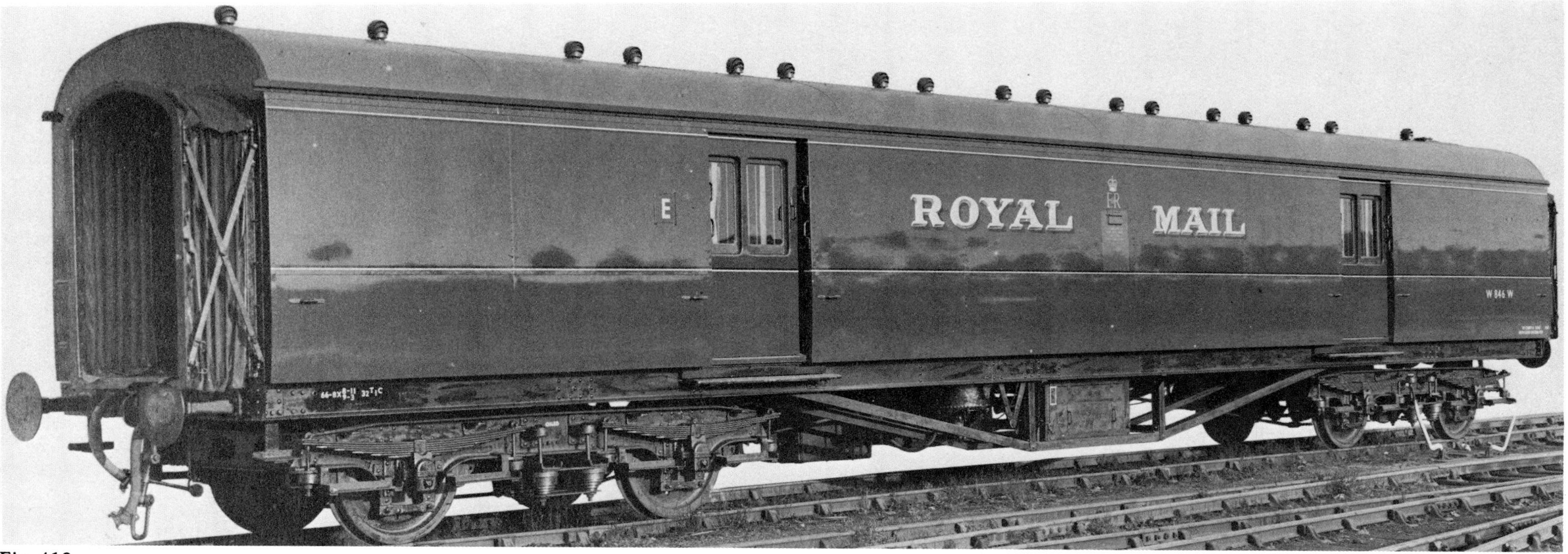

Fig. 419

*DIAGRAM L25*

**Figs. 419 & 420** show two final views of No. 846 after shopping at Swindon in 1954.

Fig. 420

*DIAGRAM M2*
Newspaper Van
Lot 444
Running number: 785
Dimensions: 40ft. 0¾in. x 8ft. 0¾in.

*DIAGRAM M3*
Parcels Van
Lot 493
Running number: 866
Dimensions: 46ft. 6¾in. x 8ft. 0¾in.
Three sliding doors on eachside. The vehicle was Condemned in 1934

*DIAGRAM M8*
Post Office Sorting Slip Van
Lot 1061 of 1904
Running number: 837
Dimensions: 68ft. 0in. x 9ft. 6¾in.

*DIAGRAM M2*
**Fig. 421** shows the vehicle at Paddington in 1932. The low roof and Dean 6ft. 4in. bogies can be seen, also the absence of gangways. The van was condemned in 1933. **Fig. 422** is interesting in that the van has been fitted with postal type side gangways. Unfortunately the number is indecipherable.

**Fig. 421**

*DIAGRAM M4*
Parcels Van
Lot 550 of 1891
Running number: 867
Dimensions: 40ft. 0¾in. x 8ft. 0¾in.
This was a conversion from No. 1047, a *Diagram K4* brake van with three sliding doors each side. The vehicle was condemned in 1934.

*DIAGRAM M6*
Parcels Van
Lot 550 of 1891
Running numbers: 1019 and 1023
Dimensions: 40ft. 0¾in. x 8ft. 0¾in.
Also conversions from *Diagram K4* brake vans, these vans had hinged doors.

*DIAGRAM M7*
Newspaper Van
Lot 960 of 1900
Running numbers: 868–9
Lot 995 of 1902
Running numbers: 870–3
Dimensions: 46ft. 6¾in. x 8ft. 0¾in.
Three sliding doors were fitted at each side and a photograph of this vehicle can be seen in *GW Coaches, Part I, page 103.*

*DIAGRAM M8*
This diagram was given to the solitary vehicle on Lot 1061 (No. 837) seen in **Fig. 423 (bottom photograph)**. It was built with a low clerestory rooflight, a guard's compartment and lavatory. The rooflight was removed in 1933. The photograph was taken at Old Oak Common in 1952. A picture of the van in use, in its original condition, can be seen in *GW Coaches, Part I, page 230,* and in *GW Coaches, Part II, page 10.*

**Fig. 422**

**Fig. 423**

*DIAGRAMS M9 & M10*
These vehicles were of similar design, the only distinction being in the official diagram book which shows No. 823 as *Diagram M9*, being distinguished by a small guard's compartment. Postal type side gangways were fitted and the vans were originally mounted on 9ft. 'American' bogies. **Fig. 424** shows No. 821 at Old Oak Common in 1949 still carrying the old GWR colour. In **Fig. 425** the guard's compartment end of No. 823 can be seen. It is noticeable that both vehicles are now mounted on 9ft. plate bogies and that the gangways have been blanked off (see also *GW Coaches, Part I, page 231*).

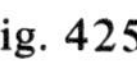

**Fig. 425**

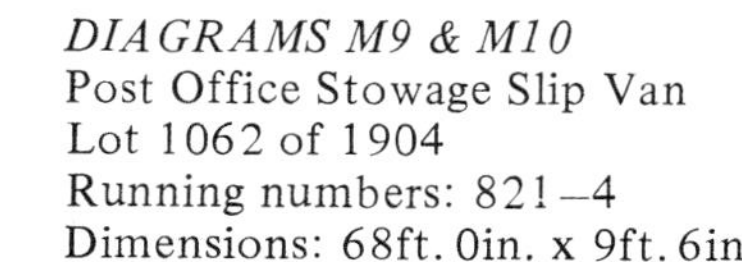

*DIAGRAMS M9 & M10*
Post Office Stowage Slip Van
Lot 1062 of 1904
Running numbers: 821–4
Dimensions: 68ft. 0in. x 9ft. 6in.

*DIAGRAM M11*
Parcels Van
Lot 1091 of 1905
Running numbers: 825–9
Dimensions: 70ft. 0in. x 8ft. 6¾in.

**Fig. 426**

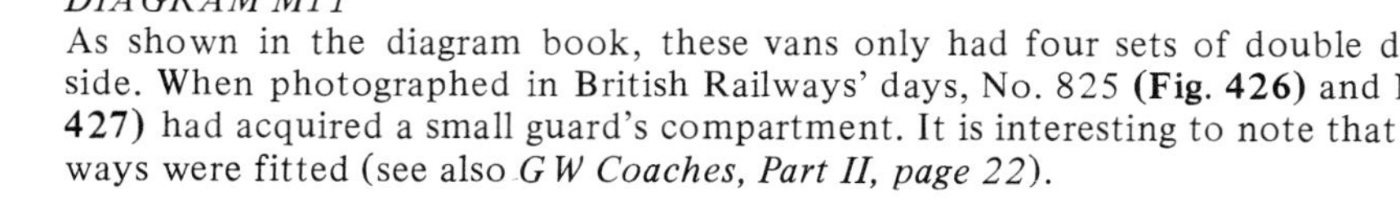

*DIAGRAM M11*
As shown in the diagram book, these vans only had four sets of double doors on each side. When photographed in British Railways' days, No. 825 **(Fig. 426)** and No. 826 **(Fig. 427)** had acquired a small guard's compartment. It is interesting to note that central gangways were fitted (see also *GW Coaches, Part II, page 22*).

**Fig. 427**

Fig. 428

*DIAGRAM M10*

**Figs. 428 & 429** show two superb official views of No. 822 taken at Paddington when the vehicle was carrying the full crimson lake livery. The 'Ocean Mails' inscription was gold, shaded red. The roof was white and the underframe and vehicle ends were black. The similarity to contemporary 'Dreadnought' stock is obvious.

Fig. 429

823

**Fig. 430 (opposite page)** illustrates the use to which the large sliding doors were put when the vehicles were loaded at Plymouth Millbay Ocean Quay with the transatlantic mails. Mailbags were transferred from the liners lying in the Sound to GWR mail tenders and thence, by electric conveyor seen in the photograph, to the railway vehicles. The date is 1927 and the vehicle is No. 823, the only van to *Diagram M9*.

*DIAGRAM M12*
Post Office Stowage Van
Lot 1144 of 1908
Running numbers: 874–5
Dimensions: 70ft. 0in. x 9ft. 0in.

*DIAGRAM M13*
Parcels Van
Lot 1165 of 1908
Running number: 833
Dimensions: 70ft. 0in. x 8ft. 11in.

*DIAGRAM M12*
**Fig. 431** depicts No. 874 at Old Oak Common with the guard's compartment nearest the camera. These vans were intended for Fishguard 'Ocean Mails' traffic.

*DIAGRAM M13*
A one-off outside-framed van of which photographs and a diagram can be found in *GW Coaches, Part II, pages 61 & 62.*

**Fig. 432**

**Fig. 433**

*DIAGRAM M14*
Parcels Van
Lot 1178 of 1910
Running numbers: 876–7
Dimensions: 70ft. 0in. x 9ft. 0in.

*DIAGRAM M14*
Built for newspaper and parcels traffic on the Fishguard Boat Train, these vans had four sliding doors each side and a guard's compartment. They were unusual in that they were mounted on six-wheeled bogies, as can be seen in **Figs. 432 & 433**, taken in 1951 and showing No. 876.

Fig. 434

**Fig. 434** shows another view of No. 876 at Old Oak Common. The vehicle is branded 'Paddington and Carmarthen' with 'Newspapers' on the waist panel.

*DIAGRAM M15*
Post Office Stowage Vans
Lot 1185 of 1910
Running numbers: 1201–6
Dimensions: 70ft. 0in. x 9ft. 0in.

Fig. 435

*DIAGRAM M15*
Once again these were massive vehicles built to the limits of the loading gauge and running on six-wheeled bogies. Nos. 1201 and 1206 were built without partitions and used as luggage vans and Nos. 1202–5 were fitted with hinged partitions and were used for 'Ocean Mails' traffic. **Fig. 435** is taken from the guard's compartment end of No. 1201 in 1950 and **Fig. 436** shows the opposite end of the vehicle in 1949. The lettering 'luggage' can be seen on the sliding doors.

Fig. 436

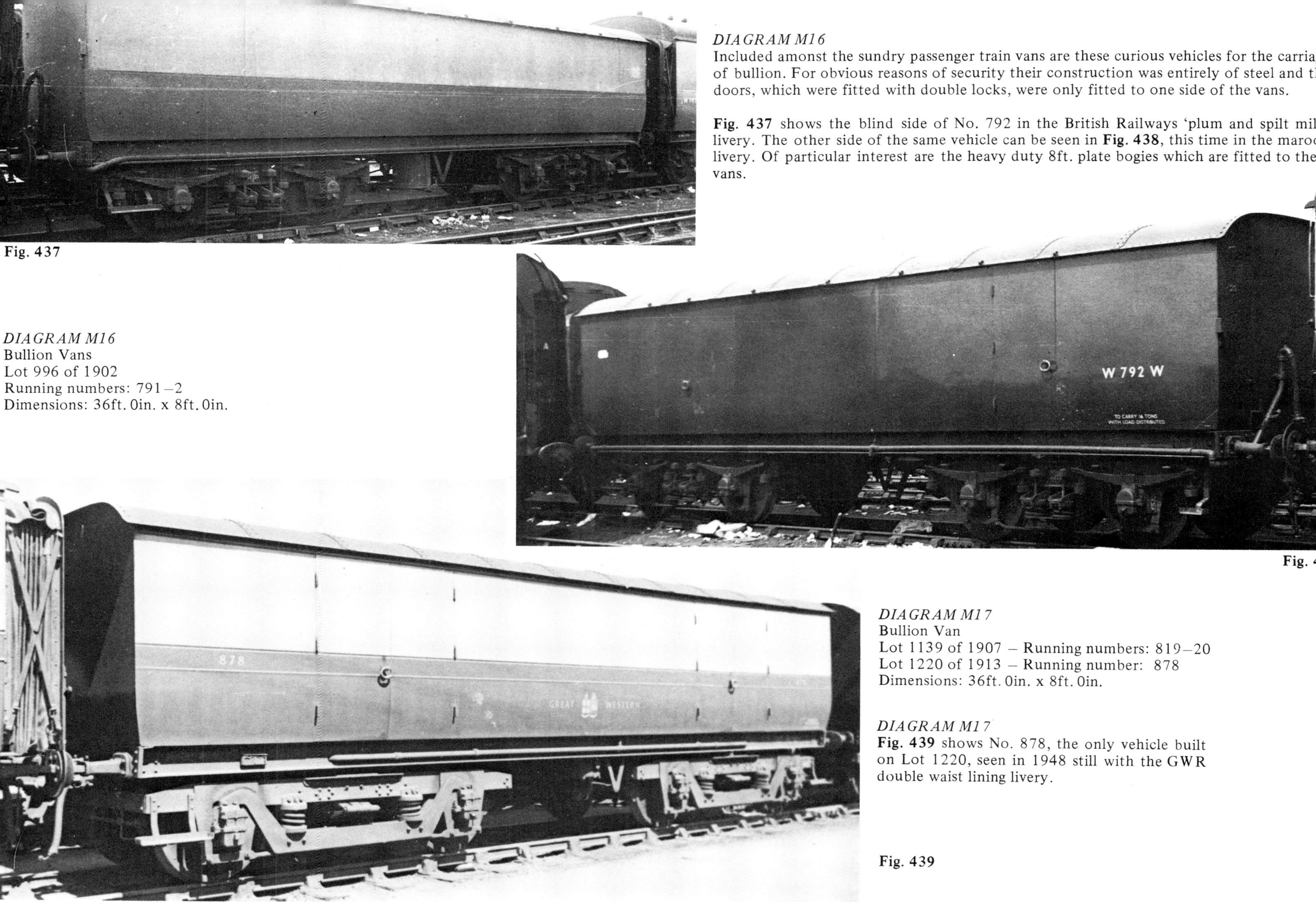


*DIAGRAM M16*
Included amonst the sundry passenger train vans are these curious vehicles for the carriage of bullion. For obvious reasons of security their construction was entirely of steel and the doors, which were fitted with double locks, were only fitted to one side of the vans.

**Fig. 437** shows the blind side of No. 792 in the British Railways 'plum and spilt milk' livery. The other side of the same vehicle can be seen in **Fig. 438**, this time in the maroon livery. Of particular interest are the heavy duty 8ft. plate bogies which are fitted to these vans.

**Fig. 437**

*DIAGRAM M16*
Bullion Vans
Lot 996 of 1902
Running numbers: 791–2
Dimensions: 36ft. 0in. x 8ft. 0in.

**Fig. 438**

*DIAGRAM M17*
Bullion Van
Lot 1139 of 1907 – Running numbers: 819–20
Lot 1220 of 1913 – Running number: 878
Dimensions: 36ft. 0in. x 8ft. 0in.

*DIAGRAM M17*
**Fig. 439** shows No. 878, the only vehicle built on Lot 1220, seen in 1948 still with the GWR double waist lining livery.

**Fig. 439**

Fig. 440

*DIAGRAM M17*
**Figs. 440 & 441** show both sides of these vans. The 9ft. 'American' bogies look a little overscale on so short a vehicle, and the coat of arms on the blind side looks decidedly lonely in the middle of such a large expanse of flat metal (see also *G W Coaches, Part II, page 52*).

*DIAGRAM M22*
Stowage vans Nos. 1202 & 1203 converted to luggage vans in 1925 and *Diagram M15* revised to M22.

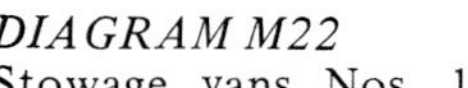

Fig. 441

Fig. 442

Fig. 443

Breakdown vans for Locomotive Dept.
Dimensions: 62ft. x 8ft. 0in. on 9ft. volute bogies
Built 1890 under Lot 542
No. 130 allotted to Old Oak Common in 1906
No. 131 allotted to Slough
No. 132 allotted to Swindon factory in 1909
**Fig. 442** shows No. 130 at Paddington in 1947
**Fig. 443** shows No. 131 at Slough in 1947
**Fig. 444** is also of No. 131 but illustrates the opposite end
**Fig. 445** is an inside view of these self-contained tool-cum-workshops
The GWR livery of these vans was chocolate sides, grey roof, black chassis, and the end was bright post office red. All lettering was in straw-coloured yellow.

Fig. 445

Fig. 444

Fig. 446

Fig. 447

**Fig. 446** shows No. 26 built under Lot 782, originally as 'Tender', and rostered for Birkenhead as at 1914.

Breakdown vans, Pilot and Tender, Twin Sets
Pilot vans were the four wheel (sometimes six wheel) vehicles built and used as travelling tool rooms for derailments or accidents. Tender vans ran with their twin 'Pilot' vans and were built and used as mess rooms, with full length bunks, for possible use as sleeping accommodation if necessary.

**Fig. 447** is of the twin vehicle No. 25, the pilot van, also destined for Birkenhead as at 1914.

Fig. 448

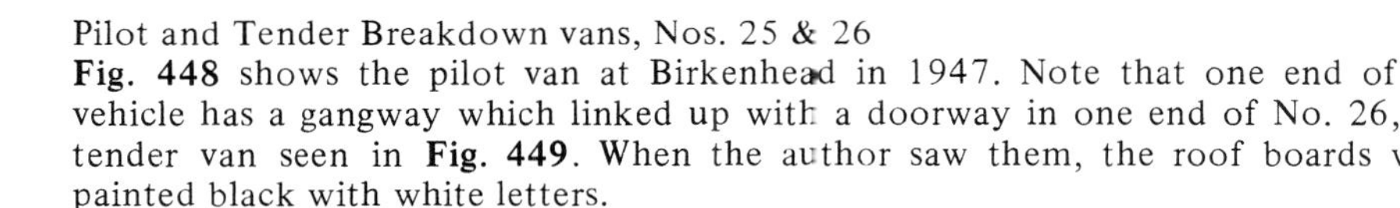

Pilot and Tender Breakdown vans, Nos. 25 & 26

**Fig. 448** shows the pilot van at Birkenhead in 1947. Note that one end of the vehicle has a gangway which linked up with a doorway in one end of No. 26, the tender van seen in **Fig. 449**. When the author saw them, the roof boards were painted black with white letters.

Fig. 449

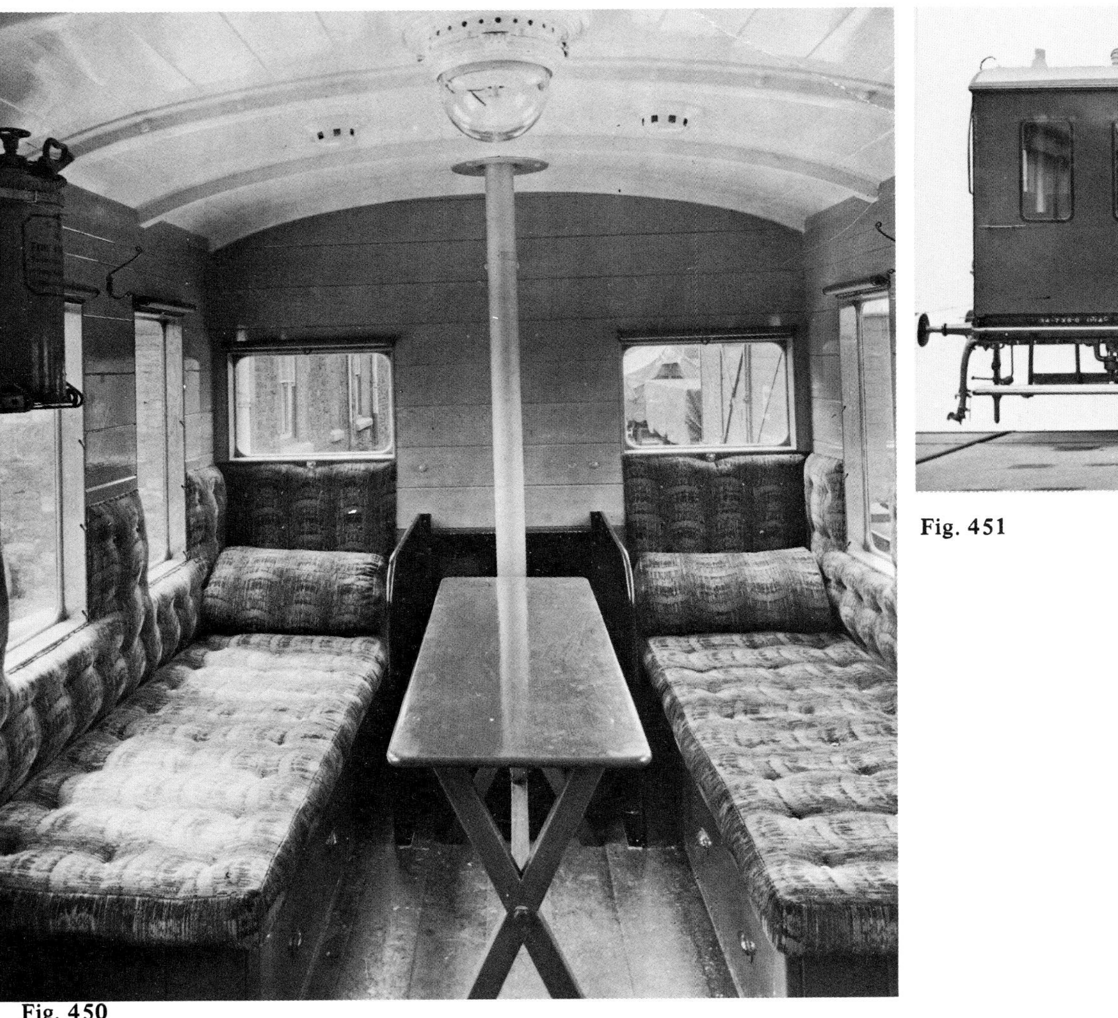

Fig. 450

Fig. 451

Fig. 452

Breakdown Tender vans (four wheel) for Newton Abbot

These two official photographs of No. 103 were taken at Swindon in 1938, and show the exterior in **Fig. 451** and the interior in **Fig. 450**. This view is of the sleeping compartment, which was furnished with two long upholstered couches, a small stove, and a long narrow table. All the windows were fitted with blinds, and the decor was cream walls with white ceiling. The trim was in brown moquette.

**Fig. 452** is a close-up view of the end section of No. 103 van. This was the end with the sleeping accommodation, and therefore was without a communicating gangway or door. Note the two small gas pipes over each buffer, which, if necessary, could be connected to portable gas flares at the scene of an accident. This large flat end was painted in post box red, whilst the sides were the usual GWR milk chocolate shade. Windows, handrails, corners and chassis were all painted black.

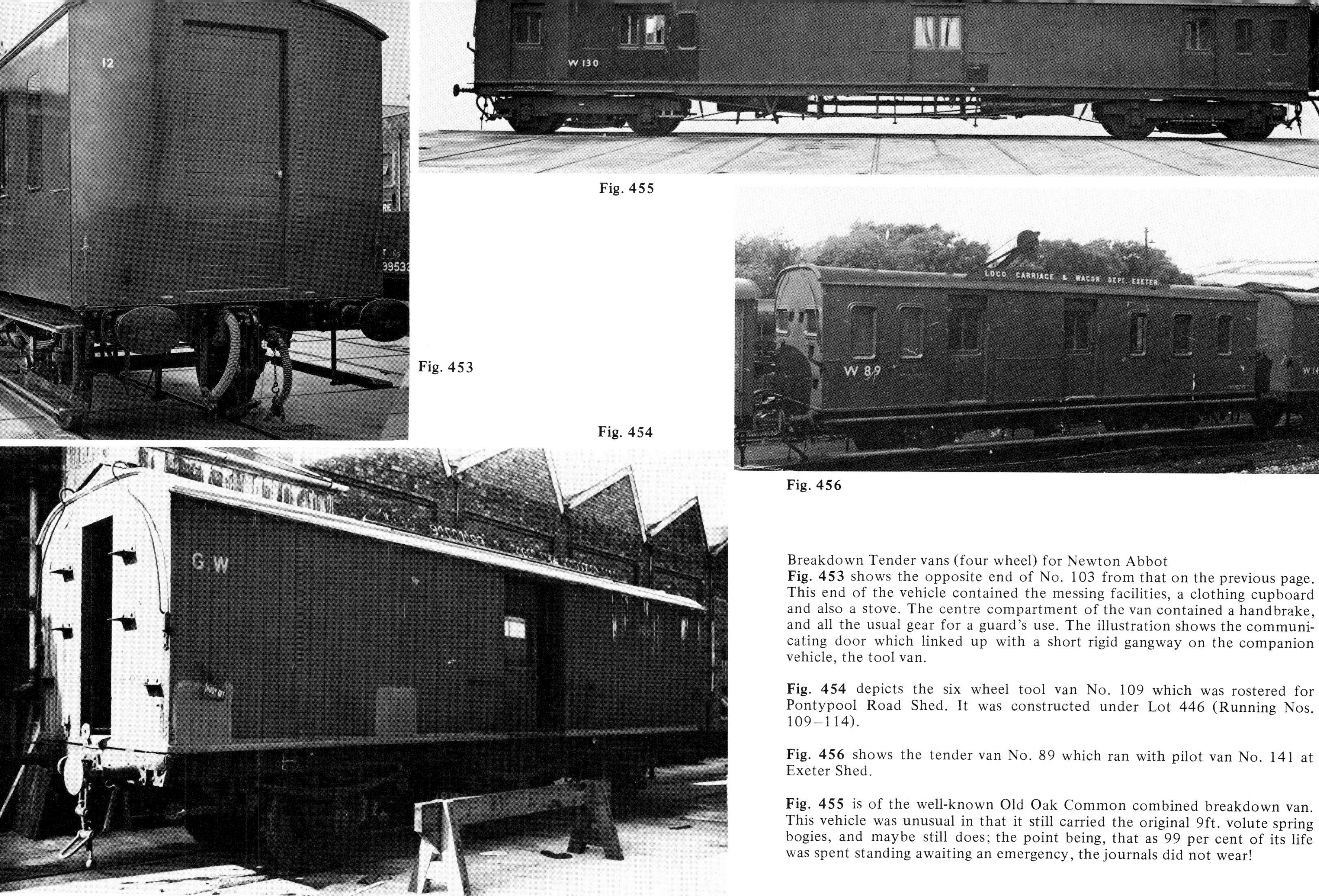


Fig. 453

Fig. 455

Fig. 454

Fig. 456

Breakdown Tender vans (four wheel) for Newton Abbot
**Fig. 453** shows the opposite end of No. 103 from that on the previous page. This end of the vehicle contained the messing facilities, a clothing cupboard and also a stove. The centre compartment of the van contained a handbrake, and all the usual gear for a guard's use. The illustration shows the communicating door which linked up with a short rigid gangway on the companion vehicle, the tool van.

**Fig. 454** depicts the six wheel tool van No. 109 which was rostered for Pontypool Road Shed. It was constructed under Lot 446 (Running Nos. 109–114).

**Fig. 456** shows the tender van No. 89 which ran with pilot van No. 141 at Exeter Shed.

**Fig. 455** is of the well-known Old Oak Common combined breakdown van. This vehicle was unusual in that it still carried the original 9ft. volute spring bogies, and maybe still does; the point being, that as 99 per cent of its life was spent standing awaiting an emergency, the journals did not wear!

Fig. 457

Two photographs of the Old Oak Common breakdown van, No. 130, in British Rail ownership, showing both sides of the vehicle. In **Fig. 457** the official photograph, taken at Swindon in 1951, illustrates the guard's compartment end, with its single droplight window.

In **Fig. 458** the opposite end is seen, with its gangway bellows for connecting with other service vehicles fitted with corridors. This end contained an 11ft. 6in. compartment detailed for use as an ambulance room with all the first aid equipment, etc.

Fig. 458

Van Conversions

**Fig. 459** shows a self-contained electric generating plant. Van No. 2 was originally passenger brake van No. 1113 *(Diagram K29)*.

Wagon Lot 1460 of 1944

This vehicle contained a large diesel-electric generator with attendants' compartment adjacent, and at each end of the van, two battery rooms each containing 52 cells, which necessitated the ventilating louvres in the vehicle's sides.

**Fig. 460** In 1945 the GWR, in conjunction with St. Mary's Hospital W2, staged a travelling exhibition to instruct and promote interest in the use of penicillin in general medicine. Two Siphon Gs, Nos. 2773 and 2787, were specially converted and linked for this purpose, and painted white with blue lettering.

The GWR was an early exponent of the railmotor and eventually operated the largest fleet in the country. Consequent on the construction of these vehicles were trailers, to increase their carrying capacity. The first two vehicles, Nos. 1 and 2 were given *Diagrams A & B* respectively. Drawings and photographs of *Diagram A* may be found in *G W Coaches, Part II.* Briefly details are as follows:

*DIAGRAM A*
Auto Trailer
Lot 1055 of 1904
Running number: 1
Dimensions: 59ft. 6in. x 8ft. 6in.

*DIAGRAM B*
Auto Trailer
Lot 1055 of 1904
Running number: 2
Dimensions: 70ft. 0¾in. x 8ft. 6in.

In 1905 further vehicles were built to *Diagram B* as follows:

*DIAGRAM B*
Auto Trailer
Lot 1081 of 1905
Running numbers: 3–6
Dimensions: 70ft. 0in. x 9ft. 0in.

The vehicles were originally mounted on Churchward 9ft. volute bogies, as can be seen in **Fig. 461**. This photograph of No. 4, as built, also shows that this second batch of trailers was built in the conventional panelled manner, the first two vehicles having been of matchboard construction. Entry was by doors at each end of the vehicle (see also *G W Coaches, Part II, page 18*).

*DIAGRAM C*
Auto Trailer
Lot 1087 of 1905
Running numbers: 7–8
Dimensions: 59ft. 6in. x 9ft. 0in.

*DIAGRAM D*
Auto Trailer
Lot 1090 of 1905
Running numbers: 9–10
Dimensions: 70ft. 0in. x 9ft. 0in.

**Fig. 461**

*DIAGRAM E/F*
Auto Trailer
Lot 1097 of 1905
Running numbers: 11–13 (see also *G W Coaches, Part II, page 28*)
Dimensions: 70ft. 0in. x 9ft. 0in.

*DIAGRAM G/G1/H*
These were conversions from clerestory thirds. A drawing and photograph can be seen in *G W Coaches, Part II, page 29.*

*DIAGRAM G/G1/H*
Auto Trailer
Lot 1097 of 1905
Running numbers: 14–17
Dimensions: 52ft. 0¾in. x 8ft. 6¾in.

*DIAGRAM J/J1*
Auto Trailer
Lot 1102 of 1906
Running numbers: 19–24
Dimensions: 59ft. 6in. x 9ft. 0in.

*DIAGRAM K/K1*
Auto Trailer
Lot 1103 of 1905
Running numbers: 25–8
Dimensions: 70ft. 0in. x 9ft. 0in.

*DIAGRAM L*
Auto Trailer
Lot 1108 of 1905 – Running numbers: 29–34
Lot 1127 of 1906 – Running numbers: 42–47
Lot 1141 of 1908 – Running numbers: 53–58
Lot 1143 of 1908 – Running numbers: 59–70
Dimensions: 70ft. 0in. x 9ft. 0in.

Fig. 462

Mounted on 9ft. 'American' bogies these trailers were designed to seat 76 passengers. Entry was by centre doors as can be seen in **Fig. 462**, showing No. 53 at Slough in 1950 and in **Fig. 463** showing No. 33 at Bourne End. No. 32 was fitted with a centre gangway at one end for communication with the railmotor, and Nos. 29 and 45 were fitted with through regulator gear for use with more than one trailer (see also *GW Coaches, Part II, pages 28 & 45*).

Fig. 463

Fig. 464 ▶

*DIAGRAM M/M1*
Auto Trailer
Lot 1108 of 1905
Running numbers: 18 and 35
Dimensions: 54ft. 0¾in. x 8ft. 6¾in.

These vehicles were also conversions from clerestory thirds.

*DIAGRAM N*
Auto Trailer
Lot 1126 of 1907
Running numbers: 36–41
Dimensions: 59ft. 6in. x 9ft. 0in.

**Fig. 464** shows No. 41 at Old Oak Common in 1950 mounted on 8ft. 'American' bogies. A drawing can be found in *GW Coaches, Part II, page 44*.

**Fig. 465**

*DIAGRAM R*
Auto Trailer
Lot 1161 of 1909 – Running numbers: 73–4
Lot 1225 of 1913 – Running numbers: 96–3
Dimensions: 70ft. 0in. x 9ft. 0in.

*DIAGRAM 0 (opposite page)*
Auto Trailer
Lot 1128 of 1908
Running number: 48
Dimensions: 70ft. 0in. x 9ft. 0in.

This vehicle was built as an experiment to see if centrally placed seating and side gangways, with a number of sliding doors on each side, would be beneficial on suburban services. The scheme was not a success and No. 48 was subsequently altered to a more conventional arrangement with a centre gangway and entry by end doors only. **Figs. 465 & 466** show the vehicle as built and mounted on 9ft. volute bogies. The eleven sliding doors can be clearly seen. A drawing of this vehicle can be found in *GW Coaches, Part II, page 46*.

**Fig. 467**

*DIAGRAM Q (above)*
Auto Trailer
Lot 1160 of 1909 – Running numbers: 71–2
Lot 1224 of 1913 – Running numbers: 93–5
Dimensions: 70ft. 0in. x 9ft. 0in.

*DIAGRAM P*
Auto Trailer
Lot 1130 of 1907
Running numbers: 49–52
Dimensions: 70ft. 0in. x 9ft. 0in.

These vehicles were intended to run in pairs on Plymouth local services. As built, they were mounted on 'American' style bogies and were lit by gas. Later they were converted to electric lighting. Entry was by end doors (see also *GW Coaches, Part II, page 81*). **Fig. 467** shows No. 94, as built, in 1913 in the crimson lake livery.

*DIAGRAM A3 (below)*
Clifton Down auto sets were conversions of low-roofed brake thirds of *Diagram D27* built on Lot 872. The conversion was carried out in 1913 and the vehicles were renumbered 3331–2 and 3335–8.

**Fig. 468** is the official photograph of the Clifton Down auto set, consisting of trailer brake third, composite, engine No. 833 of the '517' class, composite, and trailer brake third No. 3332. The whole unit could be driven from either trailer car. The livery is crimson lake.

**Fig. 468**

Fig. 469

*DIAGRAM T*
Auto Trailer
Lot 1190 of 1911
Running numbers: 75–80
Dimensions: 70ft. 0in. x 9ft. 0in.

These vehicles were built with centre door entry and a gangway at one end. They were mounted on 9ft. 'American' bogies and were originally gas lit. Conversion to electric lighting was as follows: No. 76 in 1929, No. 77 in 1930 and Nos. 75, 78, 79 and 80 in 1931. Nos. 75, 78 and 80 were fitted with wicket gates in the gangways. The vehicles to this diagram were condemned in December 1960.

**Fig. 469** depicts No. 80 at Reading in 1950. The livery is British Railways 'plum and spilt milk'.

Fig. 470

*DIAGRAM U*
Auto Trailer
Lot 1198 of 1912
Running numbers: 81–92
Dimensions: 70ft. 0in. x 9ft. 0in.

This series, too, was mounted on 9ft. 'American' bogies and was originally gas lit. Conversion to electric lighting was as follows: Nos. 81–3, 86, 88 and 89 in 1930, Nos. 84, 91 and 92 in 1931 and Nos. 85 and 87 in 1932. The series was condemned in August 1963. In **Fig. 470**, the gangway end of No. 83 is seen as the vehicle stands outside the old locomotive shed at Banbury in 1950. In **Fig. 471**, No. 90 is seen, partially obscured by travelling gas tank No. 2. The underframe of this vehicle is from a condemned four-wheeled coach (see also *GW Coaches, Part II, page 72*).

Fig. 471

*DIAGRAM A10*

Trailer cars were conversions of steam railmotors which were originally built on Lot 1078 in 1905. Conversion took place between 1915 and 1936. Renumbering on conversions were as follows:

Steam railmotor No. 29 became trailer No. 125
Steam railmotor No. 31 became trailer No. 129
Steam railmotor No. 32 became trailer No. 128
Steam railmotor No. 33 became trailer No. 130
Steam railmotor No. 34 became trailer No. 131
Steam railmotor No. 35 became trailer No. 132
Steam railmotor No. 36 became trailer No. 133

**Fig. 472**

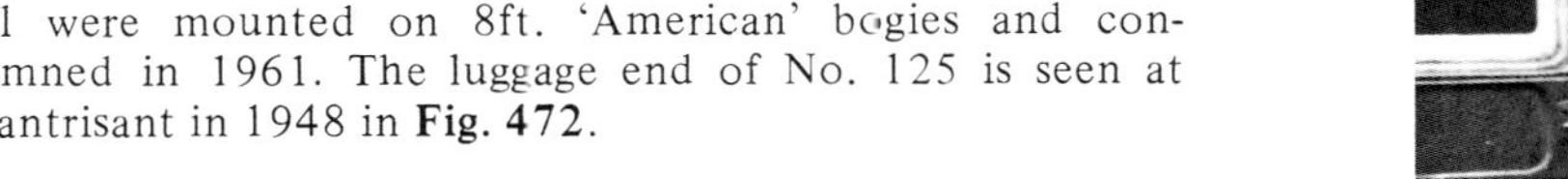

All were mounted on 8ft. 'American' bogies and condemned in 1961. The luggage end of No. 125 is seen at Llantrisant in 1948 in **Fig. 472**.

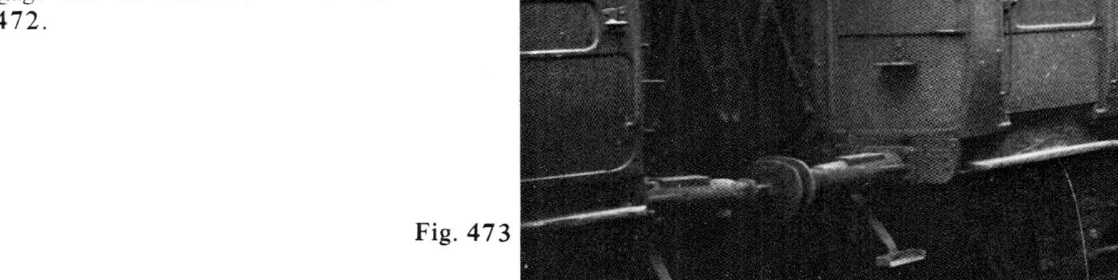


**Fig. 473**

*DIAGRAM A21 (above)*

This trailer car was ex-Cardiff Railway composite No. 3. In 1925 the vehicle was given the number 143 by the GWR and reclassified as an 'all third' on conversion. Condemnation took place in March 1957 and **Fig. 473** shows the vehicle at Cardiff in 1952.

*DIAGRAM A22*

The trailer cars which were ex-Cardiff Railway composites Nos. 4 and 5 were renumbered, in 1925 on conversion, to 144 and 155 and the vehicles were condemned in March 1957. **Fig. 474** was also taken at Cardiff in 1952 and shows No. 144

**Fig. 474**

*DIAGRAM A26 (below)*
Trailer cars which were converted from steam railmotors had three compartments, a small saloon, a vestibule and a large smoke saloon. Renumbering on conversion was as follows:

Steam railmotor No. 53 became trailer No. 199
Steam railmotor No. 54 became trailer No. 181
Steam railmotor No. 56 became trailer No. 182
Steam railmotor No. 57 became trailer No. 149
Steam railmotor No. 58 became trailer No. 200
Steam railmotor No. 84 became trailer No. 183
Steam railmotor No. 85 became trailer No. 154
Steam railmotor No. 86 became trailer No. 206
Steam railmotor No. 87 became trailer No. 155
Steam railmotor No. 89 became trailer No. 156
Steam railmotor No. 90 became trailer No. 157
Steam railmotor No. 91 became trailer No. 210
Steam railmotor No. 93 became trailer No. 212
Steam railmotor No. 94 became trailer No. 185
Steam railmotor No. 95 became trailer No. 184
Steam railmotor No. 96 became trailer No. 213
Steam railmotor No. 97 became trailer No. 214
Steam railmotor No. 98 became trailer No. 215
Steam railmotor No. 99 became trailer No. 158

**Fig. 476**

*DIAGRAM A23 (top)*
Trailer cars converted from steam railmotors were as follows:

Steam railmotor No. 40 became trailer No. 198
Steam railmotor No. 39 became trailer No. 197
Steam railmotor No. 38 became trailer No. 146

Originally, the converted trailers were mounted on 7ft. 'American' bogies and later these were changed to 9ft. 'American' pattern bogies. Entry to the trailers was by a centre door. In **Fig. 475** No. 198 is seen

**Fig. 476** depicts No. 200 as converted from steam railmotor No. 58 in 1933 (see also *G W Coaches, Part II, pages 165, 166 & 195*).

*DIAGRAM A26*
Trailer cars (centre door entry). **Fig. 477 (opposite page)** is a full page illustration of the side seated small saloon in vehicle No. 200. The view through the car is via the smaller saloon, the vestibule and the large smoking saloon, to the driving compartment at the other end.

*DIAGRAM A26*

**Fig. 478 (opposite page)** shows the view in the reverse direction to the previous illustration, taken from the driving compartment and looking right through the vehicle to the luggage compartment at the opposite end. The hanging straps for standing passengers are clearly shown, a facility to increase the vehicle's capacity for suburban work.

**Fig. 479**

*DIAGRAM A27 (above)*
Auto Trailer
Lot 1394 of 1929
Running numbers: 159–70
Dimensions: 59ft. 6in. x 9ft. 0in.

This series of vehicles was designed specifically for branch line work and was mounted on 7ft. plate bogies. On these vehicles, electric lighting was provided from the start.

**Fig. 479** is an official photograph, taken at Swindon in 1929, of No. 163, as built, with the roof painted white. The luggage end is fitted with end lights which was the case on several vehicles, but on others the openings were plated over. Access was by centre doors and the vehicles seated 72 passengers (see also *GW Coaches, Part II, pages 145 & 146*).

**Fig. 480**

*DIAGRAM A28*
Auto Trailer
Lot 1410 of 1930
Running numbers: 171–180
Dimensions: 59ft. 6in. x 9ft. 0in.

The trailers built to *Diagram A28* differed from the previous series only by having a larger smoking saloon (35ft. 11in. as against 33ft. 5in.) and the non-smoking saloon 6in. larger than before. The extra passenger space was gained at the expense of the luggage compartment.

In **Fig. 480**, No. 174 is seen at Princes Risborough in 1952 (see also *GW Coaches, Part II, pages 151 & 152*).

*Diagram A29* was given to further conversions of 70ft. steam railmotors (see also *GW Coaches, Part II, page 218* ).

*DIAGRAM A30*
Auto Trailer
Lot 1480 of 1933
Running numbers: 187–96
Dimensions: 62ft. 8in. x 9ft. 0in.

Mounted on 9ft. plate bogies these slightly larger vehicles were designed for branch line work.

**Fig. 481** shows No. 189 at Brent in 1950 and illustrates the luggage end with the windows plated over (see also *GW Coaches, Part II, page 181*).

**Fig. 482 (below)** is a picture of the Great Western modeller's ubiquitous branch line train. Engine No. 4844 is sandwiched between auto trailers 179 *(Diagram A28)* and 194 *(Diagram A30)* on a High Wycombe to Maidenhead train in 1937.

*DIAGRAM A31*
This diagram for an auto trailer was given to more conversions of steam railmotors. Dimensions were 59ft. 6in. x 9ft. and they were mounted on 7ft. plate and 8ft. 'American' bogies. Nos. 204, 205, 206 and 210 had single centre doors, whereas the others in the series had double doors. Seating was provided for 67 passengers. Conversion took place as follows:

Lot 1511 of 1933 – Steam railmotor Nos. 73/4/82–3 became trailers Nos. 202–5
Lot 1521 of 1934 – Steam railmotors Nos. 75/78/79 became trailers Nos. 207–9
Lot 1542 of 1935 – Steam railmotor No. 81 became trailer No. 211
Lot 1542 of 1935 – Steam railmotor No. 76 became Trailer No. 219
All were condemned in March 1959.

**Fig. 483 (below)** illustrates No. 205 as converted in 1933 (see also *GW Coaches, Part II, page 195*).

**Fig. 484 (opposite page)** This full page photograph shows the interior of car No. 187 *(Diagram A30)* looking down the vehicle from the driver's end, through the large smoking saloon, the guard's vestibule and the small smoking saloon to the luggage section with its barred windows. Electric lighting

**Fig. 485** shows No. 221, as built, carrying the British Railways 'plum and spilt milk' livery. This vehicle eventually became *Wren* and, with a different seating arrangement, was allocated *Diagram A40*. In **Fig. 486**, the driving end of the series is seen. No. 232 is photographed standing at Paddington (Suburban) in 1952.

*DIAGRAMS A32, A33 & A34*
These diagrams were non-corridor brake thirds and brake composites which were converted for use as auto trailers by the installation of driving gear in the brake ends.

*DIAGRAM A38*
Auto Trailer
Lot 1736 of 1951
Running numbers: 222–34
Dimensions: 64ft 0in x 8ft 11in

Fig. 486

*DIAGRAM A39 (above)*
Auto Trailer
Lot 1736 of 1951

Only one vehicle, No. 220, was built to this diagram which was dimensionally identical to *Diagram A38*. The vehicle is shown, w.th the driving end at the right, in **Fig. 487**. No. 221 was condemned in 1964.

*DIAGRAMS A35 & A36* were given ex-Taff Vale trailers, Nos. 2506, 2507, 2521 and 6422.

*DIAGRAM A40 (below)*
Auto Trailer
Lot 1736 of 1951

This was another diagram with only one vehicle, No. 221. The seating plan was different again to *Diagrams A38 & A39* although, externally, the dimensions were the same. **Fig. 488** is the official broadside view.

Fig. 489

**Figs. 489 & 490** are official views of No. 220 *(Diagram A39)* and show the vehicle after it had been given the name *Thrush*. No. 220 only had a working life of thirteen years, being built in 1951 and taken out of service in November 1964.

Fig. 490

*DIAGRAM A41*
These were auto trailers which were converted, in 1953, from *Diagram C75* thirds, Nos. 435/458/1415/1417/1678/1690/1692/1695/1699/1707 and 1709.

*DIAGRAM A42*
These were auto trailers which were converted, in 1953, from *Diagram C66* thirds, Nos. 4030, 4043, 4282, 5461, 5466, 5473 and 5481.

*DIAGRAM A43*
Auto Trailer
Lot 1766 of 1954
Running numbers: 235–44
Dimensions: 63ft. 0in. x 9ft. 0in.

*DIAGRAM A44*
These were auto trailers which were converted, in 1955, from various brake thirds as follows:

Lot 1493 – Nos. 5491 and 5495 became Nos. 245 and 246
Lot 1552 – Nos. 4015, 4016 4005 and 4019 became Nos. 247–50
Lot 1507 – Nos. 5871 and 5875 became Nos. 252 and 254
Lot 1525 – Nos. 4358, 4351 and 4345 became Nos. 253, 255 and 256

fitting of a bulkhead which formed a separate driver's compartment. A large single window was cut in the end and a regulator and warning gong were fitted. Livery was British Railways crimson with yellow lettering.

Fig. 495

**Figs. 495 & 496** show the final two pictures in this section of diesel-engined motor brake second SC79095 as turned out of Swindon in 1956, and illustrate the development of the short-haul, medium load motor trains. The prominent 'cat's whiskers' on the gangway blanking board are worthy of note.

Fig. 496

**Fig. 497** *DIAGRAM N10* Horse Box
Lot 1132 of 1907
Running numbers: 842–8
Dimensions: 21ft. 0in. x 8ft. 6in.
Wheelbase: 12ft. 0in.

**Fig. 497** shows No. 842 of this series as it appeared in 1910. The livery is chocolate brown and the large 24in. letters are in chrome yellow. The underframe and ends of the body are black. The centres of the Mansell wheels are probably red oxide and the roof is white. The vehicle has a steam heating pipe and dual brake pipes for vacuum and Westinghouse braking system.

In **Fig. 498**, No. 846 is seen in British Railways' ownership in 1949 and some of the wooden panelling has been replaced by steel panelling over the years. The horizontal planking on the ends of the vehicle is clearly shown.

Fig. 499

Several hundred of these vehicles were built between 1907 and 1926, all of similar design and dimensions. The diagrams ran from *N11 to N15*, the only differences being a few inches in external dimensions.

Lot numbers were as follows:

*DIAGRAM N11*

| | | |
|---|---|---|
| Lot 1132 of 1907 | Lot 1184 of 1910 | Lot 1221 of 1913 |
| Lot 1163 of 1909 | Lot 1205 of 1912 | Lot 1222 of 1913 |

**Figs. 499 & 500** show Nos. 345 and 221 of this series and the planked end can be seen. Further details are given in *GW Coaches, Part I, pages 163 & 164.*

**Fig. 500**

*DIAGRAM N12*

Lot 1242 of 1914
Lot 1245 of 1915
Lot 1243 of 1916
Lot 1254 of 1918
(see *GW Coaches, Part II, page 88*)

*DIAGRAM N13*

Lot 1267 of 1922
Lot 1268 of 1922
Lot 1408 of 1930
Lot 1367 of 1925
Lot 1379 of 1926
Lot 1386 of 1928
Lot 1397 of 1928

*DIAGRAM N14*

Lot 1268 of 1920
Running numbers: 227, 230 and 238

**Fig. 501** shows No. 390 of this series and **Fig. 502** shows No. 420. It can be seen that flush steel panelling has been adopted for the construction of these vehicles. An excellent view of the interior arrnagement of this series, which differed little from the others, can be found in *GW Coaches, Part II, page 96*.

**Fig. 501**

**Fig. 502**

Lot 1444 of 1930 Lot 1461 of 1931

A diagram of this series can be found in *GW Coaches, Part II, page 171.*

*DIAGRAM N16*
**Fig. 503 (above)** gives a full broadside view of No. 546 as built in 1937. The distinguishing feature of this diagram is the complete lack of any tumblehome. Livery is still chocolate brown, although the 'roundel' has replaced the lettering GW. It is also noticeable that the corner angle irons and door hinges are painted black (see also *GW Coaches, Part II, page 228*).

*DIAGRAM N16*
Horse Box
Running numbers: 507, 509, 516, 519, 522, 524, 526, 527, 532, 535, 538, 540, 543, 546–8, 551, 554–6, 559, 562, 570–1, 573–4, 579, 582–588, 590 to 719
Dimensions: 21ft. 0in. x 8ft. 8in.
Wheelbase: 12ft. 0in.

**Fig. 504** shows a perspective view of No. 546 which displays part of the interior. These boxes could accommodate three horses with the two partitions in place. An alternative arrangement was to remove the partitions and stow them in the small compartment behind the passenger cabin, so that the whole area could be used as a loose box for a mare and foal, for example. for example.

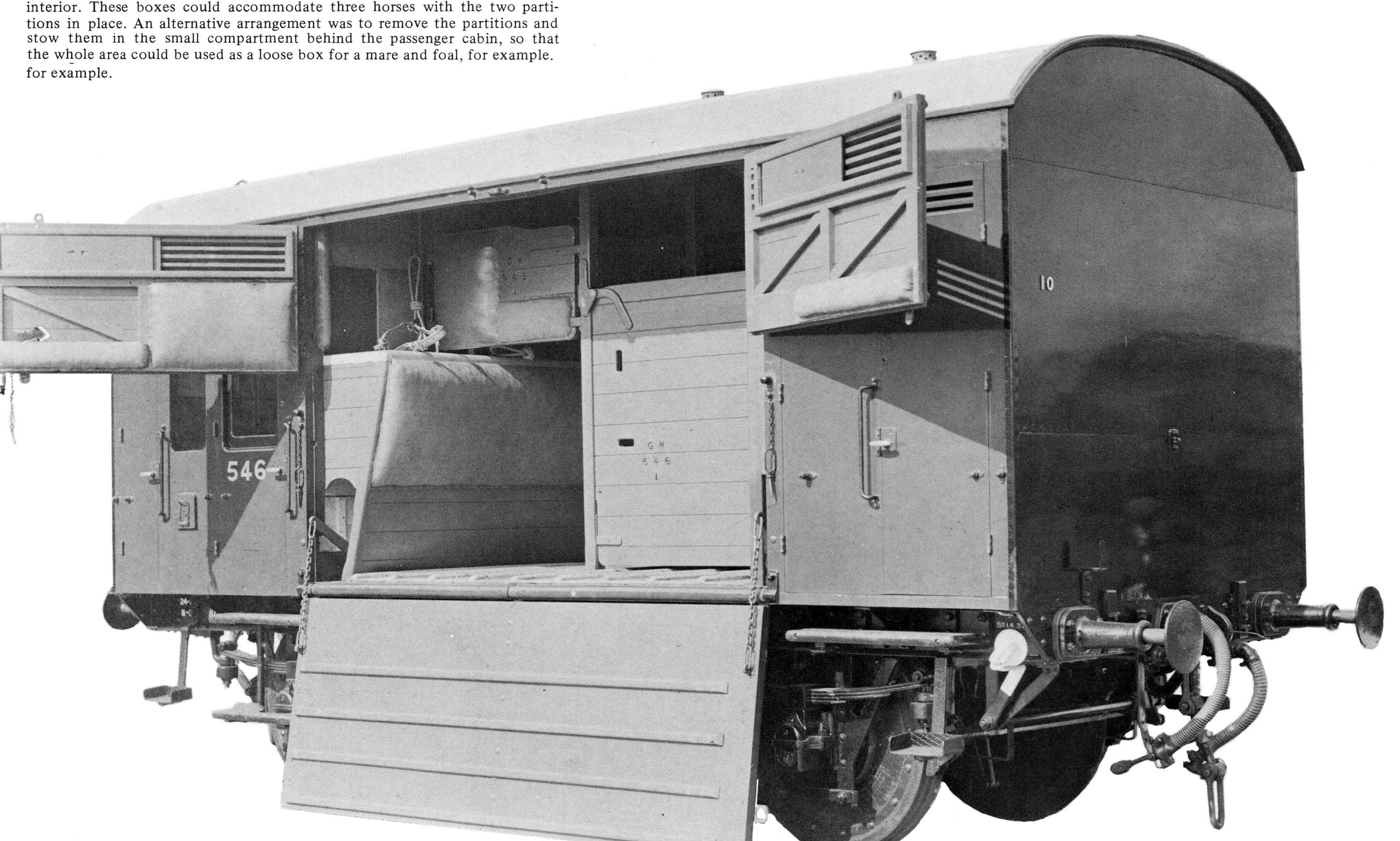

**Fig. 505** shows No. 2481, one of a series of vehicles built on Lot 1664 in 1954 for British Railways (Western Region). The view is taken from the fodder end of the vehicle and shows it as built, in 1954, bearing the British Railways maroon livery. The critical dimensions and branding can be clearly seen, as can the short lever handbrake in the nearside corner. The vehicle was 24ft. long.

VB
RETURN TO DIDCOT
W2481E
XP

**Fig. 506 (opposite page)** shows another view of No. 2481, taken from the opposite end. In this design, a lavatory was provided for the attendant or groom. The piping for filling the cistern can be seen running down the end of the vehicle to the outside corners of the chassis.

In **Fig. 507**, a final view is seen of No. 2481 with the doors open, to show the interior of the stock compartment.

**Fig. 508** shows No. 1870, in British Railways' ownership, in 1952.

The slatted milk van, given the telegraphic code name 'Siphon' is almost as much a part of the Great Western scene as was chocolate and cream livery and green locomotives. The earliest designs were four-wheeled, and later six-wheeled vehicles appeared in line with contemporary carriage underframes.

*DIAGRAM 01*
This was a four-wheeled design (18ft. x 8ft.) with a double door in the middle of each side. Sixty seven vehicles were built on three lots between 1873 and 1879. A drawing and photograph can be found in *GW Coaches, Part I, page 29.*

*DIAGRAM 02*
This was a longer, six-wheeled version of *Diagram 01* and had two double doors on each side. The body was 27ft. 6in. long and 8ft. wide. A drawing can be found in *GW Coaches, Part I, page 41.*

*DIAGRAM 03*
This was originally given to a series of vehicles built on Lots 535, 547 and 690 between 1889 and 1893. When the original *Diagram 01* vehicles were condemned, these vehicles were reallocated to *Diagram 01*. Consequently *Diagram 03* was then given to vehicles built on Lots 710, 741 and 770 between 1893 and 1895.

*DIAGRAM 04*
This was the final design of 'low siphon', these being vehicles with a body height of 6ft. 3in. or, as in this case 6ft. 8in. The body was 27ft. 6in. long and 8ft. wide and the wheelbase was 19ft. This series had three double doors on each side. A drawing is shown in *GW Coaches, Part I, page 11.* Large numbers of vehicles to this diagram, with minor variations in measurements, were built between 1896 and 1903 on Lots 788, 800, 822, 825, 835, 848, 856, 857, 868, 880, 930, 942, 943, 951, 961, 979, 993, 1016 and 1043.

Fig. 509

*DIAGRAM 05*

Basically similar to *Diagram 04*, this series had a higher 7ft. 6in. body. Seventy five vehicles were built on two lots, Lots 1039 of 1903 and Lot 1044 of 1904. A drawing can be found in *G W Coaches, Part I, page 214*. The official drawing notes these as being fish vans.

*DIAGRAM 06*

This series was similar to *Diagram 05* but had end doors so that vehicles could be loaded into the van. These vehicles were built on Lot 1082 between 1904 and 1905 and there were nine vehicles in all, which were built as milk vans (see also *G W Coaches, Part I, pages 215 & 216*).

*DIAGRAM 07*
Milk Van (Closed)
Lot 1124 of 1907
Running numbers: 1543–8
Dimensions: 40ft. 0in. x 8ft. 0in.

*DIAGRAM 07*

This series of bogie Siphons was built with gas lighting. **Fig. 509** shows No. 1546 at Banbury in 1948 and the side panel is painted cream with brown lettering. **Fig. 510** shows the same vehicle at Old Oak Common in 1952. In this case, the side panel is in brown with cream lettering. The roof board reads 'Harris Bacon and Wiltshire Sausages. Calne and Newcastle via Banbury'.

The 8ft. 'American' bogies of these vehicles can be clearly seen in both pictures. When the telegraphic coding was given, this series was coded 'Siphon F' (see also *G WCoaches, Part I, pages 42 & 43*).

*DIAGRAM 08*

A shorter, four-wheeled, version of the Siphon F, a vehicle coded as 'Siphon C'. The body was 28ft. 6in. long as was the subsequent *Diagram 09*. They were built on Lot 1125 of 1906/7 (Nos. 1525–42) and Lot 1133 of 1907 (Nos. 1515–18). Reference should be made to *G W Coaches, Part I, page 50*.

Fig. 510

*DIAGRAM 09*
**Fig. 511** shows No. 1496 again carrying Harris Bacon boards, but routes are the same as that shown on the side panel. These small vans were favourites for this traffic.

*DIAGRAM 09* **Fig. 512**
Milk Van (Closed)
Lot 1133 of 1907 (last six)
Running numbers: 1519–24
Lot 1162 of 1909
Running numbers: 1503–14
Lot 1183 of 1910
Running numbers: 1482–1501
Dimensions: 28ft. 6in. x 8ft. 6in.

In **Figs. 512 & 513**, No. 1519 is seen in 1923. These pictures show how the lettering was placed on these vans.

*DIAGRAM 011*
Milk Van (Closed)
Lot 1211 of 1912/13 – Running numbers: 1462–81
Lot 1264 of 1915/16 – Running numbers: 1442–61
Lot 1316 of 1922/23 – Running numbers: 1345–64
Lot 1347 of 1924/25 – Running numbers: 1290–1309
Lot 1368 of 1925/26 – Running numbers: 1271–89
Lot 1378 of 1926/27 – Running numbers: 1240–69
Dimensions: 50ft. 0in. x 8ft. 6in.

Fig. 515

Fig. 514

*DIAGRAM 011*
When built, some of these vehicles were mounted on 9ft. volute bogies and **Fig. 515** shows No. 1448 as built in 1927. Others were mounted on 9ft. 'American' bogies. **Fig. 514** was taken in 1949 at Swindon and shows No. 1303 when fitted with electric lighting. Another view of the series in British Railways' ownership is shown in **Fig. 516** taken in 1951. **Fig. 517** is a high level view of the roof of the series and show the arrangement of gas pipes when the vehicles were gas lit. In the telegraphic code system these vehicles were coded 'Siphon G' and have been known as outside-framed 'Siphon Gs' to distinguish them from the vehicles built later on *Diagrams 022, 033, 059, 062 and M34* (see also *G W Coaches, Part II, pages 73, 111 & 123*).

Fig. 516

*DIAGRAM 012*
Milk Van (Closed)
Lot 1266 of 1918–20
Running numbers: 1422–41
Dimensions: 50ft. 0in. x 8ft. 6in.

Fig. 518

Fig. 519

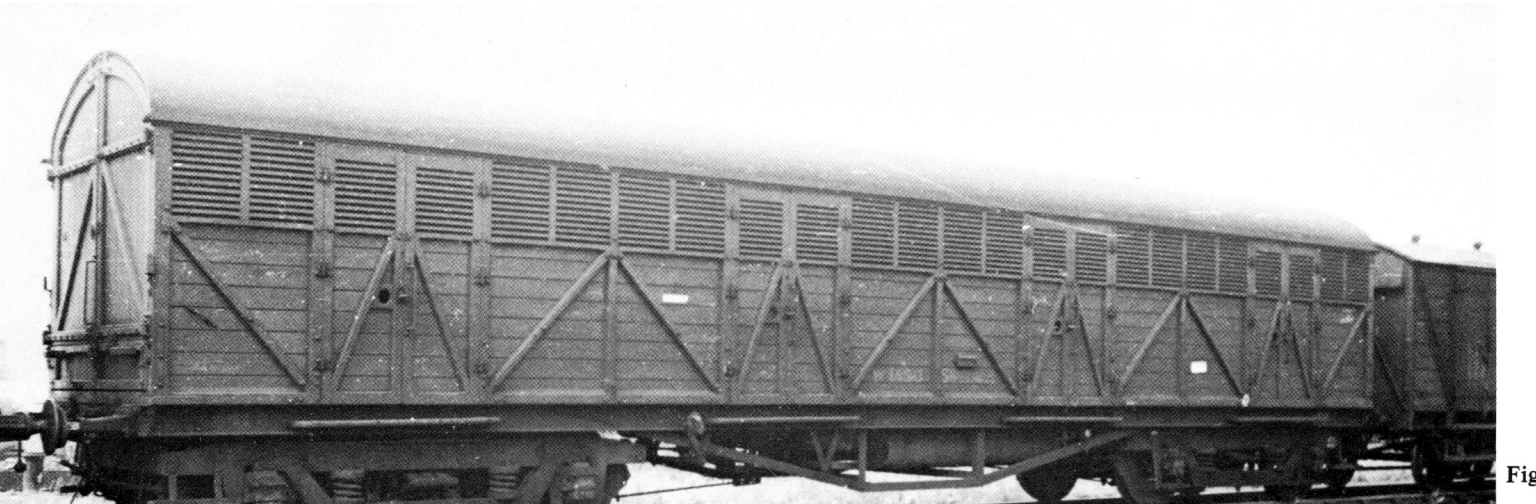

*DIAGRAM 012*
These vehicles were mounted on 9ft. 'American' bogies, as can be seen in **Figs. 518, 519 & 520**. The distinctive feature of these vans was the high cove roof, quite unlike any other series of siphon. As built, dual Westinghouse and vacuum brakes were fitted, together with a hand-brake. This series was given the telegraphic code 'Siphon H'. **Figs. 518 & 519** show No. 1426 in service in 1923. In **Fig. 520**, No. 1430 is seen in British Railways' ownership in 1952. A drawing and photograph can be found in *GW Coaches, Part II, pages 94 & 95.*

Fig. 520

*DIAGRAM 022 (above)* **Fig. 521**
Milk Van (Closed)
Lot 1370 of 1926 – Running number: 1270
Lot 1385 of 1927 – Running numbers: 1223–37
Lot 1396 of 1928/9 – Running numbers: 1186–1200
Dimensions: 50ft. 0in. x 8ft. 6in.

*DIAGRAM 022*
These vehicles are effectively outside-framed Siphon Gs turned inside out. Indeed, the vehicles even had horizontal planking and **Fig. 521** shows No. 1270 as built (see also *GW Coaches, Part II, page 135*).

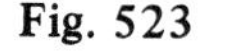

**Fig. 523**

The next series of inside-framed Siphon Gs were built with vertical planking. **Fig. 522** shows No. 2937 as outshopped in 1947 by Swindon, and bears comparison with **Fig. 521**. Differences, apart from the planking, are the bogies, suspended gangways and electric lighting instead of gas lighting. In **Fig. 523**, No. 2796 is seen in British Railways' days at Old Oak Common. During World War II, some of these vehicles were modified by plating over the louvres, for service in ambulance trains. Shell ventilators were fitted to provide ventilation. After the war some vehicles were converted back to Siphon Gs and given the new *Diagram 059*. The remaining vehicles were converted to parcels vans, the louvres were plated over externally and windows were fitted. Steam heating pipes were also fitted and the vans were given *Diagram M34*. They were, however, still called Siphon Gs. Reference should be made to *GW Coaches, Part II, pages 180 & 229*.

*DIAGRAM 033* Milk Vans
Lot 1441 of 1929/30 – Running numbers: 2051–70
Lot 1578 of 1936/7 – Running numbers: 2751–2800
Lot 1651 of 1938–40 – Running numbers: 2917–2931
Lot 1644 of 1940–5 – Running numbers: 2937–2946, 2975–78, 2985–94

**Fig. 524 (opposite page)** shows an excellent view of the interior of No. 2937. Points of interest include gas lighting, let-down racks for parcels or perishables, composition floors with drain gullies down the centre, and iron deckle plates at the doorways.

**Fig. 526**

**Fig. 525** shows the end of Siphon G No. 2789. The picture was taken at Swindon in 1937 and illustrates the suspended gangways and the small electric light switch.

**Fig. 526** shows one of the same series as converted for service in ambulance trains. The livery was War Department olive green with a red cross on a white ground.

*DIAGRAM 047*
Two of these vans were built for use at Dudley by Messrs Palethorpes for the carriage of their products. Note the ice box on the roof at the far end. These vehicles were also fitted with battery and regulator boxes, together with a dynamo, to supply power for refrigerating the van. **Fig. 527** is an

*DIAGRAM 047*
Sausage Vans (six-wheeled)
Lot 1584 of 1936

**Fig. 528** is a companion photograph to **Fig. 527** showing No. 2801 after overhaul in 1952.

**Fig. 529** shows No. 2758, a Siphon G, after return from war service and conversion to a parcels van to *Diagram M34*. The panel on the side reads 'Paddington and Carmarthen'.

Fig. 530

*DIAGRAMS 031 & 040*
Milk Van (Siphon J)
Lot 1409 of 1930 – Running numbers: 1215–22 *(Diagram 031)*
Lot 1463 of 1931 – Running numbers: 2024–50 *(Diagram 031)*
Lot 1496 of 1932–4 – Running numbers: 2518–27 *(Diagram 040)*
Dimensions: 50ft. 0in. x 8ft. 8in.

*DIAGRAMS 031 & 040*
These vehicles were readily identified by their vertical planking and total absence of windows and louvres. They were insulated vehicles and were fitted with internal ice tanks. One end was fitted with steps and electric light switchgear, as seen in **Fig. 531** and the other was completely bare. In **Fig. 530** No. 2049 is seen still running in GWR colours in 1949 (see also *GW Coaches, Part II, page 150*).

*DIAGRAMS 013 to 021* were given to various four-wheeled milk and fruit vans converted from saloon coaches and similar stock returned from War Department service after World War I. **Fig. 532** shows No. 1399 of *Diagram 013* series converted in 1921 on Lot 1299 in 1921. There were three vehicles numbered 1379–99, which were 30ft. x 8ft. 11¾in. on a 19ft. wheelbase (see also *GW Coaches, Part II, page 102*).

**Fig. 532**

Fig. 533

*DIAGRAM 062*
Milk Vans (Siphon G)
Lot 1721 of 1947–50 – Running numbers: 1310–39
Lot 1751 of 1951 – Running numbers: 1001–30
Lot 1755 of 1951 – Running numbers: 2295–2326
Lot 1765 of 1952 – Running numbers: 2332–91
Lot 1768 of 1955 – Running numbers: 1031–51
Dimensions: 50ft. 0in. x 8ft. 8in.

*DIAGRAM 062*
These vehicles were built at Swindon by British Railways (Western Region) and were little different to earlier Siphon Gs. The most noticeable difference is the sliding shutters on the lower body which can be clearly seen in **Figs. 533 & 534**, the official Swindon views of the series (see also *G W Coaches, Part II, page 262*).

Fig. 534

Fig. 535

The carriage of milk by road tankers raised the question of their transportation, mainly associated with traffic to Park Royal Depot. An additional use for these vehicles was for the transport of other tankers and some, for instance, were used to carry Guinness tankers. Photographs showing details of the loading of tankers can be found in *GW Wagons Appendix, page 84.*

**Fig. 535** depicts No. 3107, which was built at Swindon in 1949 and **Fig. 536** shows No. B748830 of a later series built in 1954.

**Fig. 536**

bars.

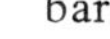

*DIAGRAM 039*
Milk Tank
Lot 1497 of 1934 – Running numbers: 2512–17
Lot 1517 of 1934 – Running numbers: 2531–36
Lot 1585 of 1937 – Running numbers: 2587–92
Dimensions: 20ft. 6in. x 8ft. 0in.

*DIAGRAM 039*
**Fig. 538** shows No. 2591 as built, at Swindon in 1937.

effects of the sun and the tanks were made of stainless steel. The vehicles were mounted on heavy duty 'W' irons and **Fig. 539** is the official view taken in 1937.

Lot 1561 of 1935–9 – Running numbers: 2561–3
Lot 1607 of 1935–9 – Running numbers: 2593–4
Lot 1613 of 1935–9 – Running numbers: 2595–8
Dimensions: 20ft. 6in. x 7ft. 9in.

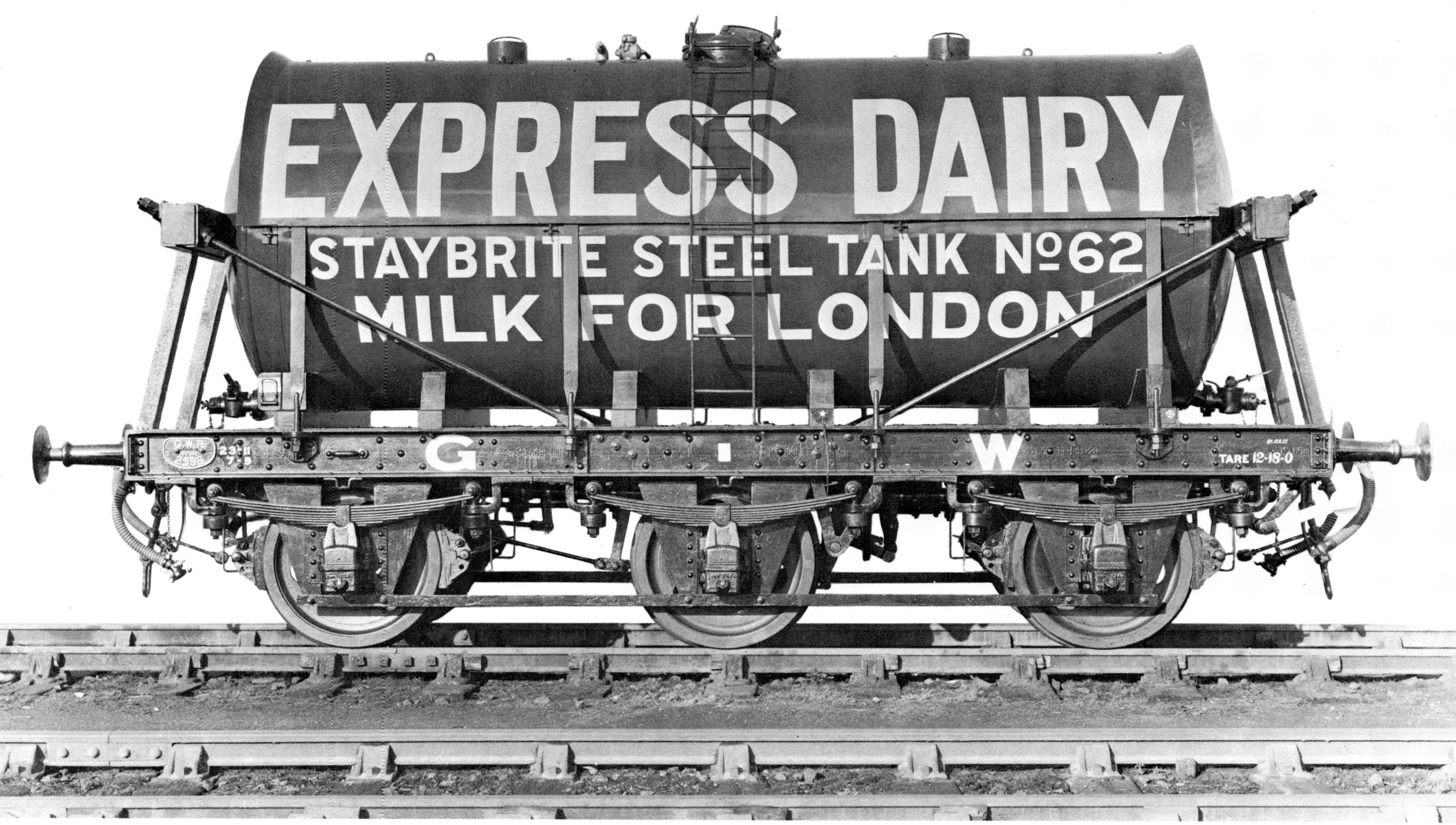

**Fig. 540 (above)** gives a clear view of the end of this series of tankers. The drain cock and outer skin can clearly be seen. This is the same vehicle, No. 2596, as that in **Fig. 539**. It is worthy of note that the tank is numbered separately (No. 62).

**Fig. 341** shows No. 1957, as built, in 1944 for the Co-operative Wholesale Society Ltd.

Lot 1678 of 1944
Running numbers: 1955–7
Dimensions: 21ft. 6in. x 7ft. 6in.

*DIAGRAM 054*
Milk Tank
Lot 1696 of 1946
Running numbers: 1968–77

*DIAGRAM 054*
**Fig. 542** shows No. 1970 carrying tank No. 95 in 1946.

Milk Tank
Lot 1697 of 1946 – Running numbers: 1978–83
Lot 1698 of 1946 – Running numbers: 1984/5
Lot 1699 of 1946 – Running numbers: 1986–95
Dimensions: 20ft. 6in. x 7ft. 9in.

*DIAGRAM 055*
**Fig. 543** shows No. 1985 at Swindon in 1946.

*DIAGRAM 058*

**Fig. 544** is the official photograph of No. 3028 taken in 1948. This tank has two compartments and the plate on the side of the wagon instructs that the tanks are to be evenly loaded when the wagon is to be moved.

*DIAGRAM 058*
Milk Tank
Lot 1717 of 1947 – Running numbers: 3023–8
Lot 1742 of 1950 – Running numbers: 3120–3
Dimensions: 21ft. 6in. x 7ft. 6½in.

The earliest vehicles of this type were built in 1870 to *Diagram P1*. They were covered vehicles and some lasted until 1907 and some may have been converted to open vehicles. The next series, *Diagram P2*, started off as open vehicles and details of these and the previous diagram may be found in *G W Coaches, Part I, page 55.*

*DIAGRAM P6* vehicles were built in 1889 and 1890 and there were only two vehicles. A drawing is shown in *G W Coaches, Part I, page 144*. Another series of short vehicles was *Diagram P7* and reference should be made to the drawing in *G W Coaches, Part I, page 142* and *Diagram P10* which is illustrated on *page 146* of that publication.

*DIAGRAM P13*
Carriage Truck (Python)
Lot 1106 of 1905
Running numbers: 521–30
Dimensions: 27ft. 4½in. x 8ft. 6in.

*DIAGRAM P13*
**Fig. 545** shows No. 523 at Paddington in 1947 still carrying GWR colours and lettering. In 1951, one of the series was overhauled and fitted out as a travelling workshop for Messrs Pooley & Sons. This firm was the manufacturer of most of the weighbridges on the GWR and they were under contract to maintain them and check their accuracy at regular intervals. **Fig. 546** illustrates this vehicle (see also *G W Coaches, Part I, page 175*).

**Fig. 546**

*DIAGRAM P14*
Carriage Truck (Python)
Lot 1134 – Running numbers: 531–40
Lot 1197 – Running numbers: 541–60
Dimensions: 27ft. 4½in. x 8ft. 6in.

**Fig. 547**

*DIAGRAM P14*
These vehicles had a 19ft. wheelbase, an extension of 12in. over the previous *Diagram P13*. The vehicles to Lot 1197 were dual-fitted. In later years many covered carriage trucks were converted for the carriage of electric batteries and accumulators and **Fig. 547** shows No. 183 in this guise after numbering. In **Fig. 548**, No. 180 is seen at Swindon in 1952 (see also *G W Coaches, Part II, pages 71, 251 & 252*).

*DIAGRAM P15 (below)*
Carriage Truck (Scorpion)
Lot 1158 * – Running numbers: 443–47/449–51
Lot 1206 * – Running numbers: 110–11/113–16/119/122–25/128–31/134–37/142
Lot 1216 – Running numbers: 149–52/155/157–58/161/163/165/171/175
Lot 1217 * – Running numbers: 454–7
Lot 1244 – Running numbers: 121/139–141/146–7/153/164/166/178–81/183/186
Lot 1245 * – Running numbers: 468–82
Lot 1255 – Running numbers: 187–91/193–5/198/200/202/204–5/208–9
Various building dates between 1909 and 1915
Dimensions: 21ft. 0in. x 8ft. 6in.

*DIAGRAM P15*
The lots marked * were built with dual brakes and were coded 'Scorpion B', the other lots were vacuum-fitted only and were given the code 'Scorpion D'. The wheelbase of these vehicles was 13ft. and they ran on carriage type Mansell wheels.

**Fig. 548**

**Figs. 549 & 550** show details of the chains and bars that were used to secure the wheels of the vehicles being carried. In **Fig. 551**, No. 442 is seen at Banbury in 1952 (see also *GW Coaches, Part I, pages 172 & 173 and GW Coaches, Part II, pages 77 & 92*).

**Fig. 550**

*DIAGRAM P12*
Carriage Truck (Scorpion)
Lot 1026 of 1903 – Running numbers: 427–8/432
Lot 1105 of 1906 – Running numbers: 433/435/441
Dimensions: 21ft. 0in. x 7ft. 8½in.

*DIAGRAM P12*
This earlier series had a 12ft. wheelbase and is illustrated in **Fig. 552**, taken at Banbury in 1950.

**Fig. 551**

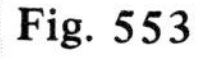

Fig. 553

*DIAGRAM P16*
The impressive lines of these outside-framed vehicles can be seen in **Fig. 553** and a drawing is provided in *GW Coaches, Part II, page 70*. In spite of being classed as carriage trucks, the principal use of these, and the other similar vehicles, was by touring theatre companies for carrying scenery.

Fig. 554

*DIAGRAM P18*
These vehicles were very similar to the previous series, although, like a Siphon G, there has been a transposition of the frames from outside to inside. The vehicles were also fitted with end gangways as can be seen in **Figs. 554 & 555**. The former picture was taken in 1947 at Old Oak Common and shows the vehicle still carrying GWR colours, and the latter picture, taken in 1951, shows the opposite side of the vehicle (see also *GW Coaches, Part II, pages 220 & 263*).

Fig. 555

*DIAGRAM P16*
Carriage Truck (Monster)
Lot 1191 of 1911
Running numbers: 490–2
Dimensions: 50ft. 0in. x 8ft. 6in.

*DIAGRAM P18*
Carriage Truck (Giant)
Lot 1265 of 1920
Running numbers: 581–2/584–92/594–5
Dimensions: 50ft. 0in. x 8ft. 10in.

*DIAGRAM P22*
Carriage Truck (Python B)
Lot 1650 of 1940
Running numbers: 1–6
Dimensions: 30ft. 6in. x 8ft. 10in.

*DIAGRAM P22*
**Fig. 556** is the official broadside view of No. 4, as built. Of particular interest are the self-contained buffers and the long lever handbrake.

*DIAGRAM P21*
Carriage Truck (Monster)
Lot 1498 of 1932
Running numbers: 486 and 489
Dimensions: 50ft. 0in. x 8ft. 10in.

*DIAGRAM P21*
These two 'Monsters' were rebuilt in 1932 from the 'Giants' built on Lot 1191 in 1910, and they remained mounted on the 9ft. 'American' bogies. **Fig. 557** shows No. 489 as rebuilt (see also *GW Coaches, Part II, page 187*).

**Fig. 557**

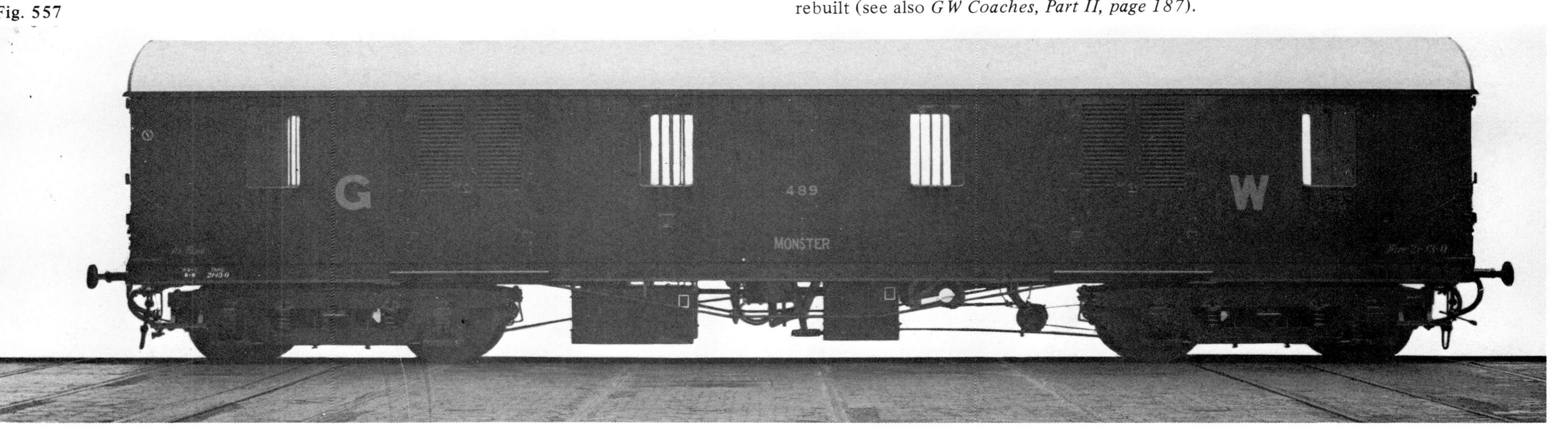

*DIAGRAM P23*
This was a Great Western design that was built in British Railways' days and, in this later guise, the vehicles were electrically lit and mounted on 9ft. pressed-steel bogies.

**Fig. 558** is an official view of No. 494 taken at Swindon when the vehicle was built (see also *GW Coaches, Part II, page 263*).

*DIAGRAM P23*
Scenery Truck (Monster)
Lot 1753 of 1953
Running numbers: 439–8
Dimensions: 50ft. 0in. x 8ft. 10in.

**Figs. 559 & 560** show two more official views of 'Monsters' built in British Railways days, in this case No. 597 (see also *GW Coaches, Part II, page 263*).

*DIAGRAM P24*
Scenery & Motor Car Van (Monster C)
Lot 1769 of 1954
Running numbers: 596–600
Dimensions: 50ft. 0in. x 8ft. 10in.

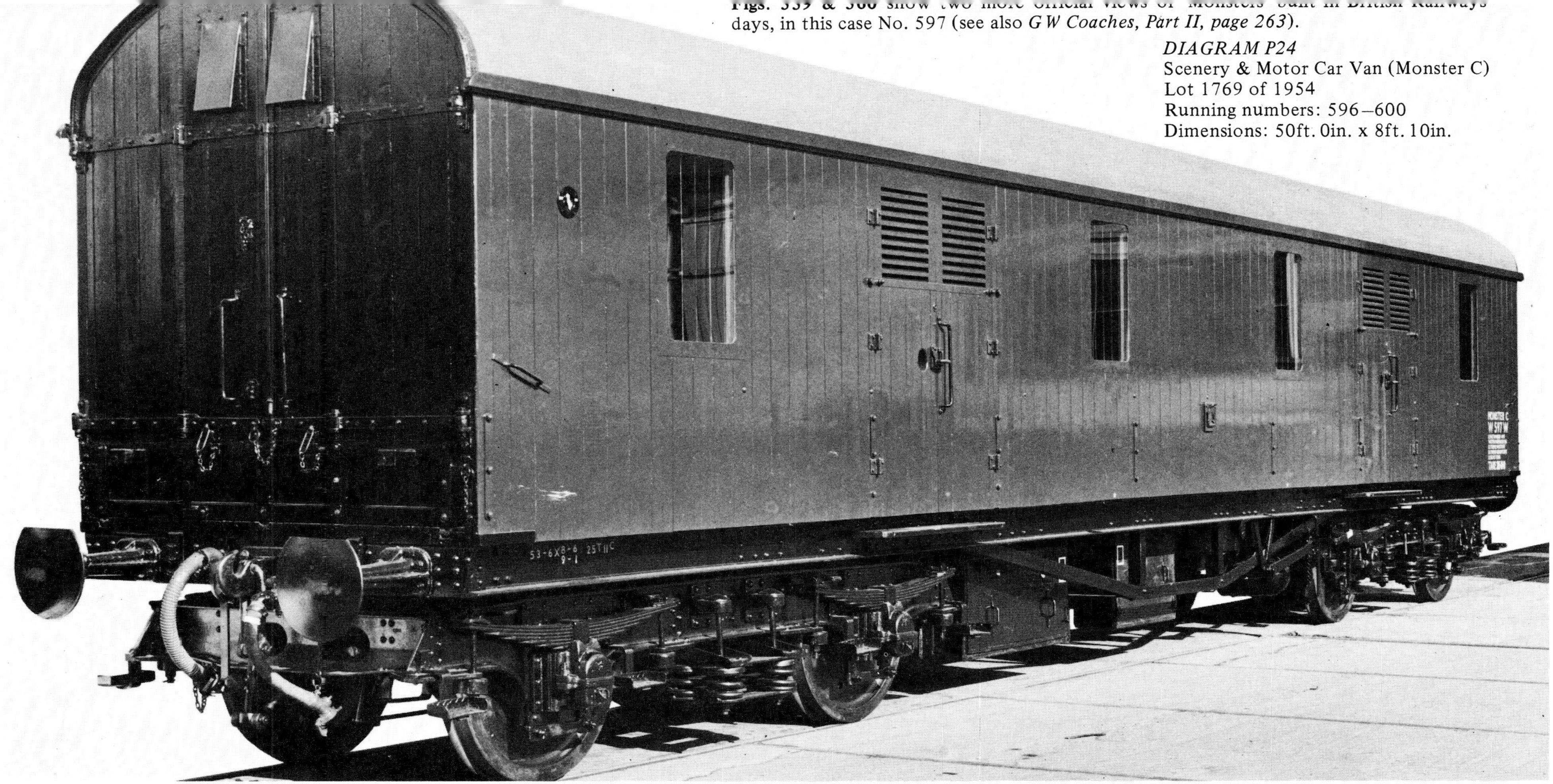

*DIAGRAM P25*
This was a British Railways' design built at Swindon and **Fig. 561** shows No. 37237 as built in 1957. The end doors are hinged in two halves to allow them to be opened even when the vehicles are coupled in a train, thus permitting through loading of vehicles without complicated shunting.

*DIAGRAM P25*
Covered Carriage Truck (CCT)
Lot 1773 of 1957
Dimensions: 30ft. 2in. x 9ft. 0½in.
Height: 12ft. 0in.

. 562

These vehicles, for use by the various engineering department as they made inspections of the tracks and structures of the railway, were often conversions of elderly service stock. As will be seen on the following pages, the GWR also made use of some of the older and more unusual stock that they acquired by the absorption of other railway companies.

*DIAGRAM Q1*
Inspection Saloon
Lot 1170 of 1910
Running number: 6479 (later Service No. 80977)
Dimensions: 43ft. 6in. x 8ft. 0¼in.

*DIAGRAM Q1*
**Fig. 562** shows this vehicle which was reconstructed in 1910 for the Taunton Division Engineering Department, as the legend in the waist panel declares. The original vehicle was probably a composite and the conversion involved the provision of two identical saloon compartments, one at each end with a linking corridor, and a guard's compartment and lavatory in the centre of the vehicle. It is mounted on Dean 8ft. 6in. bogies and carries the crimson lake livery. The picture was taken in 1910 when the conversion was outshopped. Of particular interest are the windows in the end of the vehicle and the steps beneath the doors that allow the engineers to climb up from track level.

Observation Saloon

The scene value of the coastal run from Pwllheli, via Barmouth to Machynlleth was realized by the Cambrian Railways and they built an observation saloon to capitalize on this. This vehicle was taken over at the Grouping by the GWR and the service continued. In 1929 the vehicle passed through Swindon Carriage Works and emerged painted in chocolate and cream. **Fig. 563** was taken when the vehicle emerged and the roof boards clearly proclaim the purpose of the vehicle, and it is interesting to note that it has retained the ribbed Cambrian buffers and distinctive hornguides outside the springs.

**Fig. 563**

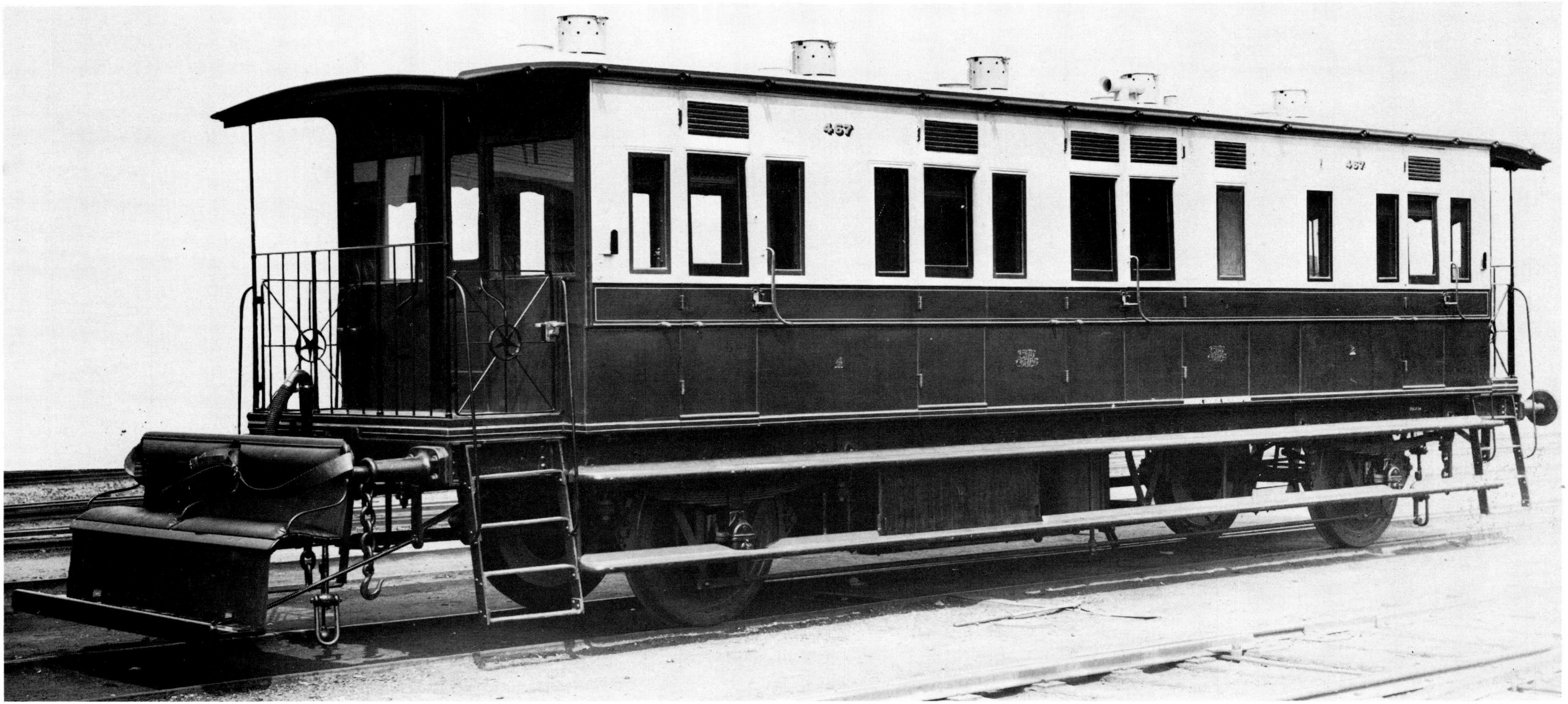

**Fig. 564**

## Inspection Cars for Civil Engineers

Dimensions 30ft. 0in. x 8ft. 0¾in.

These double-ended saloons were built in 1894, or before, (the photographs are dated 1894) and were for the Civil Engineers. No. 467, seen in **Figs. 564 & 565**, was intended for the Wolverhampton Division. Perhaps the most striking point in the photographs is the seat which slotted over the leading buffers from which the track could be closely inspected.

**Fig. 565**

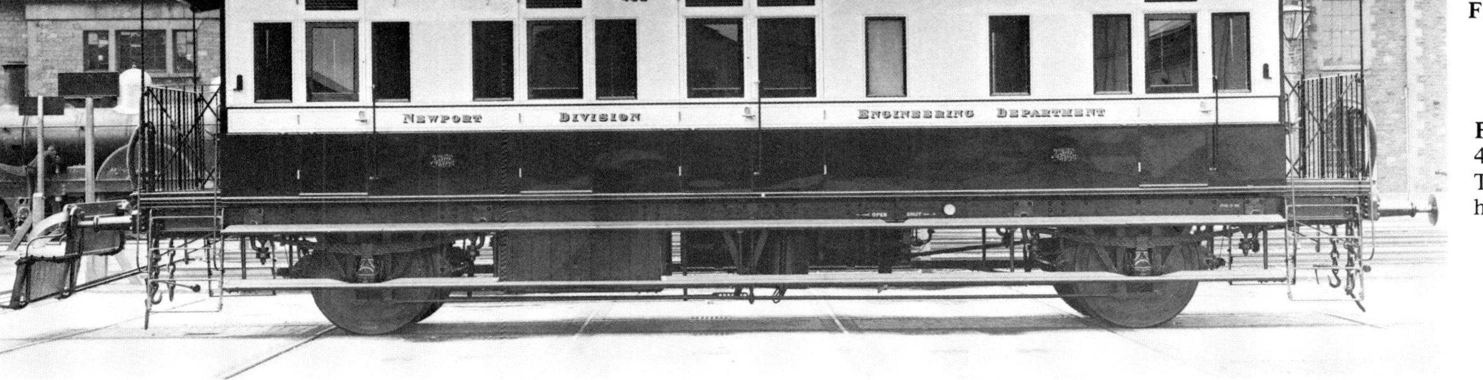


Fig. 566

**Figs. 566 & 567** show two views, dated 1896, of No. 462, a similar vehicle built for the Newport Division. The outside inspection seat can again be seen. They must have been hardy men, those engineers!



Fig. 567

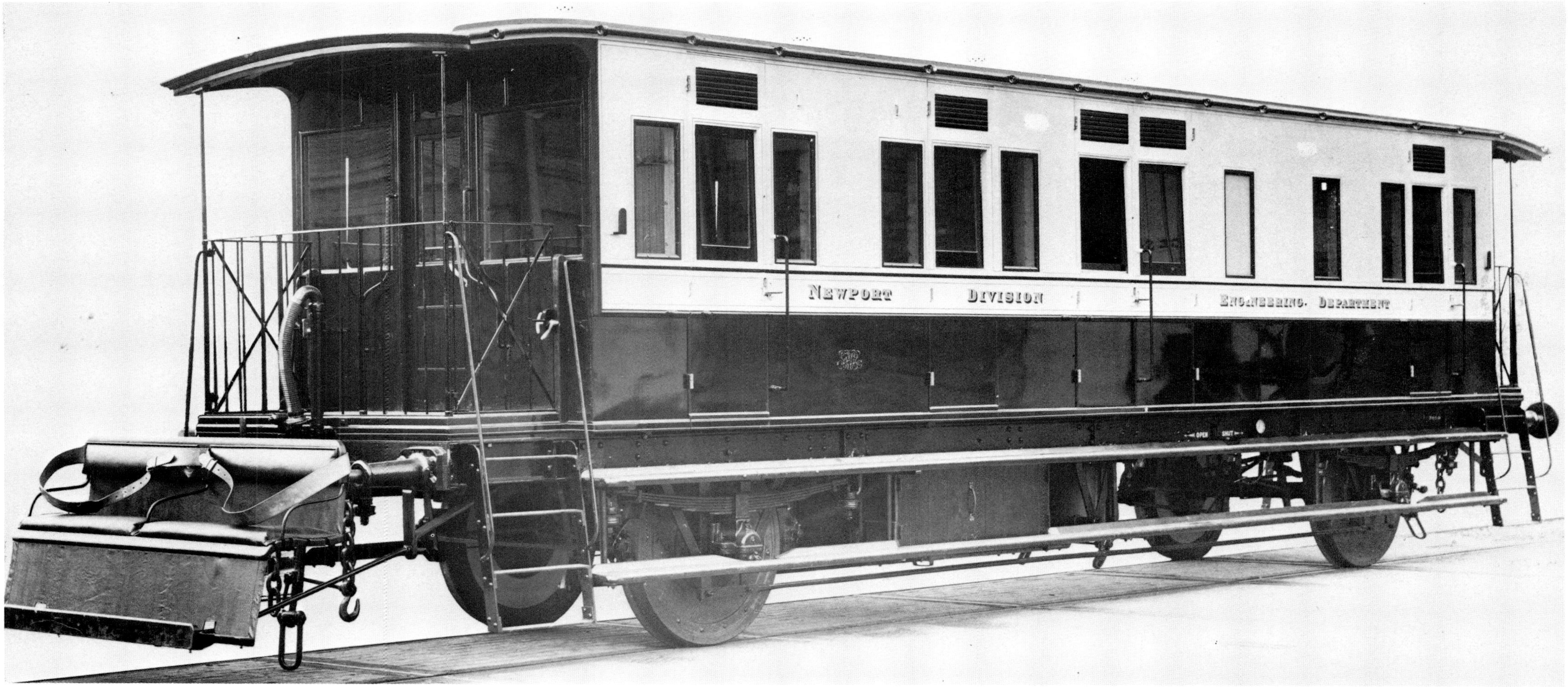

**Fig. 568** shows the Civil Engineer, himself, standing alongside one of these inspection saloons. The gas flare lamps mounted on each end of the roof, were for the inspection of tunnels and the undersides of bridges.

**Fig. 569 (below)** illustrates a March 1923 view of GWR No. 80944, a four-wheeled, single veranda inspection saloon that was taken over from the Brecon & Merthyr Railway.

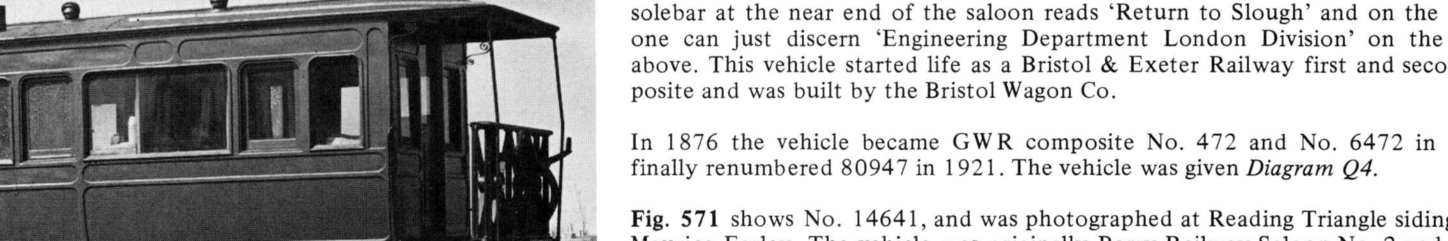

**Fig. 570** shows a fine study of No. 80974 coupled to engine No. 2026. The brand on the solebar at the near end of the saloon reads 'Return to Slough' and on the original print one can just discern 'Engineering Department London Division' on the beading just above. This vehicle started life as a Bristol & Exeter Railway first and second class composite and was built by the Bristol Wagon Co.

In 1876 the vehicle became GWR composite No. 472 and No. 6472 in 1907. It was finally renumbered 80947 in 1921. The vehicle was given *Diagram Q4*.

**Fig. 571** shows No. 14641, and was photographed at Reading Triangle sidings in 1951 by Maurice Earley. The vehicle was originally Barry Railway Saloon No. 2 and passed to the GWR at the Grouping.

Fig. 571

Fig. 572

**Figs. 572 & 573** illustrate the vehicle in use. In the former picture a 'King' class locomotive is being tested with a 20 coach train and in the latter, a British Railways Class 4 locomotive hauls the train.

*DIAGRAM Q20*

**Fig. 574** shows the vehicle in British Railways' ownership in 1950 and gives a good view of the layout of the vehicle. The 'ninth wheel' used for recording purposes can clearly be seen. A drawing can be found in *GW Coaches, Part I, page 184*.

Inspection & Dynamometer Car
Wagon Lot 293 of 1900
Running number: 790 (later No. W7)
Dimensions: 45ft. 0¾in. x 8ft. 10¾in.

Fig. 574

Fig. 575

**Figs. 575 & 576** show the interior of the dynamometer car and the bewildering array of instruments therein.

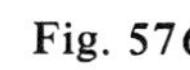

Fig. 576

Fig. 577

Fig. 578



**Figs. 577 & 578** are two more interior photographs, **Fig. 577** illustrating the pyrometer equipment used for measuring the locomotives efficiency and **Fig. 578** showing the time and distance logs.

**Fig. 579** shows No. W14476 in 1949, originally a 40ft. passenger brake numbered 222, after conversion for use as a tunnel inspection vehicle. Decking was provided on the roof to enable a close survey of tunnel brickwork, which must have been a dirty job in the days of steam! The loading gauges were fitted so that any distortion of the roof arches would be immediately noticed.

Lot 1701 of 1948
Running numbers: 80943/69/70/74/75/82
Dimensions: 52ft. 0in. x 8ft. 11in.

This series of vehicles was specially constructed at Swindon for the Engineer's Department. Each end had observation windows, and there were facilities for light meals. **Fig. 580** illustrates No. 80943.

**Fig. 581**, taken in 1961, illustrates another inspection saloon, No. 150266, which was rebuilt from restaurant car No. 9580, built originally on Lot 1349 in 1935 to *Diagram H33*.

**Fig. 581**

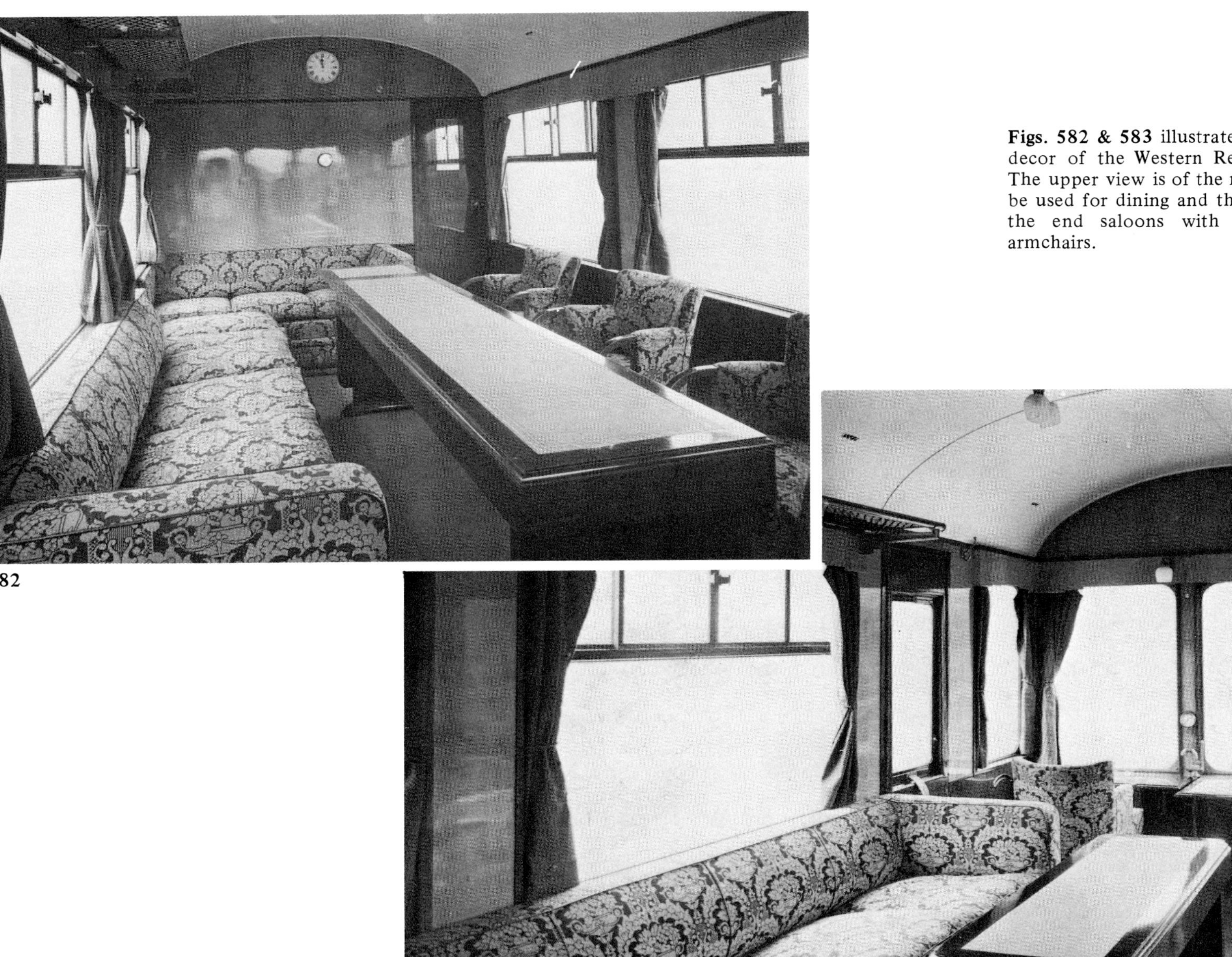

Fig. 582

Fig. 583

**Figs. 582 & 583** illustrate the interior fittings and decor of the Western Region inspection saloons. The upper view is of the main saloon, which could be used for dining and the lower view is of one of the end saloons with its large windows and armchairs.

Fig. 584

## FISH WAGONS

The following pages give a very brief glimpse of the smaller brown vehicles of the GWR which, although not on the carriage or van lists were nevertheless designed for, and mostly ran with, passenger-rated trains or to passenger speeds.

*DIAGRAM S2*
Bogie Fish Wagon (Open)
Lot 473 of 1889
Running numbers: 11210–6
Dimensions: 40ft. 0in.

*DIAGRAM S2*
These vehicles were originally broad gauge vehicles and they were transferred to the narrow gauge wagon list and given Nos. 42801–7. Finally, they were transferred to the van list and renumbered again to Nos. 2001–6. It was at this time that they were painted brown, having, until then, been grey.

**Figs. 584 & 585** illustrate the vehicles in broad gauge days. The bogies had a 5ft. wheelbase and were mounted at 27ft. centre. The vehicles illustrated were built as brake vans, hence the 'caboose'. There were similar vehicles without the caboose built to *Diagram S1*. The open fish vehicles were given the code 'Tadpole' and were eventually superseded when refrigeration became more common (see also *GW Coaches, Part I, pages 38, 39 & 40*).

Fig. 585

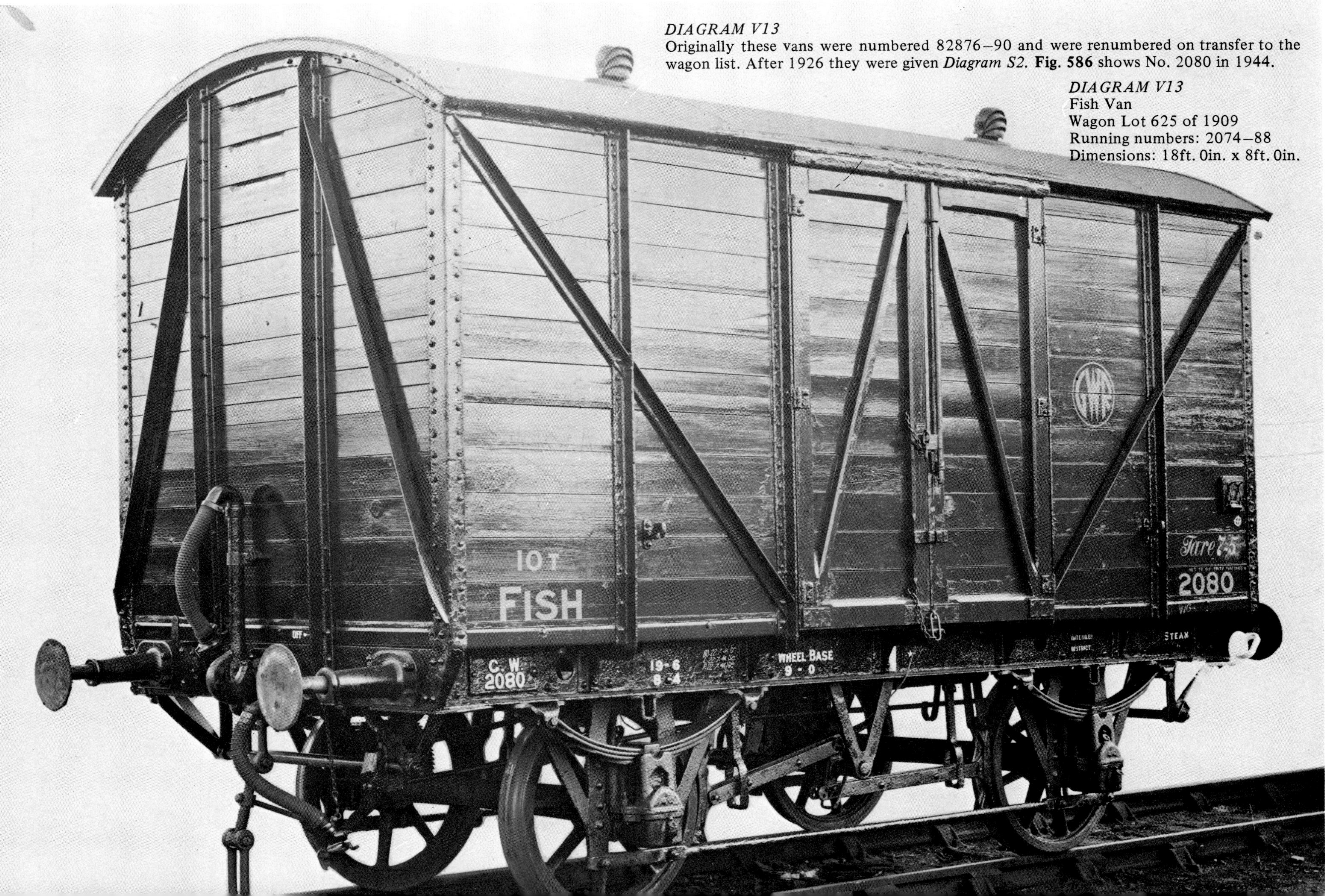


*DIAGRAM V13*
Originally these vans were numbered 82876–90 and were renumbered on transfer to the wagon list. After 1926 they were given *Diagram S2*. **Fig. 586** shows No. 2080 in 1944.

*DIAGRAM V13*
Fish Van
Wagon Lot 625 of 1909
Running numbers: 2074–88
Dimensions: 18ft. 0in. x 8ft. 0in.

Fig. 587

*DIAGRAM S6*
Fish Van
Lot 700 of 1912
Running numbers: 2089–113
Dimensions: 21ft. 0in. x 8ft. 4in.

*DIAGRAM S6*
These 12ft. wheelbase vans were originally numbered 85831–55. **Fig. 587** shows No. 2101 branded to work from Cardiff General.

Fig. 588

*DIAGRAM S8*
Fish Van (Bloater)
Lot 1258 of 1919 – Running numbers: 2139–2213
Lot 1259 of 1919 – Running numbers: 2114–38
Lot 1307 of 1923 – Running numbers: 2268–88, 2601–29
Dimensions: 28ft. 6in. x 8ft. 4in.

*DIAGRAM S8*
**Fig. 588** illustrates No. 2277 of this series of 18ft. wheelbase vans and the vehicle was photographed in 1925.

**Fig. 589** illustrates No. 2113 of *Diagram S6* in 1949 at the end of its days at Old Oak Common. ▶

▼ **Fig. 590** was taken at Swindon in 1944 after No. 2157 *(Diagram S8)* had been overhauled. The livery is brown and the lettering is yellow.

S8 series in all respects, except for the provision of roof ventilation. It appears that some interchange took place as the vehicle in **Fig. 590** is numbered in *Diagram S8* series but has roof ventilators. The vehicle in this photograph, taken in 1950, has been fitted with disc wheels in place of the original spoked variety.

*DIAGRAM S13*
Fish Van (Insulfish)
Lot 1718 of 1948
Running numbers: 3301–50
Dimensions: 31ft. 0in. x 8ft. 8in.

**Fig. 592** shows No. 3302 of this series as built at Swindon in 1948. The wheelbase is 10ft. 6in. x 10ft. 6in. and the apparatus on the roof contains the ice boxes for refrigeration.

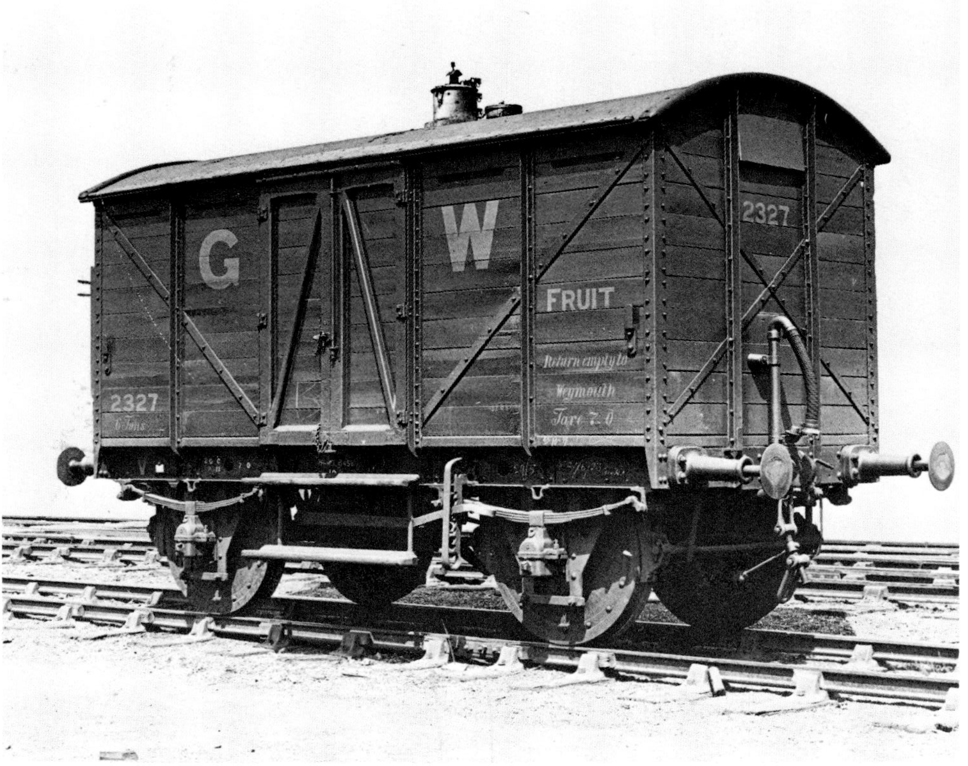


Fig. 594

# FRUIT VANS

*DIAGRAM Y2*
Fruit Van
Various Lots and numbers built between 1889 and 1900
Dimensions: 16ft. 0in. x 8ft. 8in (over steps)

*DIAGRAM Y2*
The wheelbase of these vans was 10ft. and they were mounted on Mansell coach wheels with carriage type Dean vaccum brake gear. **Figs. 593 & 594** show No. 2327 as running in 1923. This was one of the earliest of the series, being built in 1890 and the van is fitted with coach length buffers and screw couplings. In **Fig. 595**, No. 2399 is seen at Old Oak Common in 1951 and even at this late date, it still has the oil lamp on the roof.

Fig. 595

Fig. 597

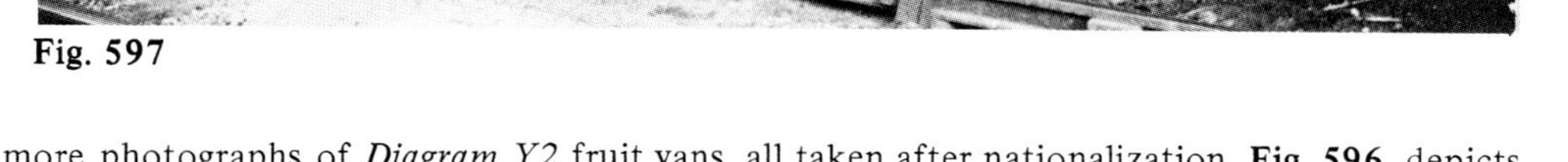

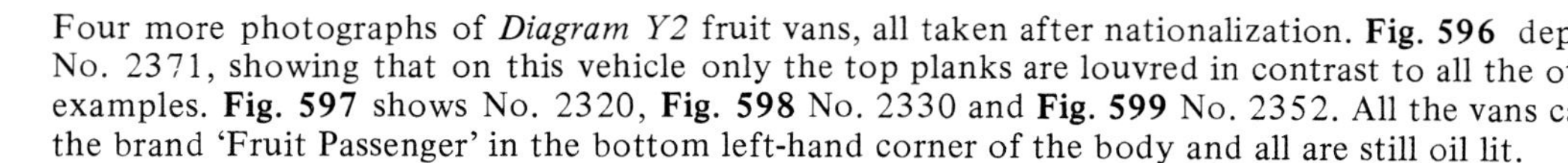

Four more photographs of *Diagram Y2* fruit vans, all taken after nationalization. **Fig. 596** depicts No. 2371, showing that on this vehicle only the top planks are louvred in contrast to all the other examples. **Fig. 597** shows No. 2320, **Fig. 598** No. 2330 and **Fig. 599** No. 2352. All the vans carry the brand 'Fruit Passenger' in the bottom left-hand corner of the body and all are still oil lit.

Fig. 598

Fig. 599

Fig. 600

Fig. 601

Fig. 602

*DIAGRAM Y3*
The next series of fruit vans followed the same lines as the fish vans, in being an extension in length of a four-wheeled van with twin double doors on each side. The wheelbase increased to 12ft. 6in.

*DIAGRAM Y3*
Fruit Van
Lot 667 of 1912 – Running numbers: 2426–2500
Lot 668 of 1912 – Running numbers: 2401–25
Dimensions: 22ft. 0in. x 8ft. 8in.

**Fig. 600** shows No. 2434 in 1923, **Fig. 601** shows No. 2466 in 1951 and in **Fig. 602**, No. 2424 is seen in 1950. Notice that this series of vans is fitted with wagon type vacuum brakes and that No. 2434 has been dual-fitted.

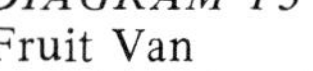

**Fig. 603** gives a good view of the end of the *Diagram Y3* series.

Fig. 603

*DIAGRAM Y9*
Fruit Van (Fruit C)
Carriage Lot 1606 of 1937 – Running numbers: 2803–32
Carriage Lot 1634 of 1938 – Running numbers: 2847–66
Dimensions: 22ft. 0in. x 8ft. 6in.

*DIAGRAM Y9*
These were similar vehicles to *Diagram Y3*, but with vented ends, upright planked doors and fewer louvres. **Fig. 604** is the official Swindon picture of No. 2803 taken in 1939.

*DIAGRAM Y11*
Fruit Van (Fruit D)
Carriage Lot 1649 of 1939
Running numbers: 2867–2916
Dimensions: 28ft 6in x 8ft 6in

*DIAGRAM Y11*
A further extension of wheelbase to 18ft. and the provision of three sets of doors each side produced the vehicles to *Diagram Y11*. No. 2885 is seen in 1941 condition in **Fig. 605**.

In 1948, with the need to carry fish declining, several of the 25ft. 6in. 'Bloaters' were given a new lease of life as parcels vans. **Fig. 606** of No. 2694 illustrates one of the vans as converted by the fitting of iron doors.

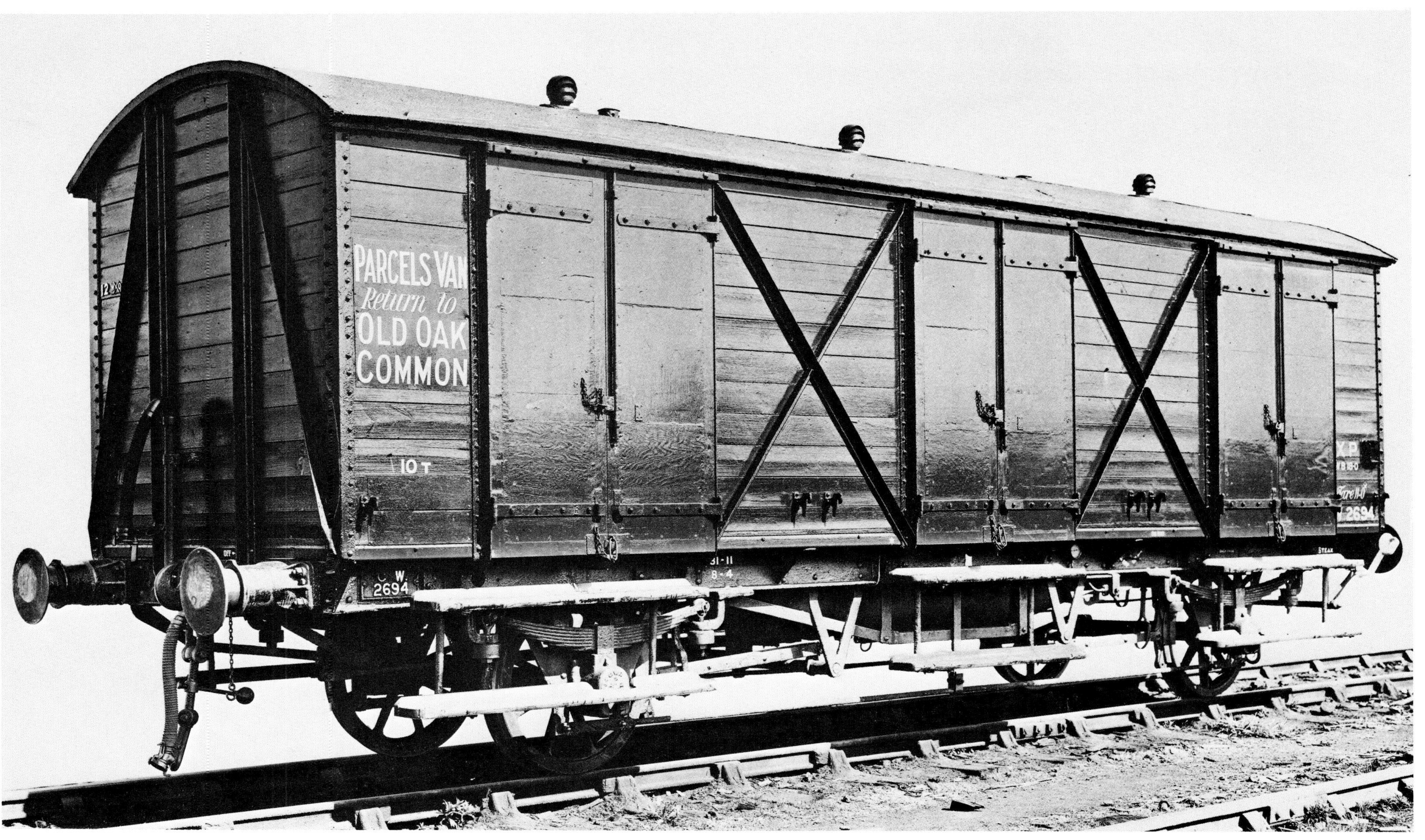

# SPECIAL CATTLE WAGONS (Beetle C)

Fig. 607

Fig. 609

Fig. 608

DIAGRAM W13

These vehicles were also known as prize cattle vans which more accurately describes their purpose, the carriage of particular animals in better conditions than would normally be found in ordinary cattle trucks and at passenger train speeds.

Vans were built to various diagrams in the 'W' series, varying little in design and appearance, for instance:

*DIAGRAM W7* on carriage Lot 1380 in 1909

*DIAGRAM W13* on carriage Lot 1467 in 1931 – Running numbers: 614–9 and 622–5

*DIAGRAM W14* on carriage Lot 1605 in 1938 – Running numbers: 720–30

*DIAGRAM W17* on carriage Lot 1728 in 1952 – Running numbers: 731–40

*DIAGRAM W17* on carriage Lot 1774 in 1952 – Running numbers: 741–60

**Fig. 607** shows No. 200 of *Diagram W13* in 1947 and **Fig. 608** shows one of *Diagram W7* series. Worthy of note are the similarities and the central drovers compartment. **Fig. 609** illustrates *Diagram W17* series which shows a slight difference in strapping and illustrates the two positions for the sliding shutters over

**Fig. 610**

Three more photographs showing closer detail of the 'Beetle C' cattle vans. **Fig. 610** shows the gas cylinder and door fastenings, **Fig. 611**, the steam pipe and drawgear and **Fig. 612** a general view of the end of the vehicle.

**Fig. 612**

# Appendix ~ Lot List

## HORSE BOX INDEX

| H'Box No. | Lot No. | Diag. No. | H'Box No. | Lot No. | Diag. No. | H'Box No. | Lot No. | Diag. No. | H'Box No. | Lot No. | Diag. No. | H'Box No. | Lot No. | Diag. No. | H'Box No. | Lot No. | Diag. No. | H'Box No. | Lot No. | Diag. No. | H'Box No. | Lot No. | Diag. No. | H'Box No. | Lot No. | Diag. No. | H'Box No. | Lot No. |
|---|---|---|---|---|---|---|---|---|---|---|---|---|---|---|---|---|---|---|---|---|---|---|---|---|---|---|---|---|
| 1 | | | 51 | | | 101 | | | 151 | | | 201 | | | 251 | 1222 | N.11 | 301 | 1221 | N.11 | 351 | 1221 | N.11 | 401 | 1267 | N.13 | 431 | |
| 2 | 1205 | N.11 | 2 | | | 2 | | | 2 | 1367 | N.13 | 2 | 1205 | N.11 | 2 | | | 2 | | | 2 | | | 2 | | | 2 | 1408 |
| 3 | | | 3 | | | 3 | | | 3 | " | " | 3 | | | 3 | 1386 | N.13 | 3 | 1267 | N.13 | 3 | | | 3 | 1267 | N.13 | 3 | " |
| 4 | | | 4 | 1205 | N.11 | 4 | | | 4 | 1254 | N.12 | 4 | 1243 | N.12 | 4 | 1222 | N.11 | 4 | 1242 | N.12 | 4 | | | 4 | " | " | 4 | |
| 5 | | | 5 | | | 5 | | | 5 | | | 5 | | | 5 | 1386 | N.13 | 5 | 1267 | N.13 | 5 | 1242 | N.12 | 5 | 1242 | N.12 | 5 | |
| 6 | | | 6 | | | 6 | | | 6 | 1367 | N.13 | 6 | | | 6 | " | " | 6 | 1397 | " | 6 | " | " | 6 | | | 6 | |
| 7 | 1254 | N.12 | 7 | | | 7 | | | 7 | " | " | 7 | 1243 | N.12 | 7 | 1222 | N.11 | 7 | 1267 | " | 7 | 1267 | N.13 | 7 | 1267 | N.13 | 7 | |
| 8 | | | 8 | | | 8 | | | 8 | " | " | 8 | " | " | 8 | 1386 | N.13 | 8 | 1221 | N.11 | 8 | " | " | 8 | " | " | 8 | |
| 9 | | | 9 | | | 9 | | | 9 | " | " | 9 | " | " | 9 | " | " | 9 | | | 9 | 1221 | N.11 | 9 | 1242 | N.12 | 9 | |
| 10 | | | 60 | | | 110 | | | 160 | " | " | 210 | | | 260 | | | 310 | 1267 | N.13 | 360 | | | 410 | 1267 | N.13 | 460 | 1408 |
| 1 | | | 1 | | | 1 | | | 1 | " | " | 1 | | | 1 | 1243 | N.12 | 1 | 1221 | N.11 | 1 | 1397 | N.13 | 1 | 1242 | N.12 | 1 | |
| 2 | | | 2 | | | 2 | | | 2 | 1254 | N.12 | 2 | 1205 | N.11 | 2 | 1222 | N.11 | 2 | | | 2 | 1221 | N.11 | 2 | 1267 | N.13 | 2 | |
| 3 | | | 3 | | | 3 | | | 3 | 1367 | N.13 | 3 | " | " | 3 | 1397 | N.13 | 3 | 1267 | N.13 | 3 | 1267 | N.13 | 3 | | | 3 | |
| 4 | | | 4 | | | 4 | | | 4 | " | " | 4 | | | 4 | " | " | 4 | 1221 | N.11 | 4 | 1221 | N.11 | 4 | 1254 | N.12 | 4 | |
| 5 | | | 5 | | | 5 | | | 5 | 1205 | N.11 | 5 | | | 5 | " | " | 5 | " | " | 5 | " | " | 5 | " | " | 5 | |
| 6 | | | 6 | | | 6 | | | 6 | 1254 | N.12 | 6 | | | 6 | " | " | 6 | | | 6 | | | 6 | 1267 | N.13 | 6 | |
| 7 | | | 7 | | | 7 | | | 7 | | | 7 | 1222 | N.11 | 7 | " | " | 7 | 1267 | N.13 | 7 | 1267 | N.13 | 7 | " | " | 7 | |
| 8 | | | 8 | | | 8 | | | 8 | 1367 | N.13 | 8 | " | " | 8 | 1222 | N.11 | 8 | 1221 | N.11 | 8 | | | 8 | " | " | 8 | |
| 9 | 1254 | N.12 | 9 | | | 9 | | | 9 | " | " | 9 | | | 9 | " | " | 9 | 1242 | N.12 | 9 | | | 9 | " | " | 9 | |
| 20 | " | " | 70 | | | 120 | | | 170 | | | 220 | | | 270 | | | 320 | | | 370 | 1242 | N.12 | 420 | | " | 470 | |
| 1 | | | 1 | | | 1 | | | 1 | | | 1 | | | 1 | 1397 | N.13 | 1 | 1267 | N.13 | 1 | 1267 | N.13 | 1 | 1408 | " | 1 | |
| 2 | | | 2 | | | 2 | | | 2 | 1205 | N.11 | 2 | | | 2 | 1222 | N.11 | 2 | " | " | 2 | " | " | 2 | 1267 | " | 2 | |
| 3 | | | 3 | | | 3 | | | 3 | 1254 | N.12 | 3 | 1268 | N.13 | 3 | 1408 | N.13 | 3 | 1242 | N.12 | 3 | " | " | 3 | 1408 | " | 3 | |
| 4 | | | 4 | | | 4 | | | 4 | " | " | 4 | | | 4 | 1397 | " | 4 | | | 4 | 1242 | N.12 | 4 | 1267 | " | 4 | |
| 5 | | | 5 | | | 5 | | | 5 | " | " | 5 | 1268 | N.13 | 5 | 1222 | N.11 | 5 | 1267 | N.13 | 5 | 1267 | N.13 | 5 | " | " | 5 | |
| 6 | 1254 | N.12 | 6 | | | 6 | | | 6 | 1379 | N.13 | 6 | | | 6 | 1397 | N.13 | 6 | 1221 | N.11 | 6 | 1242 | N.12 | 6 | 1408 | " | 6 | 1408 |
| 7 | | | 7 | | | 7 | 1205 | N.11 | 7 | 1254 | N.12 | 7 | 1268 | N.14 | 7 | | | 7 | | | 7 | " | " | 7 | 1267 | " | 7 | |
| 8 | 1254 | N.12 | 8 | | | 8 | | | 8 | " | " | 8 | " | N.13 | 8 | 1243 | N.12 | 8 | 1242 | N.12 | 8 | 1267 | N.13 | 8 | " | " | 8 | |
| 9 | | | 9 | | | 9 | | | 9 | | | 9 | 1222 | N.11 | 9 | 1222 | N.11 | 9 | 1397 | N.13 | 9 | | | 9 | " | " | 9 | |
| 30 | | | 80 | | | 130 | | | 180 | 1379 | N.13 | 230 | 1268 | N.14 | 280 | " | " | 330 | 1267 | " | 380 | 1267 | N.13 | 430 | " | " | 480 | |
| 1 | 1254 | N.12 | 1 | | | 1 | 1254 | N.12 | 1 | " | " | 1 | 1222 | N.11 | 1 | | | 1 | 1221 | N.11 | 1 | " | " | 1 | " | " | 1 | |
| 2 | | | 2 | | | 2 | 1205 | N.11 | 2 | | | 2 | 1243 | N.12 | 2 | 1222 | N.11 | 2 | " | " | 2 | " | " | 2 | " | " | 2 | |
| 3 | | | 3 | | | 3 | " | " | 3 | 1379 | N.13 | 3 | " | " | 3 | 1397 | N.13 | 3 | 1267 | N.13 | 3 | " | " | 3 | " | " | 3 | |
| 4 | 1205 | N.11 | 4 | | | 4 | 1254 | N.12 | 4 | 1254 | N.12 | 4 | " | " | 4 | " | " | 4 | " | " | 4 | 1254 | N.12 | 4 | " | " | 4 | |
| 5 | | | 5 | | | 5 | " | " | 5 | 1205 | N.11 | 5 | 1222 | N.11 | 5 | " | " | 5 | " | " | 5 | 1267 | N.13 | 5 | " | " | 5 | |
| 6 | | | 6 | | | 6 | | | 6 | 1379 | N.13 | 6 | 1268 | N.13 | 6 | | | 6 | " | " | 6 | 1397 | " | 6 | " | " | 6 | |
| 7 | | | 7 | | | 7 | | | 7 | 1205 | N.11 | 7 | " | " | 7 | 1243 | N.12 | 7 | 1397 | " | 7 | 1267 | " | 7 | " | " | 7 | |
| 8 | | | 8 | | | 8 | | | 8 | 1254 | N.12 | 8 | " | N.14 | 8 | 1397 | N.13 | 8 | | | 8 | | | 8 | " | " | 8 | |
| 9 | 1254 | N.12 | 9 | | | 9 | | | 9 | 1379 | N.13 | 9 | " | N.13 | 9 | 1243 | N.12 | 9 | 1221 | N.11 | 9 | | | 9 | " | " | 9 | 1444 |
| 40 | | | 90 | | | 140 | | | 190 | " | " | 240 | " | " | 290 | " | " | 340 | | | 390 | | | 440 | 1408 | " | 490 | " |
| 1 | | | 1 | | | 1 | 1205 | N.11 | 1 | | | 1 | 1386 | " | 1 | 1397 | N.13 | 1 | 1242 | N.12 | 1 | | | 1 | " | " | | " |
| 2 | | | 2 | | | 2 | | | 2 | 1254 | N.12 | 2 | 1254 | N.12 | 2 | " | " | 2 | 1267 | N.13 | 2 | | | 2 | " | " | 2 | " |
| 3 | | | 3 | | | 3 | 1254 | N.12 | 3 | " | " | 3 | 1222 | N.11 | 3 | " | " | 3 | 1221 | N.11 | 3 | | | 3 | " | " | 3 | " |
| 4 | | | 4 | | | 4 | 1367 | N.13 | 4 | " | " | 4 | 1386 | N.13 | 4 | " | " | 4 | 1267 | N.13 | 4 | 1408 | N.13 | 4 | " | " | 4 | |
| 5 | | | 5 | | | 5 | | | 5 | " | " | 5 | 1222 | N.11 | 5 | " | " | 5 | 1221 | N.11 | 5 | " | " | 5 | " | " | 5 | 1444 |
| 6 | | | 6 | | | 6 | 1367 | N.13 | 6 | | | 6 | " | " | 6 | 1243 | N.12 | 6 | 1267 | N.13 | 6 | 1267 | " | 6 | " | " | 6 | " |
| 7 | | | 7 | | | 7 | 1379 | " | 7 | | | 7 | 1386 | N.13 | 7 | " | " | 7 | | | 7 | " | " | 7 | " | " | 7 | " |
| 8 | | | 8 | | | 8 | " | " | 8 | 1243 | N.12 | 8 | " | " | 8 | 1397 | N.13 | 8 | 1242 | N.12 | 8 | " | " | 8 | " | " | 8 | |
| 9 | | | 9 | | | 9 | 1205 | N.11 | 9 | 1379 | N.13 | 9 | " | " | 9 | " | " | 9 | 1267 | N.13 | 9 | " | " | 9 | | | 9 | |
| 50 | | | 100 | | | 150 | 1254 | N.12 | 200 | | | 250 | 1222 | N.11 | 300 | " | " | 350 | 1221 | N.11 | 400 | " | " | 450 | 1408 | N.13 | 500 | 1444 |

| H'Box No. | Lot No. | Diag. No. | H'Box No. | Lot No. | Diag. No. | H'Box No. | Lot No. | Diag. No. | H'Box No. | Lot No. | Diag. No. | H'Box No. | Lot No. | Diag. No. | H'Box No. | Lot No. | Diag. No. | H'Box No. | Lot No. | Diag. No. | H'Box No. | Lot No. | Diag. No. | H'Box No. | Lot No. | Diag. No. | H'Box No. | Lot No. |
|---|---|---|---|---|---|---|---|---|---|---|---|---|---|---|---|---|---|---|---|---|---|---|---|---|---|---|---|---|
| 501 | 1444 | N.15 | 551 | 1577 | N.16 | 601 | 1577 | N.16 | 651 | 1577 | N.16 | 701 | 1577 | N.16 | 751 | | | 801 | | | 851 | 1132 | N.11 | 901 | 1367 | N.13 | 951 | |
| 2 | " | " | 2 | 1461 | N.15 | 2 | " | " | 2 | " | " | 2 | " | " | 2 | | | 2 | | | 2 | " | " | 2 | " | " | 2 | |
| 3 | | | 3 | " | " | 3 | " | " | 3 | " | " | 3 | " | " | 3 | | | 3 | | | 3 | " | " | 3 | " | " | 3 | |
| 4 | 1444 | N.15 | 4 | 1577 | N.16 | 4 | " | " | 4 | " | " | 4 | " | " | 4 | | | 4 | | | 4 | " | " | 4 | | | 4 | |
| 5 | " | " | 5 | " | " | 5 | " | " | 5 | " | " | 5 | " | " | 5 | | | 5 | | | 5 | " | " | 5 | 1367 | N.13 | 5 | |
| 6 | " | " | 6 | " | " | 6 | " | " | 6 | " | " | 6 | " | " | 6 | | | 6 | | | 6 | | | 6 | " | " | 6 | |
| 7 | 1577 | N.16 | 7 | 1461 | N.15 | 7 | | | 7 | " | " | 7 | " | " | 7 | | | 7 | | | 7 | | | 7 | " | " | 7 | |
| 8 | 1444 | N.15 | 8 | " | " | 8 | 1577 | N.16 | 8 | " | " | 8 | " | " | 8 | | | 8 | | | 8 | 1132 | N.11 | 8 | " | " | 8 | |
| 9 | 1577 | N.16 | 9 | 1577 | N.16 | 9 | " | " | 9 | " | " | 9 | " | " | 9 | | | 9 | | | 9 | " | " | 9 | " | " | 9 | |
| 510 | 1444 | N.15 | 560 | 1461 | N.15 | 610 | " | " | 660 | " | " | 710 | " | " | 760 | | | 810 | | | 860 | " | " | 910 | " | " | 960 | |
| 1 | " | " | 1 | " | " | 1 | " | " | 1 | " | " | 1 | " | " | 1 | | | 1 | | | 1 | " | " | 1 | " | " | 1 | |
| 2 | " | " | 2 | 1577 | N.16 | 2 | " | " | 2 | " | " | 2 | " | " | 2 | | | 2 | | | 2 | | | 2 | " | " | 2 | |
| 3 | " | " | 3 | 1461 | N.15 | 3 | " | " | 3 | " | " | 3 | " | " | 3 | | | 3 | | | 3 | 1163 | N.11 | 3 | " | " | 3 | |
| 4 | " | " | 4 | " | " | 4 | | | 4 | " | " | 4 | " | " | 4 | | | 4 | | | 4 | " | " | 4 | " | " | 4 | |
| 5 | 1461 | " | 5 | " | " | 5 | | | 5 | " | " | 5 | " | " | 5 | | | 5 | | | 5 | " | " | 5 | " | " | 5 | |
| 6 | 1577 | N.16 | 6 | " | " | 6 | | | 6 | " | " | 6 | " | " | 6 | | | 6 | | | 6 | " | " | 6 | " | " | 6 | |
| 7 | 1461 | N.15 | 7 | " | " | 7 | | | 7 | " | " | 7 | " | " | 7 | | | 7 | | | 7 | " | " | 7 | " | " | 7 | |
| 8 | " | " | 8 | " | " | 8 | | | 8 | " | " | 8 | " | " | 8 | | | 8 | | | 8 | " | " | 8 | " | " | 8 | |
| 9 | 1577 | N.16 | 9 | " | " | 9 | | | 9 | " | " | 9 | " | " | 9 | | | 9 | | | 9 | " | " | 9 | " | " | 9 | |
| 520 | " | " | 570 | 1577 | N.16 | 620 | 1577 | N.16 | 670 | " | " | 720 | | | 770 | | | 820 | | | 870 | | | 920 | " | " | 970 | |
| 1 | 1461 | N.15 | 1 | " | " | 1 | " | " | 1 | " | " | 1 | | | 1 | | | 1 | | | 1 | 1163 | N.11 | 1 | " | " | 1 | |
| 2 | 1577 | N.16 | 2 | 1461 | N.15 | 2 | | | 2 | " | " | 2 | | | 2 | | | 2 | | | 2 | 1184 | " | 2 | " | " | 2 | |
| 3 | 1461 | N.15 | 3 | 1577 | N.16 | 3 | | | 3 | " | " | 3 | | | 3 | | | 3 | | | 3 | | | 3 | " | " | 3 | |
| 4 | 1577 | N.16 | 4 | " | " | 4 | | | 4 | " | " | 4 | | | 4 | | | 4 | | | 4 | 1184 | N.11 | 4 | " | " | 4 | |
| 5 | 1461 | N.15 | 5 | 1461 | N.15 | 5 | | | 5 | " | " | 5 | | | 5 | | | 5 | | | 5 | | | 5 | " | " | 5 | |
| 6 | 1577 | N.16 | 6 | " | " | 6 | 1577 | N.16 | 6 | " | " | 6 | | | 6 | | | 6 | | | 6 | | | 6 | " | " | 6 | |
| 7 | " | " | 7 | " | " | 7 | " | " | 7 | " | " | 7 | | | 7 | | | 7 | | | 7 | 1184 | N.11 | 7 | " | " | 7 | |
| 8 | 1461 | N.15 | 8 | " | " | 8 | " | " | 8 | " | " | 8 | | | 8 | | | 8 | | | 8 | " | " | 8 | | | 8 | |
| 9 | " | " | 9 | 1577 | N.16 | 9 | " | " | 9 | " | " | 9 | | | 9 | | | 9 | | | 9 | " | " | 9 | | | 9 | |
| 530 | " | " | 580 | 1461 | N.15 | 630 | " | " | 680 | " | " | 730 | | | 780 | | | 830 | | | 880 | " | " | 930 | | | 980 | |
| 1 | " | " | 1 | " | " | 1 | " | " | 1 | " | " | 1 | | | 1 | | | 1 | | | 1 | " | " | 1 | | | 1 | |
| 2 | 1577 | N.16 | 2 | 1577 | N.16 | 2 | " | " | 2 | " | " | 2 | | | 2 | | | 2 | | | 2 | " | " | 2 | | | 2 | |
| 3 | 1461 | N.15 | 3 | " | " | 3 | " | " | 3 | " | " | 3 | | | 3 | | | 3 | | | 3 | " | " | 3 | | | 3 | |
| 4 | " | " | 4 | " | " | 4 | " | " | 4 | " | " | 4 | | | 4 | | | 4 | | | 4 | | | 4 | | | 4 | |
| 5 | 1577 | N.16 | 5 | " | " | 5 | " | " | 5 | " | " | 5 | | | 5 | | | 5 | | | 5 | 1184 | N.11 | 5 | | | 5 | |
| 6 | 1461 | N.15 | 6 | " | " | 6 | " | " | 6 | | | 6 | | | 6 | | | 6 | | | 6 | " | " | 6 | | | 6 | |
| 7 | " | " | 7 | " | " | 7 | " | " | 7 | 1577 | N.16 | 7 | | | 7 | | | 7 | | | 7 | " | " | 7 | | | 7 | |
| 8 | 1577 | N.16 | 8 | " | " | 8 | " | " | 8 | | | 8 | | | 8 | | | 8 | | | 8 | " | " | 8 | | | 8 | |
| 9 | 1461 | N.15 | 9 | 1461 | N.15 | 9 | " | " | 9 | 1577 | N.16 | 9 | | | 9 | | | 9 | | | 9 | " | " | 9 | | | 9 | |
| 540 | 1577 | N.16 | 590 | 1577 | N.16 | 640 | " | " | 690 | " | " | 740 | | | 790 | | | 840 | | | 890 | | | 940 | | | 990 | |
| 1 | 1461 | N.15 | 1 | " | " | 1 | " | " | 1 | " | " | 1 | | | 1 | | | 1 | 1184 | N.11 | 1 | | | 1 | | | 1 | |
| 2 | " | " | 2 | " | " | 2 | " | " | 2 | " | " | 2 | | | 2 | | | 2 | | | 2 | 1367 | N.13 | 2 | | | 2 | |
| 3 | 1577 | N.16 | 3 | " | " | 3 | " | " | 3 | " | " | 3 | | | 3 | | | 3 | | | 3 | " | " | 3 | | | 3 | |
| 4 | 1461 | N.15 | 4 | " | " | 4 | " | " | 4 | " | " | 4 | | | 4 | | | 4 | | | 4 | " | " | 4 | | | 4 | |
| 5 | " | " | 5 | " | " | 5 | " | " | 5 | " | " | 5 | | | 5 | | | 5 | 1132 | N.10 | 5 | " | " | 5 | | | 5 | |
| 6 | 1577 | N.16 | 6 | " | " | 6 | | | 6 | " | " | 6 | | | 6 | | | 6 | " | " | 6 | " | " | 6 | | | 6 | |
| 7 | " | " | 7 | | | 7 | 1577 | N.16 | 7 | " | " | 7 | | | 7 | | | 7 | " | " | 7 | " | " | 7 | | | 7 | |
| 8 | " | " | 8 | 1577 | N.16 | 8 | " | " | 8 | " | " | 8 | | | 8 | | | 8 | " | " | 8 | " | " | 8 | | | 8 | |
| 9 | 1461 | N.15 | 9 | " | " | 9 | " | " | 9 | " | " | 9 | | | 9 | | | 9 | " | N.11 | 9 | " | " | 9 | | | 9 | |
| 550 | " | " | 600 | | | 650 | " | " | 700 | " | " | 750 | | | 800 | | | 850 | " | " | 900 | " | " | 950 | | | 1000 | |

# CARRIACE TRUCK INDEX

| Lot No. | Diag No. | Truck No. | Lot No. | Diag No. | Truck No. | Lot No. | Diag No. | Truck No. | Lot No. | Diag No. | Truck No. | Lot No. | Diag No. | Truck No. | Lot No. | Diag No. | Truck No. | Lot No. | Diag No. | Truck No. | Lot No. | Diag No. | Truck No. | Lot No. | Diag No. | Truck No. | Lot No. | Diag No. |
|---|---|---|---|---|---|---|---|---|---|---|---|---|---|---|---|---|---|---|---|---|---|---|---|---|---|---|---|---|
| 1650 | P22 | 51 | | | 101 | | | 151 | 1216 | P.15 | 201 | | | 251 | | | 301 | | | 351 | | | 401 | | | 451 | 1158 | P.15 |
| " | " | 2 | | | 2 | | | 2 | - | " | 2 | 1255 | P.15 | 2 | | | 2 | | | 2 | | | 2 | | | 2 | | |
| " | " | 3 | | | 3 | | | 3 | 1244 | " | 3 | | | 3 | | | 3 | | | 3 | | | 3 | | | 3 | | |
| " | " | 4 | | | 4 | | | 4 | | | 4 | 1255 | P.15 | 4 | | | 4 | | | 4 | | | 4 | | | 4 | 1217 | P.15 |
| " | " | 5 | | | 5 | | | 5 | 1216 | P.15 | 5 | " | " | 5 | | | 5 | | | 5 | | | 5 | | | 5 | " | - |
| " | " | 6 | | | 6 | | | 6 | | | 6 | | | 6 | | | 6 | | | 6 | | | 6 | | | 6 | " | - |
| | | 7 | | | 7 | | | 7 | 1216 | P.15 | 7 | | | 7 | | | 7 | | | 7 | | | 7 | | | 7 | - | - |
| | | 8 | | | 8 | | | 8 | " | " | 8 | 1255 | P.15 | 8 | | | 8 | | | 8 | | | 8 | | | 8 | - | - |
| | | 9 | | | 9 | | | 9 | | | 9 | " | " | 9 | | | 9 | | | 9 | | | 9 | | | 9 | | - |
| | | 60 | | | 110 | 1206 | P.15 | 160 | | | 210 | | | 260 | | | 310 | | | 360 | | | 410 | | | 460 | - | - |
| | | 1 | | | 1 | " | " | 1 | 1216 | P.15 | 1 | | | 1 | | | 1 | | | 1 | | | 1 | | | 1 | - | - |
| | | 2 | | | 2 | | | 2 | | | 2 | | | 2 | | | 2 | | | 2 | | | 2 | | | 2 | | - |
| | | 3 | | | 3 | 1206 | P.15 | 3 | 1216 | P.15 | 3 | | | 3 | | | 3 | | | 3 | | | 3 | | | 3 | - | - |
| | | 4 | | | 4 | " | " | 4 | 1244 | " | 4 | | | 4 | | | 4 | | | 4 | | | 4 | | | 4 | - | - |
| | | 5 | | | 5 | " | " | 5 | 1216 | " | 5 | | | 5 | | | 5 | | | 5 | | | 5 | | | 5 | - | - |
| | | 6 | | | 6 | " | " | 6 | 1244 | " | 6 | | | 6 | | | 6 | | | 6 | | | 6 | | | 6 | - | - |
| | | 7 | | | 7 | | | 7 | | | 7 | | | 7 | | | 7 | | | 7 | | | 7 | | | 7 | | - |
| | | 8 | | | 8 | | | 8 | 1216 | P.15 | 8 | | | 8 | | | 8 | | | 8 | | | 8 | | | 8 | 1245 | - |
| | | 9 | | | 9 | 1206 | P.15 | 9 | " | " | 9 | | | 9 | | | 9 | | | 9 | | | 9 | | | 9 | - | - |
| | | 70 | | | 120 | | | 170 | | | 220 | | | 270 | | | 320 | | | 370 | | | 420 | | | 470 | - | - |
| | | 1 | | | 1 | 1244 | P.15 | 1 | 1216 | P.15 | 1 | | | 1 | | | 1 | | | 1 | | | 1 | | | 1 | - | - |
| | | 2 | | | 2 | 1206 | " | 2 | | | 2 | | | 2 | | | 2 | | | 2 | | | 2 | | | 2 | - | - |
| | | 3 | | | 3 | " | " | 3 | | | 3 | | | 3 | | | 3 | | | 3 | | | 3 | | | 3 | | - |
| | | 4 | | | 4 | " | " | 4 | | | 4 | | | 4 | | | 4 | | | 4 | | | 4 | | | 4 | | - |
| | | 5 | | | 5 | " | " | 5 | 1216 | P.15 | 5 | | | 5 | | | 5 | | | 5 | | | 5 | | | 5 | - | - |
| | | 6 | | | 6 | | | 6 | | | 6 | | | 6 | | | 6 | | | 6 | | | 6 | | | 6 | | - |
| | | 7 | | | 7 | | | 7 | | | 7 | | | 7 | | | 7 | | | 7 | | | 7 | 1026 | P.12 | 7 | - | - |
| | | 8 | | | 8 | 1206 | P.15 | 8 | 1244 | P.15 | 8 | | | 8 | | | 8 | | | 8 | | | 8 | | - | 8 | | - |
| | | 9 | | | 9 | " | " | 9 | " | " | 9 | | | 9 | | | 9 | | | 9 | | | 9 | | | 9 | | - |
| | | 80 | | | 130 | " | " | 180 | " | " | 230 | | | 280 | | | 330 | | | 380 | | | 430 | | | 480 | | - |
| | | 1 | | | 1 | " | " | 1 | " | " | 1 | | | 1 | | | 1 | | | 1 | | | 1 | | | 1 | - | - |
| | | 2 | | | 2 | | | 2 | | | 2 | | | 2 | | | 2 | | | 2 | | | 2 | 1026 | P.12 | 2 | - | - |
| | | 3 | | | 3 | | | 3 | 1244 | P.15 | 3 | | | 3 | | | 3 | | | 3 | | | 3 | 1105 | - | 3 | 1223 | P.18 |
| | | 4 | | | 4 | 1206 | P.15 | 4 | | | 4 | | | 4 | | | 4 | | | 4 | | | 4 | | | 4 | - | - |
| | | 5 | | | 5 | " | " | 5 | | | 5 | | | 5 | | | 5 | | | 5 | | | 5 | 1105 | P.12 | 5 | - | - |
| | | 6 | | | 6 | " | " | 6 | 1244 | P.15 | 6 | | | 6 | | | 6 | | | 6 | | | 6 | | | 6 | 1498 | P.21 |
| | | 7 | | | 7 | " | " | 7 | 1255 | " | 7 | | | 7 | | | 7 | | | 7 | | | 7 | | | 7 | | |
| | | 8 | | | 8 | | | 8 | " | " | 8 | | | 8 | | | 8 | | | 8 | | | 8 | | | 8 | | |
| | | 9 | | | 9 | 1244 | P.15 | 9 | " | " | 9 | | | 9 | | | 9 | | | 9 | 891 | P.8 | 9 | | | 9 | 1498 | P.21 |
| | | 90 | | | 140 | " | " | 190 | " | " | 240 | | | 290 | | | 340 | | | 390 | - | " | 440 | | | 490 | 1191 | P.16 |
| | | 1 | | | 1 | " | " | 1 | " | " | 1 | | | 1 | | | 1 | | | 1 | | | 1 | 1105 | P.12 | 1 | - | |
| | | 2 | | | 2 | 1206 | " | 2 | | | 2 | | | 2 | | | 2 | | | 2 | | | 2 | | | 2 | | |
| | | 3 | | | 3 | | | 3 | 1255 | P.15 | 3 | | | 3 | | | 3 | | | 3 | | | 3 | 1158 | P.15 | 3 | 1753 | P23 |
| | | 4 | | | 4 | | | 4 | " | " | 4 | | | 4 | | | 4 | | | 4 | | | 4 | - | - | 4 | - | |
| | | 5 | | | 5 | 1216 | P.15 | 5 | " | " | 5 | | | 5 | | | 5 | | | 5 | | | 5 | - | - | 5 | - | - |
| | | 6 | | | 6 | 1244 | - | 6 | | | 6 | | | 6 | | | 6 | | | 6 | | | 6 | - | - | 6 | - | |
| | | 7 | | | 7 | - | " | 7 | | | 7 | | | 7 | | | 7 | | | 7 | 891 | P.8 | 7 | - | - | 7 | - | |
| | | 8 | | | 8 | | | 8 | 1255 | P.15 | 8 | | | 8 | | | 8 | | | 8 | | | 8 | | | 8 | - | |
| | | 9 | | | 9 | 1216 | P.15 | 9 | | | 9 | | | 9 | | | 9 | | | 9 | | | 9 | 1158 | P.15 | 9 | | |
| | | 100 | | | 130 | " | " | 200 | 1255 | P.15 | 250 | | | 300 | | | 350 | | | 400 | | | 450 | - | - | 500 | | |

| Lot No. | Diag No. | Truck No. | Lot No. | Diag No. | Truck No. | Lot No. | Diag No. | Truck No. | Lot No. | Diag No. | Truck No. | Lot No. | Diag No. | Truck No. | Lot No. | Diag No. | Truck No. | Lot No. | Diag No. | Truck No. | Lot No. | Diag No. | Truck No. | Lot No. | Diag No. | Truck No. | Lot No. | Diag No. |
|---|---|---|---|---|---|---|---|---|---|---|---|---|---|---|---|---|---|---|---|---|---|---|---|---|---|---|---|---|
| | | 551 | 1197 | P.14 | 601 | | | 651 | | | 701 | | | 751 | | | 801 | | | 851 | | | 901 | | | 951 | | |
| | | 2 | " | " | 2 | | | 2 | | | 2 | | | 2 | | | 2 | | | 2 | | | 2 | | | 2 | | |
| | | 3 | " | " | 3 | | | 3 | | | 3 | | | 3 | | | 3 | | | 3 | | | 3 | | | 3 | | |
| | | 4 | " | " | 4 | | | 4 | | | 4 | | | 4 | | | 4 | | | 4 | | | 4 | | | 4 | | |
| | | 5 | " | " | 5 | | | 5 | | | 5 | | | 5 | | | 5 | | | 5 | | | 5 | | | 5 | | |
| | | 6 | " | " | 6 | | | 6 | | | 6 | | | 6 | | | 6 | | | 6 | | | 6 | | | 6 | | |
| | | 7 | " | " | 7 | | | 7 | | | 7 | | | 7 | | | 7 | | | 7 | | | 7 | | | 7 | | |
| | | 8 | " | " | 8 | | | 8 | | | 8 | | | 8 | | | 8 | | | 8 | | | 8 | | | 8 | | |
| | | 9 | " | " | 9 | | | 9 | | | 9 | | | 9 | | | 9 | | | 9 | | | 9 | | | 9 | | |
| | | 560 | " | " | 610 | | | 660 | | | 710 | | | 760 | | | 810 | | | 860 | | | 910 | | | 960 | | |
| | | 1 | 1238 | P.19 | 1 | | | 1 | | | 1 | | | 1 | | | 1 | | | 1 | | | 1 | | | 1 | | |
| | | 2 | " | " | 2 | | | 2 | | | 2 | | | 2 | | | 2 | | | 2 | | | 2 | | | 2 | | |
| | | 3 | " | " | 3 | | | 3 | | | 3 | | | 3 | | | 3 | | | 3 | | | 3 | | | 3 | | |
| | | 4 | " | " | 4 | | | 4 | | | 4 | | | 4 | | | 4 | | | 4 | | | 4 | | | 4 | | |
| | | 5 | " | " | 5 | | | 5 | | | 5 | | | 5 | | | 5 | | | 5 | | | 5 | | | 5 | | |
| | | 6 | | | 6 | | | 6 | | | 6 | | | 6 | | | 6 | | | 6 | | | 6 | | | 6 | | |
| | | 7 | 1238 | P.19 | 7 | | | 7 | | | 7 | | | 7 | | | 7 | | | 7 | | | 7 | | | 7 | | |
| | | 8 | " | " | 8 | | | 8 | | | 8 | | | 8 | | | 8 | | | 8 | | | 8 | | | 8 | | |
| | | 9 | " | " | 9 | | | 9 | | | 9 | | | 9 | | | 9 | | | 9 | | | 9 | | | 9 | | |
| | | 570 | " | " | 620 | | | 670 | | | 720 | | | 770 | | | 820 | | | 870 | | | 920 | | | 970 | | |
| | | 1 | " | " | 1 | | | 1 | | | 1 | | | 1 | | | 1 | | | 1 | | | 1 | | | 1 | | |
| | | 2 | " | " | 2 | | | 2 | | | 2 | | | 2 | | | 2 | | | 2 | | | 2 | | | 2 | | |
| | | 3 | " | " | 3 | | | 3 | | | 3 | | | 3 | | | 3 | | | 3 | | | 3 | | | 3 | | |
| | | 4 | " | " | 4 | | | 4 | | | 4 | | | 4 | | | 4 | | | 4 | | | 4 | | | 4 | | |
| | | 5 | " | " | 5 | | | 5 | | | 5 | | | 5 | | | 5 | | | 5 | | | 5 | | | 5 | | |
| | | 6 | " | " | 6 | | | 6 | | | 6 | | | 6 | | | 6 | | | 6 | | | 6 | | | 6 | | |
| | | 7 | " | " | 7 | | | 7 | | | 7 | | | 7 | | | 7 | | | 7 | | | 7 | | | 7 | | |
| | | 8 | " | " | 8 | | | 8 | | | 8 | | | 8 | | | 8 | | | 8 | | | 8 | | | 8 | | |
| | | 9 | " | " | 9 | | | 9 | | | 9 | | | 9 | | | 9 | | | 9 | | | 9 | | | 9 | | |
| | | 580 | " | P.20 | 630 | | | 680 | | | 730 | | | 780 | | | 830 | | | 880 | | | 930 | | | 980 | | |
| 1134 | P.14 | 1 | 1265 | P.18 | 1 | | | 1 | | | 1 | | | 1 | | | 1 | | | 1 | | | 1 | | | 1 | | |
| | | 2 | " | " | 2 | | | 2 | | | 2 | | | 2 | | | 2 | | | 2 | | | 2 | | | 2 | | |
| | | 3 | | | 3 | | | 3 | | | 3 | | | 3 | | | 3 | | | 3 | | | 3 | | | 3 | | |
| 1134 | P.14 | 4 | 1265 | P.18 | 4 | | | 4 | | | 4 | | | 4 | | | 4 | | | 4 | | | 4 | | | 4 | | |
| " | " | 5 | " | " | 5 | | | 5 | | | 5 | | | 5 | | | 5 | | | 5 | | | 5 | | | 5 | | |
| " | " | 6 | " | " | 6 | | | 6 | | | 6 | | | 6 | | | 6 | | | 6 | | | 6 | | | 6 | | |
| " | " | 7 | " | " | 7 | | | 7 | | | 7 | | | 7 | | | 7 | | | 7 | | | 7 | | | 7 | | |
| " | " | 8 | " | " | 8 | | | 8 | | | 8 | | | 8 | | | 8 | | | 8 | | | 8 | | | 8 | | |
| | | 9 | " | " | 9 | | | 9 | | | 9 | | | 9 | | | 9 | | | 9 | | | 9 | | | 9 | | |
| 1134 | P.14 | 590 | " | " | 640 | | | 690 | | | 740 | | | 790 | | | 840 | | | 890 | | | 940 | | | 990 | | |
| 1197 | " | 1 | " | " | 1 | | | 1 | | | 1 | | | 1 | | | 1 | | | 1 | | | 1 | | | 1 | | |
| " | " | 2 | " | " | 2 | | | 2 | | | 2 | | | 2 | | | 2 | | | 2 | | | 2 | | | 2 | | |
| " | " | 3 | | | 3 | | | 3 | | | 3 | | | 3 | | | 3 | | | 3 | | | 3 | | | 3 | | |
| " | " | 4 | 1265 | P.18 | 4 | | | 4 | | | 4 | | | 4 | | | 4 | | | 4 | | | 4 | | | 4 | | |
| " | " | 5 | " | " | 5 | | | 5 | | | 5 | | | 5 | | | 5 | | | 5 | | | 5 | | | 5 | | |
| " | " | 6 | 1769 | P.24 | 6 | | | 6 | | | 6 | | | 6 | | | 6 | | | 6 | | | 6 | | | 6 | | |
| " | " | 7 | " | " | 7 | | | 7 | | | 7 | | | 7 | | | 7 | | | 7 | | | 7 | | | 7 | | |
| " | " | 8 | " | " | 8 | | | 8 | | | 8 | | | 8 | | | 8 | | | 8 | | | 8 | | | 8 | | |
| | | 9 | " | " | 9 | | | 9 | | | 9 | | | 9 | | | 9 | | | 9 | | | 9 | | | 9 | | |
| | | 600 | " | " | 650 | | | 700 | | | 750 | | | 800 | | | 850 | | | 900 | | | 950 | | | 1000 | | |

# VAN INDEX

| VAN Nº | LOT Nº | DIAG. Nº | VAN Nº | LOT Nº | DIAG. Nº | VAN Nº | LOT Nº | DIAG. Nº | VAN Nº | LOT Nº | DIAG. Nº | VAN Nº | LOT Nº | DIAG. Nº | VAN Nº | LOT Nº | DIAG. Nº | VAN Nº | LOT Nº | DIAG. Nº | VAN Nº | LOT Nº | DIAG Nº | VAN Nº | LOT Nº | DIAG Nº | VAN Nº | LOT Nº |
|---|---|---|---|---|---|---|---|---|---|---|---|---|---|---|---|---|---|---|---|---|---|---|---|---|---|---|---|---|
| 1 | | | 51 | 1462 | K.40 | 101 | 1495 | K.41 | 151 | 1602 | K.41 | 201 | | | 251 | 1241 | K.19 | 301 | 1740 | K.45 | 351 | | | 401 | | | 451 | |
| 2 | | | 2 | | | 2 | " | " | 2 | " | " | 2 | | | 2 | " | " | 2 | " | " | 2 | | | 2 | | | 2 | |
| 3 | 1462 | K.40 | 3 | 1462 | K.40 | 3 | " | " | 3 | " | " | 3 | | | 3 | " | " | 3 | " | " | 3 | | | 3 | | | 3 | |
| 4 | " | " | 4 | | | 4 | " | " | 4 | " | " | 4 | | | 4 | " | " | 4 | " | " | 4 | | | 4 | | | 4 | |
| 5 | " | " | 5 | 1462 | K.40 | 5 | " | " | 5 | " | " | 5 | | | 5 | — | K.39 | 5 | " | " | 5 | | | 5 | | | 5 | |
| 6 | " | " | 6 | " | " | 6 | " | " | 6 | " | " | 6 | | | 6 | 1253 | K.22 | 6 | " | " | 6 | | | 6 | | | 6 | |
| 7 | | | 7 | " | " | 7 | " | " | 7 | " | " | 7 | | | 7 | 1281 | " | 7 | " | " | 7 | | | 7 | | | 7 | |
| 8 | | | 8 | | | 8 | " | " | 8 | 1604 | K.42 | 8 | | | 8 | " | " | 8 | " | " | 8 | | | 8 | | | 8 | |
| 9 | 1462 | K.40 | 9 | | | 9 | " | " | 9 | " | " | 9 | | | 9 | " | " | 9 | " | " | 9 | | | 9 | | | 9 | |
| 10 | | | 60 | | | 110 | " | " | 160 | " | " | 210 | | | 260 | " | " | 310 | " | " | 360 | | | 410 | | | 460 | |
| 1 | 1462 | K.40 | 1 | 1667 | K.44 | 1 | 1518 | " | 1 | " | " | 1 | | | 1 | " | " | 1 | " | " | 1 | | | 1 | | | 1 | |
| 2 | | | 2 | " | " | 2 | " | " | 2 | " | " | 2 | | | 2 | " | " | 2 | " | " | 2 | | | 2 | | | 2 | |
| 3 | 1462 | K.40 | 3 | " | " | 3 | " | " | 3 | " | " | 3 | | | 3 | " | " | 3 | " | " | 3 | | | 3 | | | 3 | |
| 4 | | | 4 | " | " | 4 | " | " | 4 | " | " | 4 | | | 4 | " | " | 4 | " | " | 4 | | | 4 | | | 4 | |
| 5 | | | 5 | " | " | 5 | " | " | 5 | " | " | 5 | | | 5 | " | " | 5 | " | " | 5 | | | 5 | | | 5 | |
| 6 | | | 6 | " | " | 6 | " | " | 6 | " | " | 6 | | | 6 | " | " | 6 | " | " | 6 | | | 6 | | | 6 | |
| 7 | | | 7 | " | " | 7 | " | " | 7 | " | " | 7 | | | 7 | 1288 | " | 7 | " | " | 7 | | | 7 | | | 7 | |
| 8 | | | 8 | " | " | 8 | " | " | 8 | | | 8 | | | 8 | 1665 | K.42 | 8 | " | " | 8 | | | 8 | | | 8 | |
| 9 | 1462 | K.40 | 9 | " | " | 9 | " | " | 9 | | | 9 | | | 9 | " | " | 9 | " | " | 9 | | | 9 | | | 9 | |
| 20 | | | 70 | " | " | 120 | " | " | 170 | | | 220 | | | 270 | " | " | 320 | " | " | 370 | | | 420 | | | 470 | |
| 1 | | | 1 | 1481 | K.40 | 1 | 1652 | K.42 | 1 | | | 1 | | | 1 | " | " | 1 | " | " | 1 | | | 1 | | | 1 | |
| 2 | | | 2 | " | " | 2 | " | " | 2 | | | 2 | | | 2 | " | " | 2 | " | " | 2 | | | 2 | | | 2 | |
| 3 | | | 3 | " | " | 3 | " | " | 3 | | | 3 | | | 3 | " | " | 3 | " | " | 3 | | | 3 | | | 3 | |
| 4 | | | 4 | " | " | 4 | " | " | 4 | | | 4 | | | 4 | " | " | 4 | " | " | 4 | | | 4 | | | 4 | |
| 5 | | | 5 | | | 5 | " | " | 5 | | | 5 | | | 5 | " | " | 5 | 1752 | K.46 | 5 | | | 5 | | | 5 | |
| 6 | | | 6 | 1481 | K.40 | 6 | " | " | 6 | | | 6 | | | 6 | " | " | 6 | " | " | 6 | | | 6 | | | 6 | |
| 7 | 1462 | K.40 | 7 | " | " | 7 | " | " | 7 | | | 7 | | | 7 | " | " | 7 | " | " | 7 | | | 7 | | | 7 | |
| 8 | " | " | 8 | " | " | 8 | " | " | 8 | | | 8 | | | 8 | | | 8 | " | " | 8 | | | 8 | | | 8 | |
| 9 | | | 9 | " | " | 9 | " | " | 9 | | | 9 | | | 9 | | | 9 | " | " | 9 | | | 9 | | | 9 | |
| 30 | | | 80 | " | " | 130 | " | " | 180 | | | 230 | | | 280 | | | 330 | " | " | 380 | | | 430 | | | 480 | |
| 1 | 1462 | K.40 | 1 | " | " | 1 | | | 1 | 1535 | K.41 | 1 | | | 1 | | | 1 | " | " | 1 | | | 1 | | | 1 | |
| 2 | " | " | 2 | " | " | 2 | | | 2 | " | " | 2 | | | 2 | | | 2 | " | " | 2 | | | 2 | | | 2 | |
| 3 | " | " | 3 | " | " | 3 | | | 3 | " | " | 3 | | | 3 | | | 3 | " | " | 3 | | | 3 | | | 3 | |
| 4 | " | " | 4 | " | " | 4 | | | 4 | " | " | 4 | | | 4 | | | 4 | " | " | 4 | | | 4 | | | 4 | |
| 5 | " | " | 5 | " | " | 5 | 1617 | K.43 | 5 | " | " | 5 | | | 5 | | | 5 | | | 5 | | | 5 | | | 5 | |
| 6 | " | " | 6 | | | 6 | " | " | 6 | " | " | 6 | | | 6 | | | 6 | | | 6 | | | 6 | | | 6 | |
| 7 | " | " | 7 | | | 7 | " | " | 7 | " | " | 7 | | | 7 | | | 7 | | | 7 | | | 7 | | | 7 | |
| 8 | | | 8 | | | 8 | 1562 | K.41 | 8 | " | " | 8 | | | 8 | | | 8 | | | 8 | | | 8 | | | 8 | |
| 9 | 1462 | K.40 | 9 | | | 9 | | | 9 | " | " | 9 | | | 9 | | | 9 | | | 9 | | | 9 | | | 9 | |
| 40 | | | 90 | | | 140 | 1562 | K.41 | 190 | " | " | 240 | | | 290 | 1722 | K45 | 340 | | | 390 | | | 440 | | | 490 | |
| 1 | 1462 | K.40 | 1 | 1665 | K.42 | 1 | " | " | 1 | " | " | 1 | | | 1 | " | " | 1 | | | 1 | | | 1 | | | 1 | |
| 2 | | | 2 | " | " | 2 | " | " | 2 | " | " | 2 | | | 2 | " | " | 2 | | | 2 | | | 2 | | | 2 | |
| 3 | 1462 | K.40 | 3 | " | " | 3 | " | " | 3 | " | " | 3 | | | 3 | " | " | 3 | | | 3 | | | 3 | | | 3 | |
| 4 | | | 4 | " | " | 4 | " | " | 4 | " | " | 4 | | | 4 | " | " | 4 | | | 4 | | | 4 | | | 4 | |
| 5 | | | 5 | " | " | 5 | " | " | 5 | " | " | 5 | | | 5 | " | " | 5 | | | 5 | | | 5 | | | 5 | |
| 6 | | | 6 | " | " | 6 | " | " | 6 | " | " | 6 | | | 6 | " | " | 6 | | | 6 | | | 6 | | | 6 | |
| 7 | | | 7 | " | " | 7 | " | " | 7 | " | " | 7 | | | 7 | " | " | 7 | | | 7 | | | 7 | | | 7 | |
| 8 | | | 8 | " | " | 8 | " | " | 8 | " | " | 8 | 1204 | K.18 | 8 | " | " | 8 | | | 8 | | | 8 | | | 8 | |
| 9 | | | 9 | " | " | 9 | " | " | 9 | " | " | 9 | | | 9 | " | " | 9 | | | 9 | | | 9 | | | 9 | |
| 50 | | | 100 | " | " | 150 | " | " | 200 | " | " | 250 | 1241 | K.19 | 300 | 1740 | " | 350 | | | 400 | | | 450 | | | 500 | |

| VAN Nº | LOT Nº | DIAG. Nº | VAN Nº | LOT Nº | DIAG. Nº | VAN Nº | LOT Nº | DIAG. Nº | VAN Nº | LOT Nº | DIAG. Nº | VAN Nº | LOT Nº | DIAG. Nº | VAN Nº | LOT Nº | DIAG. Nº | VAN Nº | LOT Nº | DIAG. Nº | VAN Nº | LOT Nº | DIAG. Nº | VAN Nº | LOT Nº | DIAG. Nº | VAN Nº | LOT Nº |
|---|---|---|---|---|---|---|---|---|---|---|---|---|---|---|---|---|---|---|---|---|---|---|---|---|---|---|---|---|
| 501 | | | 551 | | | 601 | | | 651 | | | 701 | | | 751 | | | 801 | 1502 | L.22 | 851 | | | 901 | | | 951 | |
| 2 | | | 2 | | | 2 | | | 2 | | | 2 | | | 2 | | | 2 | " | " | 2 | | | 2 | | | 2 | |
| 3 | | | 3 | | | 3 | | | 3 | | | 3 | | | 3 | | | 3 | " | " | 3 | | | 3 | | | 3 | |
| 4 | | | 4 | | | 4 | | | 4 | | | 4 | | | 4 | | | 4 | | | 4 | | | 4 | | | 4 | |
| 5 | | | 5 | | | 5 | | | 5 | | | 5 | | | 5 | | | 5 | | | 5 | | | 5 | | | 5 | |
| 6 | | | 6 | | | 6 | | | 6 | | | 6 | | | 6 | | | 6 | 1430 | L.18 | 6 | | | 6 | | | 6 | |
| 7 | | | 7 | | | 7 | | | 7 | | | 7 | | | 7 | | | 7 | " | " | 7 | | | 7 | | | 7 | |
| 8 | | | 8 | | | 8 | | | 8 | | | 8 | | | 8 | | | 8 | " | " | 8 | | | 8 | | | 8 | |
| 9 | | | 9 | | | 9 | | | 9 | | | 9 | | | 9 | | | 9 | | | 9 | | | 9 | | | 9 | |
| 510 | | | 560 | | | 610 | | | 660 | | | 710 | | | 760 | | | 810 | | | 860 | | | 910 | | | 960 | |
| 1 | | | 1 | | | 1 | | | 1 | | | 1 | | | 1 | | | 1 | | | 1 | | | 1 | | | 1 | |
| 2 | | | 2 | | | 2 | | | 2 | | | 2 | | | 2 | | | 2 | 1503 | L.23 | 2 | | | 2 | | | 2 | |
| 3 | | | 3 | | | 3 | | | 3 | | | 3 | | | 3 | | | 3 | " | " | 3 | | | 3 | | | 3 | |
| 4 | | | 4 | | | 4 | | | 4 | | | 4 | | | 4 | | | 4 | [illegible] | " | 4 | | | 4 | | | 4 | |
| 5 | | | 5 | | | 5 | | | 5 | | | 5 | | | 5 | | | 5 | 1504 | L.24 | 5 | | | 5 | | | 5 | |
| 6 | | | 6 | | | 6 | | | 6 | | | 6 | | | 6 | | | 6 | " | " | 6 | | | 6 | | | 6 | |
| 7 | | | 7 | | | 7 | | | 7 | | | 7 | | | 7 | | | 7 | " | " | 7 | | | 7 | | | 7 | |
| 8 | | | 8 | | | 8 | | | 8 | | | 8 | | | 8 | | | 8 | | | 8 | | | 8 | | | 8 | |
| 9 | | | 9 | | | 9 | | | 9 | | | 9 | | | 9 | | | 9 | 1139 | M.17 | 9 | | | 9 | | | 9 | |
| 520 | | | 570 | | | 620 | | | 670 | | | 720 | | | 770 | | | 820 | " | " | 870 | | | 920 | | | 970 | |
| 1 | | | 1 | | | 1 | | | 1 | | | 1 | | | 1 | | | 1 | | | 1 | | | 1 | | | 1 | |
| 2 | | | 2 | | | 2 | | | 2 | | | 2 | | | 2 | | | 2 | 1062 | M.10 | 2 | | | 2 | | | 2 | |
| 3 | | | 3 | | | 3 | | | 3 | | | 3 | | | 3 | | | 3 | " | M.9 | 3 | | | 3 | | | 3 | |
| 4 | | | 4 | | | 4 | | | 4 | | | 4 | | | 4 | | | 4 | | | 4 | 1144 | M.12 | 4 | | | 4 | |
| 5 | | | 5 | | | 5 | | | 5 | | | 5 | | | 5 | | | 5 | | | 5 | | | 5 | | | 5 | |
| 6 | | | 6 | | | 6 | | | 6 | | | 6 | | | 6 | | | 6 | 1091 | M.11 | 6 | 1178 | M.14 | 6 | | | 6 | |
| 7 | | | 7 | | | 7 | | | 7 | | | 7 | | | 7 | | | 7 | | | 7 | " | " | 7 | | | 7 | |
| 8 | | | 8 | | | 8 | | | 8 | | | 8 | | | 8 | | | 8 | 1091 | M.11 | 8 | 1220 | M.17 | 8 | | | 8 | |
| 9 | | | 9 | | | 9 | | | 9 | | | 9 | | | 9 | | | 9 | | | 9 | | | 9 | | | 9 | |
| 530 | | | 580 | | | 630 | | | 680 | | | 730 | | | 780 | | | 830 | | | 880 | | | 930 | | | 980 | |
| 1 | | | 1 | | | 1 | | | 1 | | | 1 | | | 1 | | | 1 | | | 1 | | | 1 | | | 1 | |
| 2 | | | 2 | | | 2 | | | 2 | | | 2 | | | 2 | | | 2 | | | 2 | | | 2 | | | 2 | |
| 3 | | | 3 | | | 3 | | | 3 | | | 3 | | | 3 | | | 3 | 1165 | M.13 | 3 | | | 3 | | | 3 | |
| 4 | | | 4 | | | 4 | | | 4 | | | 4 | | | 4 | | | 4 | | | 4 | | | 4 | | | 4 | |
| 5 | | | 5 | | | 5 | | | 5 | | | 5 | | | 5 | | | 5 | 1094 | L.13 | 5 | | | 5 | | | 5 | |
| 6 | | | 6 | | | 6 | | | 6 | | | 6 | | | 6 | | | 6 | | | 6 | | | 6 | | | 6 | |
| 7 | 217 | O.2 | 7 | | | 7 | | | 7 | | | 7 | | | 7 | | | 7 | 1061 | M.8 | 7 | | | 7 | | | 7 | |
| 8 | | | 8 | | | 8 | | | 8 | | | 8 | | | 8 | | | 8 | | | 8 | | | 8 | | | 8 | |
| 9 | | | 9 | | | 9 | | | 9 | | | 9 | | | 9 | | | 9 | | | 9 | | | 9 | | | 9 | |
| 540 | | | 590 | | | 640 | | | 690 | | | 740 | | | 790 | | | 840 | | | 890 | | | 940 | | | 990 | |
| 1 | | | 1 | | | 1 | | | 1 | | | 1 | | | 1 | | | 1 | | | 1 | | | 1 | | | 1 | |
| 2 | | | 2 | | | 2 | | | 2 | | | 2 | | | 2 | 996 | M.16 | 2 | | | 2 | | | 2 | | | 2 | |
| 3 | | | 3 | | | 3 | | | 3 | | | 3 | | | 3 | 1499 | L.21 | 3 | 1719 | L.25 | 3 | | | 3 | | | 3 | |
| 4 | | | 4 | | | 4 | | | 4 | | | 4 | | | 4 | " | " | 4 | " | " | 4 | | | 4 | | | 4 | |
| 5 | | | 5 | | | 5 | | | 5 | | | 5 | | | 5 | " | " | 5 | " | " | 5 | | | 5 | | | 5 | |
| 6 | | | 6 | | | 6 | | | 6 | | | 6 | | | 6 | 1500 | L.20 | 6 | " | " | 6 | | | 6 | | | 6 | |
| 7 | | | 7 | | | 7 | | | 7 | | | 7 | | | 7 | 1501 | L.22 | 7 | " | " | 7 | | | 7 | | | 7 | |
| 8 | | | 8 | | | 8 | | | 8 | | | 8 | | | 8 | " | " | 8 | 1484 | L.19 | 8 | | | 8 | | | 8 | |
| 9 | | | 9 | | | 9 | | | 9 | | | 9 | | | 9 | " | " | 9 | " | " | 9 | | | 9 | | | 9 | |
| 550 | | | 600 | | | 650 | | | 700 | | | 750 | | | 800 | " | " | 850 | | | 900 | | | 950 | | | 1000 | |

# VAN INDEX

| VAN Nº | LOT Nº | DIAG Nº | VAN Nº | LOT Nº | DIAG Nº | VAN Nº | LOT Nº | DIAG Nº | VAN Nº | LOT Nº | DIAG Nº | VAN Nº | LOT Nº | DIAG Nº | VAN Nº | LOT Nº | DIAG Nº | VAN Nº | LOT Nº | DIAG Nº | VAN Nº | LOT Nº | DIAG Nº | VAN Nº | LOT Nº | DIAG Nº | VAN Nº | LOT Nº | DIAG Nº |
|---|---|---|---|---|---|---|---|---|---|---|---|---|---|---|---|---|---|---|---|---|---|---|---|---|---|---|---|---|---|
| 1 | 1751 | 0.62 | 1051 | | | 1101 | | | 1151 | 1301 | K.22 | 1201 | 1185 | M.15 | 1251 | 1378 | 0.11 | 1301 | 1347 | 0.11 | 1351 | 1316 | 0.11 | 1401 | | | 1451 | 1264 | 0.11 |
| 2 | ″ | ″ | 2 | | | 2 | | | 2 | ″ | ″ | 2 | | | 2 | ″ | ″ | 2 | ″ | ″ | 2 | ″ | ″ | 2 | | | 2 | ″ | ″ |
| 3 | ″ | ″ | 3 | | | 3 | | | 3 | ″ | ″ | 3 | | | 3 | ″ | ″ | 3 | ″ | ″ | 3 | ″ | ″ | 3 | | | 3 | ″ | ″ |
| 4 | ″ | ″ | 4 | | | 4 | | | 4 | | | 4 | | | 4 | ″ | ″ | 4 | ″ | ″ | 4 | ″ | ″ | 4 | | | 4 | ″ | ″ |
| 5 | ″ | ″ | 5 | | | 5 | | | 5 | 1344 | K.35 | 5 | 1185 | M.23 | 5 | ″ | ″ | 5 | ″ | ″ | 5 | ″ | ″ | 5 | | | 5 | ″ | ″ |
| 6 | ″ | ″ | 6 | | | 6 | | | 6 | ″ | K.34 | 6 | | | 6 | ″ | ″ | 6 | ″ | ″ | 6 | ″ | ″ | 6 | | | 6 | ″ | ″ |
| 7 | ″ | ″ | 7 | | | 7 | | | 7 | ″ | K.36 | 7 | | | 7 | ″ | ″ | 7 | ″ | ″ | 7 | ″ | ″ | 7 | | | 7 | ″ | ″ |
| 8 | ″ | ″ | 8 | | | 8 | | | 8 | ″ | ″ | 8 | | | 8 | ″ | ″ | 8 | ″ | ″ | 8 | ″ | ″ | 8 | | | 8 | ″ | ″ |
| 9 | ″ | ″ | 9 | | | 9 | | | 9 | — | M.33 | 9 | | | 9 | ″ | ″ | 9 | ″ | ″ | 9 | ″ | ″ | 9 | | | 9 | ″ | ″ |
| 0 | ″ | ″ | 1060 | | | 1110 | | | 1160 | 1344 | K.36 | 1210 | | | 1260 | ″ | ″ | 1310 | 1721 | 0.62 | 1360 | ″ | ″ | 1410 | | | 1460 | ″ | ″ |
| 1 | ″ | ″ | 1 | | | 1 | | | 1 | | | 1 | | | 1 | ″ | ″ | 1 | ″ | ″ | 1 | ″ | ″ | 1 | | | 1 | ″ | ″ |
| 2 | ″ | ″ | 2 | | | 2 | | | 2 | 1344 | K.36 | 2 | | | 2 | ″ | ″ | 2 | ″ | ″ | 2 | ″ | ″ | 2 | | | 2 | 1211 | ″ |
| 3 | ″ | ″ | 3 | | | 3 | | | 3 | | | 3 | | | 3 | ″ | ″ | 3 | ″ | ″ | 3 | ″ | ″ | 3 | | | 3 | ″ | ″ |
| 4 | ″ | ″ | 4 | | | 4 | | | 4 | | | 4 | | | 4 | ″ | ″ | 4 | ″ | ″ | 4 | ″ | ″ | 4 | | | 4 | | |
| 5 | ″ | ″ | 5 | | | 5 | | | 5 | 1345 | K.37 | 5 | 1409 | 0.31 | 5 | ″ | ″ | 5 | ″ | ″ | 5 | | | 5 | | | 5 | 1211 | 0.11 |
| 6 | ″ | ″ | 6 | | | 6 | | | 6 | ″ | K.34 | 6 | ″ | ″ | 6 | ″ | ″ | 6 | ″ | ″ | 6 | | | 6 | | | 6 | ″ | ″ |
| 7 | ″ | ″ | 7 | | | 7 | | | 7 | ″ | ″ | 7 | ″ | ″ | 7 | ″ | ″ | 7 | ″ | ″ | 7 | | | 7 | | | 7 | ″ | ″ |
| 8 | ″ | ″ | 8 | | | 8 | | | 8 | ″ | ″ | 8 | ″ | ″ | 8 | ″ | ″ | 8 | ″ | ″ | 8 | | | 8 | | | 8 | | |
| 9 | ″ | ″ | 9 | | | 9 | | | 9 | 1346 | K.38 | 9 | ″ | ″ | 9 | ″ | ″ | 9 | ″ | ″ | 9 | | | 9 | | | 9 | 1211 | 0.11 |
| 0 | ″ | ″ | 1070 | | | 1120 | | | 1170 | ″ | ″ | 1220 | ″ | ″ | 1270 | 1370 | 0.22 | 1320 | ″ | ″ | 1370 | | | 1420 | | | 1470 | ″ | ″ |
| 1 | ″ | ″ | 1 | | | 1 | | | 1 | ″ | ″ | 1 | ″ | ″ | 1 | 1368 | 0.11 | 1 | ″ | ″ | 1 | | | 1 | | | 1 | | |
| 2 | ″ | ″ | 2 | | | 2 | | | 2 | ″ | ″ | 2 | ″ | ″ | 2 | ″ | ″ | 2 | ″ | ″ | 2 | | | 2 | 1266 | 0.12 | 2 | 1211 | 0.11 |
| 3 | ″ | ″ | 3 | | | 3 | | | 3 | ″ | ″ | 3 | 1385 | 0.22 | 3 | ″ | ″ | 3 | ″ | ″ | 3 | | | 3 | ″ | ″ | 3 | ″ | ″ |
| 4 | ″ | ″ | 4 | | | 4 | | | 4 | ″ | ″ | 4 | ″ | ″ | 4 | ″ | ″ | 4 | ″ | ″ | 4 | | | 4 | ″ | ″ | 4 | ″ | ″ |
| 5 | ″ | ″ | 5 | | | 5 | | | 5 | 1413 | K.40 | 5 | ″ | ″ | 5 | ″ | ″ | 5 | ″ | ″ | 5 | | | 5 | ″ | ″ | 5 | ″ | ″ |
| 6 | ″ | ″ | 6 | | | 6 | | | 6 | ″ | ″ | 6 | ″ | ″ | 6 | ″ | ″ | 6 | ″ | ″ | 6 | | | 6 | ″ | ″ | 6 | ″ | ″ |
| 7 | ″ | ″ | 7 | | | 7 | | | 7 | ″ | ″ | 7 | ″ | ″ | 7 | ″ | ″ | 7 | ″ | ″ | 7 | | | 7 | ″ | ″ | 7 | ″ | ″ |
| 8 | ″ | ″ | 8 | | | 8 | | | 8 | ″ | ″ | 8 | ″ | ″ | 8 | ″ | ″ | 8 | ″ | ″ | 8 | | | 8 | ″ | ″ | 8 | ″ | ″ |
| 9 | ″ | ″ | 9 | 865 | K.25 | 9 | 1301 | K.22 | 9 | ″ | ″ | 9 | ″ | ″ | 9 | ″ | ″ | 9 | ″ | ″ | 9 | | | 9 | ″ | ″ | 9 | | |
| 0 | ″ | ″ | 1080 | | | 1130 | ″ | ″ | 1180 | ″ | ″ | 1230 | ″ | ″ | 1280 | ″ | ″ | 1330 | ″ | ″ | 1380 | | | 1430 | ″ | ″ | 1480 | 1211 | 0.11 |
| 1 | | | 1 | | | 1 | ″ | ″ | 1 | ″ | ″ | 1 | ″ | ″ | 1 | ″ | ″ | 1 | ″ | ″ | 1 | | | 1 | ″ | ″ | 1 | ″ | ″ |
| 2 | | | 2 | | | 2 | ″ | ″ | 2 | ″ | ″ | 2 | ″ | ″ | 2 | ″ | ″ | 2 | ″ | ″ | 2 | | | 2 | ″ | ″ | 2 | | |
| 3 | | | 3 | | | 3 | ″ | ″ | 3 | ″ | ″ | 3 | ″ | ″ | 3 | | | 3 | ″ | ″ | 3 | | | 3 | ″ | ″ | 3 | | |
| 4 | | | 4 | | | 4 | ″ | ″ | 4 | ″ | ″ | 4 | ″ | ″ | 4 | 1368 | 0.11 | 4 | ″ | ″ | 4 | | | 4 | | | 4 | | |
| 5 | | | 5 | | | 5 | ″ | ″ | 5 | | | 5 | ″ | ″ | 5 | ″ | ″ | 5 | ″ | ″ | 5 | | | 5 | 1266 | 0.12 | 5 | 1183 | 0.9 |
| 6 | | | 6 | | | 6 | ″ | ″ | 6 | 1396 | 0.22 | 6 | ″ | ″ | 6 | ″ | ″ | 6 | ″ | ″ | 6 | | | 6 | ″ | ″ | 6 | ″ | ″ |
| 7 | | | 7 | | | 7 | ″ | ″ | 7 | ″ | ″ | 7 | ″ | ″ | 7 | ″ | ″ | 7 | ″ | ″ | 7 | | | 7 | ″ | ″ | 7 | | |
| 8 | | | 8 | | | 8 | ″ | ″ | 8 | ″ | ″ | 8 | | | 8 | ″ | ″ | 8 | ″ | ″ | 8 | | | 8 | ″ | ″ | 8 | | |
| 9 | | | 9 | | | 9 | ″ | ″ | 9 | ″ | ″ | 9 | | | 9 | ″ | ″ | 9 | ″ | ″ | 9 | | | 9 | ″ | ″ | 9 | | |
| 0 | | | 1090 | | | 1140 | ″ | ″ | 1190 | ″ | ″ | 1240 | 1378 | 0.11 | 1290 | 1347 | ″ | 1340 | | | 1390 | | | 1440 | ″ | ″ | 1490 | | |
| 1 | | | 1 | | | 1 | ″ | ″ | 1 | ″ | ″ | 1 | ″ | ″ | 1 | ″ | ″ | 1 | | | 1 | | | 1 | ″ | ″ | 1 | 1183 | 0.9 |
| 2 | | | 2 | | | 2 | ″ | ″ | 2 | ″ | ″ | 2 | ″ | ″ | 2 | ″ | ″ | 2 | | | 2 | | | 2 | 1264 | 0.11 | 2 | | |
| 3 | | | 3 | | | 3 | ″ | ″ | 3 | ″ | ″ | 3 | ″ | ″ | 3 | ″ | ″ | 3 | | | 3 | | | 3 | ″ | ″ | 3 | | |
| 4 | | | 4 | | | 4 | ″ | ″ | 4 | ″ | ″ | 4 | ″ | ″ | 4 | ″ | ″ | 4 | | | 4 | | | 4 | ″ | ″ | 4 | 1183 | 0.9 |
| 5 | | | 5 | | | 5 | ″ | ″ | 5 | ″ | ″ | 5 | ″ | ″ | 5 | ″ | ″ | 5 | 1316 | 0.11 | 5 | | | 5 | ″ | ″ | 5 | | |
| 6 | | | 6 | | | 6 | ″ | ″ | 6 | ″ | ″ | 6 | ″ | ″ | 6 | ″ | ″ | 6 | ″ | ″ | 6 | | | 6 | ″ | ″ | 6 | 1183 | 0.9 |
| 7 | | | 7 | | | 7 | ″ | ″ | 7 | ″ | ″ | 7 | ″ | ″ | 7 | ″ | ″ | 7 | ″ | ″ | 7 | 1299 | 0.13 | 7 | ″ | ″ | 7 | | |
| 8 | | | 8 | | | 8 | ″ | ″ | 8 | ″ | ″ | 8 | ″ | ″ | 8 | ″ | ″ | 8 | ″ | ″ | 8 | ″ | ″ | 8 | ″ | ″ | 8 | | |
| 9 | | | 9 | | | 9 | ″ | ″ | 9 | ″ | ″ | 9 | ″ | ″ | 9 | ″ | ″ | 9 | ″ | ″ | 9 | ″ | ″ | 9 | ″ | ″ | 9 | | |
| 0 | | | 1100 | | | 1150 | ″ | ″ | 1200 | ″ | ″ | 1250 | ″ | ″ | 1300 | ″ | ″ | 1350 | ″ | ″ | 1400 | | | 1450 | ″ | ″ | 1500 | 1183 | 0.9 |

| VAN No. | LOT No. | DIAG. No. | VAN No. | LOT No. | DIAG. No. | VAN No. | LOT No. | DIAG. No. | VAN No. | LOT No. | DIAG. No. | VAN No. | LOT No. | DIAG. No. | VAN No. | LOT No. | DIAG. No. | VAN No. | LOT No. | DIAG. No. | VAN No. | LOT No. | DIAG. No. | VAN No. | LOT No. | DIAG. No. | VAN No. | LOT No. | DIAG. No. |
|---|---|---|---|---|---|---|---|---|---|---|---|---|---|---|---|---|---|---|---|---|---|---|---|---|---|---|---|---|---|
| 1 | | | 1551 | | | 1601 | | | 1651 | | | 1701 | | | 1751 | | | 1801 | | | 1851 | | | 1901 | | | 1951 | 1679 | 0.52 |
| 2 | 1164 | 0.10 | 2 | | | 2 | | | 2 | | | 2 | | | 2 | | | 2 | | | 2 | | | 2 | | | 2 | ″ | ″ |
| 3 | | | 3 | | | 3 | | | 3 | | | 3 | | | 3 | | | 3 | | | 3 | | | 3 | | | 3 | ″ | ″ |
| 4 | | | 4 | | | 4 | | | 4 | | | 4 | | | 4 | | | 4 | | | 4 | | | 4 | | | 4 | ″ | ″ |
| 5 | | | 5 | | | 5 | | | 5 | | | 5 | | | 5 | | | 5 | | | 5 | | | 5 | | | 5 | 1678 | 0.53 |
| 6 | | | 6 | | | 6 | | | 6 | | | 6 | | | 6 | | | 6 | | | 6 | | | 6 | | | 6 | ″ | ″ |
| 7 | | | 7 | | | 7 | | | 7 | | | 7 | | | 7 | | | 7 | | | 7 | | | 7 | | | 7 | ″ | ″ |
| 8 | | | 8 | | | 8 | | | 8 | | | 8 | | | 8 | | | 8 | | | 8 | | | 8 | | | 8 | 1680 | 0.52 |
| 9 | 1162 | 0.9 | 9 | | | 9 | | | 9 | | | 9 | | | 9 | | | 9 | | | 9 | | | 9 | | | 9 | ″ | ″ |
| 0 | | | 1560 | | | 1610 | | | 1660 | | | 1710 | | | 1760 | | | 1810 | | | 1860 | | | 1910 | | | 1960 | ″ | ″ |
| 1 | 1162 | 0.9 | 1 | | | 1 | | | 1 | | | 1 | | | 1 | | | 1 | | | 1 | | | 1 | | | 1 | | |
| 2 | | | 2 | | | 2 | | | 2 | | | 2 | | | 2 | | | 2 | | | 2 | | | 2 | | | 2 | | |
| 3 | | | 3 | 1044 | 0.5 | 3 | | | 3 | | | 3 | | | 3 | | | 3 | | | 3 | | | 3 | | | 3 | 1680 | 0.52 |
| 4 | 1162 | 0.9 | 4 | | | 4 | | | 4 | | | 4 | | | 4 | | | 4 | | | 4 | | | 4 | | | 4 | ″ | ″ |
| 5 | | | 5 | | | 5 | | | 5 | | | 5 | | | 5 | | | 5 | | | 5 | | | 5 | | | 5 | ″ | ″ |
| 6 | | | 6 | | | 6 | | | 6 | | | 6 | | | 6 | | | 6 | | | 6 | | | 6 | | | 6 | 1681 | 0.49 |
| 7 | | | 7 | | | 7 | | | 7 | | | 7 | | | 7 | | | 7 | | | 7 | | | 7 | | | 7 | 1695 | ″ |
| 8 | 1133 | 0.8 | 8 | | | 8 | | | 8 | | | 8 | | | 8 | | | 8 | | | 8 | | | 8 | | | 8 | 1696 | 0.54 |
| 9 | | | 9 | | | 9 | | | 9 | | | 9 | | | 9 | | | 9 | | | 9 | | | 9 | | | 9 | ″ | ″ |
| 0 | | | 1570 | | | 1620 | | | 1670 | | | 1720 | | | 1770 | | | 1820 | | | 1870 | 800 | 0.4 | 1920 | | | 1970 | ″ | ″ |
| 1 | | | 1 | | | 1 | | | 1 | | | 1 | | | 1 | | | 1 | | | 1 | | | 1 | | | 1 | ″ | ″ |
| 2 | | | 2 | | | 2 | | | 2 | | | 2 | | | 2 | | | 2 | | | 2 | | | 2 | | | 2 | ″ | ″ |
| 3 | 1133 | 0.9 | 3 | | | 3 | | | 3 | | | 3 | | | 3 | | | 3 | | | 3 | | | 3 | | | 3 | ″ | ″ |
| 4 | | | 4 | | | 4 | | | 4 | | | 4 | | | 4 | | | 4 | | | 4 | | | 4 | | | 4 | ″ | ″ |
| 5 | | | 5 | | | 5 | | | 5 | | | 5 | | | 5 | | | 5 | | | 5 | | | 5 | | | 5 | ″ | ″ |
| 6 | | | 6 | | | 6 | | | 6 | | | 6 | | | 6 | | | 6 | | | 6 | | | 6 | | | 6 | ″ | ″ |
| 7 | 1125 | 0.8 | 7 | | | 7 | | | 7 | | | 7 | | | 7 | | | 7 | | | 7 | | | 7 | | | 7 | ″ | ″ |
| 8 | | | 8 | | | 8 | | | 8 | | | 8 | | | 8 | | | 8 | | | 8 | | | 8 | | | 8 | 1697 | 0.55 |
| 9 | | | 9 | | | 9 | | | 9 | | | 9 | | | 9 | | | 9 | | | 9 | | | 9 | | | 9 | ″ | ″ |
| 0 | | | 1580 | | | 1630 | | | 1680 | | | 1730 | | | 1780 | | | 1830 | | | 1880 | | | 1930 | | | 1980 | ″ | ″ |
| 1 | | | 1 | | | 1 | | | 1 | | | 1 | | | 1 | | | 1 | | | 1 | | | 1 | | | 1 | ″ | ″ |
| 2 | | | 2 | | | 2 | | | 2 | | | 2 | | | 2 | | | 2 | | | 2 | | | 2 | | | 2 | ″ | ″ |
| 3 | | | 3 | | | 3 | | | 3 | | | 3 | | | 3 | | | 3 | | | 3 | | | 3 | | | 3 | ″ | ″ |
| 4 | | | 4 | | | 4 | | | 4 | | | 4 | | | 4 | | | 4 | | | 4 | | | 4 | | | 4 | 1698 | ″ |
| 5 | 1125 | 0.8 | 5 | | | 5 | | | 5 | | | 5 | | | 5 | | | 5 | | | 5 | | | 5 | | | 5 | ″ | ″ |
| 6 | | | 6 | | | 6 | | | 6 | | | 6 | | | 6 | | | 6 | | | 6 | | | 6 | | | 6 | 1699 | ″ |
| 7 | 1125 | 0.8 | 7 | | | 7 | | | 7 | | | 7 | | | 7 | | | 7 | | | 7 | | | 7 | | | 7 | ″ | ″ |
| 8 | | | 8 | | | 8 | | | 8 | | | 8 | | | 8 | | | 8 | | | 8 | | | 8 | | | 8 | ″ | ″ |
| 9 | | | 9 | | | 9 | | | 9 | | | 9 | | | 9 | | | 9 | | | 9 | | | 9 | | | 9 | ″ | ″ |
| 0 | | | 1590 | | | 1640 | | | 1690 | | | 1740 | | | 1790 | | | 1840 | | | 1890 | | | 1940 | | | 1990 | ″ | ″ |
| 1 | | | 1 | 1044 | 0.5 | 1 | | | 1 | | | 1 | | | 1 | | | 1 | | | 1 | | | 1 | | | 1 | ″ | ″ |
| 2 | | | 2 | | | 2 | | | 2 | | | 2 | | | 2 | | | 2 | | | 2 | | | 2 | | | 2 | ″ | ″ |
| 3 | | | 3 | | | 3 | | | 3 | | | 3 | 943 | 0.4 | 3 | | | 3 | | | 3 | | | 3 | | | 3 | ″ | ″ |
| 4 | | | 4 | | | 4 | | | 4 | | | 4 | | | 4 | | | 4 | | | 4 | | | 4 | | | 4 | ″ | ″ |
| 5 | | | 5 | | | 5 | | | 5 | | | 5 | | | 5 | | | 5 | | | 5 | | | 5 | | | 5 | ″ | ″ |
| 6 | 1124 | 0.7 | 6 | | | 6 | | | 6 | | | 6 | | | 6 | | | 6 | | | 6 | | | 6 | | | 6 | | |
| 7 | | | 7 | | | 7 | | | 7 | | | 7 | | | 7 | | | 7 | | | 7 | | | 7 | | | 7 | | |
| 8 | 1124 | 0.7 | 8 | | | 8 | | | 8 | | | 8 | | | 8 | | | 8 | | | 8 | | | 8 | | | 8 | | |
| 9 | | | 9 | | | 9 | | | 9 | | | 9 | | | 9 | | | 9 | | | 9 | | | 9 | | | 9 | | |
| 50 | | | 1600 | | | 1650 | | | 1700 | | | 1750 | | | 1800 | | | 1850 | | | 1900 | | | 1950 | | | 2000 | | |